Handbook of
Data Communications

PUBLISHED BY NCC PUBLICATIONS

Keywords for information retrieval (drawn from *NCC Thesaurus of Computing Terms*): data transmission

Published and printed in the United Kingdom of Great Britain and Northern Ireland by NCC Publications The UK National Computing Centre Limited Oxford Road, Manchester M1 7ED

ISBN 0 85012 121 3

Set in 10/12 point Times Roman and printed by Wright's (Sandbach) Limited, Sandbach, Cheshire, England

D
621·3802'8
POS

HANDBOOK OF DATA COMMUNICATIONS

Computer and telecommunications technologies are becoming increasingly convergent and the UK Post Office, in conjunction with the National Computing Centre Limited, has produced this Handbook as a contribution to a greater understanding of their interdependence by students of both disciplines.

Based on Post Office Data Communications Courses, the subjects covered are those which we have found from several years' teaching experience to be the ones needed by the average student. The Handbook should be of value to systems analysts, systems programmers and systems engineers, although it should also be a good reference source for management and newcomers to computing.

Apart from giving particular attention to the facilities available in the UK and the Post Office's role in data communications, the book provides an insight to the facilities available internationally.

Preface

Today, we take for granted the worldwide network of telegraph, telephone, radio and television systems upon which so much of the structure of modern civilisation depends. In recent years, the function of this complex of telecommunications systems has been extended even further by the development of the electronic digital computer. The computer is now an essential component of business, industry, government and education and, in becoming a vital tool for managers, engineers, researchers and administrators, wherever they may be situated, has created a new communications need – between man and computer and between computers themselves – data communications.

This new communications need has posed certain problems for telecommunication authorities throughout the world. Public networks which have evolved over the last century were specifically designed for telephony and low speed telegraph transmission, but sheer economics dictated that they be also utilised for data transmission when this need arose. The present range of services available throughout the world demonstrate how successfully telecommunications engineers have adapted these networks to carry this new form of traffic. However, the existing telecommunications networks do impose certain limitations on the range, performance and economics of data transmission services; but, the advent of digital transmission and switching systems will enable telecommunications administrations to provide networks in the future more suited to the special needs of data transmission. Moreover, these systems will themselves use computers and computer technology.

Computer and telecommunications technologies are, therefore, becoming increasingly convergent and the UK Post Office, in conjunction with the National Computing Centre, has produced this handbook as a contribution to a greater understanding of their interdependence by students of both disciplines.

It is not feasible in a book of this size to examine in great detail all the possible facets of both telecommunications and computer systems which the reader may need. We have, therefore, concentrated on the essential aspects of the interface between the two disciplines. The subjects covered are those which we have found from several years' teaching experience to be the ones needed by the average student. If the reader finds that some topics start at too elementary a level, we ask him to be patient with his less fortunate colleagues and proceed to the next. Conversely, if the reader finds a topic not dealt with in sufficient depth to meet his needs, we hope that the guidance given in the bibliography will lead him to other more detailed sources.

The inter-related nature of the subject makes it difficult to present a general handbook in a simple serial form, so, a few words here on the structure of the book may help the reader. To begin with, Chapters 2, 3 and 4 describe the basic features of the telecommunications networks available and how they can be used for data transmission. These are followed in Chapters 5, 6 and 7 with information on the types of devices which can be connected to these networks and how they must interface with them. Subsequent chapters look at various aspects of the operation of a data communications system, what can be achieved and the limitations.

Although the book originates in the UK and many examples quoted are from UK practice, most of the material dealt with in Chapters 1 to 10 is largely independent of local practice in individual countries. Chapter 11 deals specifically with the data communications facilities available in the UK whilst Chapter 12 looks at the international scene from a UK viewpoint.

The original text of this handbook was prepared by Mr Bernard Cullen of the Data Communications Division in the Marketing Department of the UK Post Office. Mr J J Soulsby of the same Division researched much of the material on which it is based, whilst many others, both in the PO and the National Computing Centre, contributed by reviewing the manuscripts.

G DALE

Head of Data Communications Division
Marketing Department
UK PO Telecommunications HQ

Contents

1 The Origins and Nature of Data Communications

Until the advent of electronic computers, man's progress can be measured by his ability to communicate information between people through time and over distance. The efficient recording of information allowing communication with successive generations was a major problem until Caxton developed the printing press in 1473. The problem of moving information rapidly over distance has taxed the ingenuity of man throughout the ages. For most of history, communication over distance has involved travel and the faithful horse governed its speed until the invention of the steam engine. In the many other different and novel methods of communication over distance which have been tried in the past lie the origins of our sophisticated communications system of today.

Developments in Communications

Our inability to make our voices heard beyond a very limited distance is something we all learn as children. Most of man's attempts at rapid communication beyond voice range have therefore necessitated using some form of telegraphy, which means the conveyance of messages using signalling symbols or codes. Fiery beacons, for example, used to be a very popular method of communicating impending danger. Homer, describing the fall of Troy in the 11th Century BC spoke of a chain of flaring beacons which brought the news to Argos. In 1588, warning of the Spanish Armada was given by a chain of beacons throughout the length and breadth of Britain. Smoke signalling was used widely by the North American Indians. How much information could be conveyed accurately by such means obviously depended on weather conditions and it is reasonable to conclude that the Indians had a few error control problems! The tom-tom is one of the most ancient methods employed and is still in use today by the natives of Africa, South America and Polynesia. Little is known about the codes used but it is interesting to reflect that such primitive peoples, by inventing suitable codes and the means to transmit and relay information, have communicated effectively and rapidly over considerable distances since before the time of Christ.

In more recent history, signalling systems have been developed using the movements of human or mechanical arms (semaphore) or reflected light (heliograph) and these systems are still effective today where no alternative form of communication is possible. Since electrical telegraphic communication began in 1837 there have been many ingenious machines using various codes and signals. Although the first reliable machine for sending letters and figures was invented by Wheatstone in 1840, we owe much to Baudot, Hughes, Morkrum and others for their pioneering work in electrical telegraphy.

Since the telephone was invented by Bell in 1876, two completely different but complementary methods of fast communication over distance have developed, both reaching a high level of sophistication. Telecommunications has effectively removed the problem of the limited range of the human voice and apart from the enormous social benefits and changes it has brought, it has also enabled man to advance more rapidly by breaking down the main barrier to the exchange of ideas over distance.

Telegraphic communication through telegram services, privately rented telegraph circuits and the dialled Telex has developed more modestly to enable the rapid worldwide communication of graphic information, or information which is to be printed. It may be regarded as remote typewriting using teleprinter machines and the transmission speed of telegraphy is closely allied to the keying speed of teleprinter operators. Telegraphic communication is normally used for messages rather than conversation and provides a faster alternative to the postal services.

It is doubtful if any new development in recent time has had such a widespread effect on industry, commerce or the general public as the development of the electronic computer. The advent of the computer is also a milestone in the history of communications.

Man's future progress will depend to a great extent on how successfully he can communicate with computers and how efficiently they can be made to communicate with one another.

The Advent of the Computer

Much has been written about the early history of computing and this fascinating study is beyond the scope of this book. However, it is interesting to note that Charles Babbage, now widely recognised as being the father of computing, was working on the first of his mechanical calculating machines, the Difference Engine, in the early 1820s – long before the first electrical telegraph message was transmitted. Ironically it was in 1842 – only two years after Wheatstone invented the first reliable teleprinter – that the British government wrote to Babbage withdrawing all support for the development of his calculating machines. Although this may have been due to a lack of understanding on the part of government officials, it is fair to say that Babbage's ideas were too far in advance of the current technology to be of obvious practical value. However, in the concept of one of Babbage's machines, the unfinished Analytical Engine, can be seen the key elements of the modern computer. It is perhaps a measure of his genius that Babbage's ideas would lie in limbo for nearly a century until technology would allow the construction of the first automatic computer.

The modern history of digital computers began in 1939 with the work done by Howard Aiken and his associates at Harvard University. Work on their electro-mechanical Sequence Control Calculator began in 1939 and was completed in 1944. The machine was primarily designed to solve differential equations and the Mark 1 followed a sequence of programmed instructions stored on punched paper tape. A number of automatic machines of this type were constructed in universities in the early days of computing. Although they performed many useful functions, their speed of calculation was seriously limited by the relays and other electro-mechanical equipment which they used.

The second key development was the construction of the ENIAC (Electronic Numerical Integrator and Calculator) as a joint project between the University of Pennsylvania and the United States Army. This machine, which was completed in 1946, used thermionic valves rather than electro-magnetic relays and was the forerunner of the first generation of electronic digital computers. Until the discovery of the germanium transistor in 1947, electronic computers were like very large furnaces, consuming enormous quantities of electrical power and, because they were unreliable, tended to produce more heat than processed information. The ENIAC computer, for example, weighed 30 tons and occupied 1500 square feet of floor space. Its short lived 18,000 vacuum tubes produced 150 kilowatts of heat and the environment created would be more familiar to the stoker than the computer operator of today.

The early machines using valves were employed mainly for scientific and experimental work and there was then very little desire to add to the hazards of computing by passing information remotely over telegraph and telephone lines.

The next generation of electronic computers emerged in the mid-1950s. These were 'stored program' machines holding programming instructions in the main memory of the computer rather than externally on punched cards or tape. They used transistors instead of valves, had more efficient storage and consumed less power and were faster and more reliable than their predecessors. The work by Birkbeck College, London, in the development of magnetic drum storage contributed to this area of development, reflecting earlier contributions by Cambridge University and J Lyons & Co Ltd who introduced the first computer for commercial use, LEO (Lyons Electronic Office, 1951). Because they could store and process more information faster, computers were increasingly being developed for commercial data processing. The growth in the processing power of these computers was rapid and as programming skills grew an increasing number of tasks were undertaken by the computer. Many of these computer jobs such as payroll, billing, statistics and customer records were not time critical within a few days. When information for processing originated at sites remote from the central computer, the source documents were usually sent by post to the computer centre where the information was converted into a machine readable coded form and held on punched paper tape or punched cards for processing at some later, scheduled time.

Later in the 1950s, as the volume of the information grew and as jobs became more time critical, people turned towards the existing telegraph circuits and the Telex system as faster alternatives to the post for collecting information 'off-line'. This was a natural development as business people had for many years been able to automatically transmit information held on punched paper tape at 400 characters per minute and reproduce the tape if required at the distant end using standard telegraph facilities. It was also the beginning of 'data' communications as we know it today.

No infant prodigy can ever have entered the stage so modestly for there was apparently nothing dramatically new about this rather odd requirement which appeared merely to be a novel form of telegraphy. At that time few could see through the disguise and recognise that this new communication need would eventually provide, in terms of both complexity and volume of information transmitted, one of the biggest problems ever faced by communication authorities throughout the world.

Today it is possible to obtain a computer with a greater processing capability than ENIAC which can be fitted into a desk drawer. This is a measure of the advance in the technology which has taken place in the intervening years. The computer has become an integral part of the organisation of businesses of all sizes and types. A complete spectrum of types exists from the pocket calculator, through the desk-sized 'visible record computer', to machines which still need vast halls to house them.

Communicating with Computers

Complementing the development of computer systems has been the utilisation of communications to extend the power of the computer beyond the computer room, thereby allowing the benefits of the system to be more widely available geographically. This mixture of computers and communications gives the benefits of computer facilities at one's fingertips regardless of location whilst preserving on one site the expertise needed to operate the system.

A simple example is of a person dialling a connection over the telephone network to interconnect his terminal with the facilities available at the computer.

As the 'art' has developed, the communication systems have become more sophisticated and dedicated communication networks have been designed and installed.

A typical involvement with data communications is shown by the example of a large firm with numerous branch offices and several factories (*see* figure 1.1). Each of the factories could have its own medium-sized computer

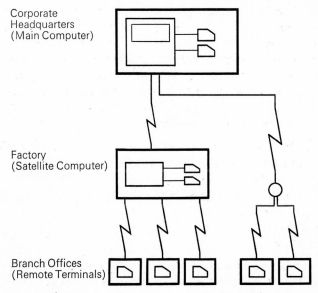

Figure 1.1   Simplified configuration of a business data communication network

which would be linked to terminals within the factory and also at adjacent branch offices. Further communications links could exist between these machines and a larger machine at the corporate headquarters. The individual terminals would be used for the collection and dissemination of the user data with the 'satellite' computer collating and editing this data and carrying out much of the local minor data processing. Major computation and corporate matters would be passed into the large headquarters' machine.

This blend of computers and communications is now taken for granted in a rapidly growing proportion of business organisations. Even the most unsophisticated of users may unconsciously be using very complex systems. For example, a small business in Manchester, England, may have a fairly simple terminal which is connected, via a local telephone call, into a computer service bureau to use one of the facilities offered by that bureau.

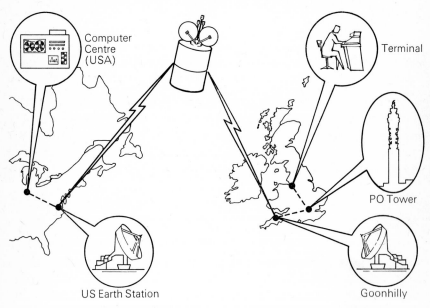

Figure 1.2   International Data Communications Connection

Unknown to the user, however, his local call takes him a very long way from home (*see* figure 1.2). His connection is to a small communications computer in Manchester which concentrates his data along with that from other local users and passes it to a larger computer in London. Here, because of the particular services being used, it is passed via a communications satellite in orbit above the Atlantic, to the service company's main computer centre in the USA. The results come back over the same links giving the user the impression that his bureau is just next door.

Some Definitions

Before considering the nature of communication with computers it is necessary to consider first of all the meaning of the terms data, information, data transmission and data communications.

Data and information

The term 'data'[1] can be defined as 'any representation, such as a figure or a letter, to which meaning can be ascribed'. 'Information' has a number of meanings; to the communications theorist, for example, it means 'any organised signal' (*see* Chapter 3). Generally, however, the term is understood to describe something which is meaningful.

A somewhat tenuous distinction can be made between data and information on the basis that 'data' is not always meaningful. For example, the group of alphanumeric characters HTG675D can be regarded as data if their significance is not understood, or information if it is recognised by someone in the UK as being the registration number of a rather ancient car which was bought in Cardiff. More precisely, statisticians use the qualified term 'raw' data to distinguish it from information which they regard as the knowledge derived from 'raw' data after it has been processed. There is, however, very little value in distinguishing between 'data' and 'information' in a book of this kind and indeed it can be confusing as we will later be concerned with transmission both prior to and after processing. The two terms will therefore be regarded as being synonymous and will be used interchangeably in this book.

Data transmission

Data transmission can be defined as 'the movement of information in coded form over some kind of electrical transmission system'. To distinguish it from telegraph transmission we may usefully add 'prior to or after processing by a computer'.

Data communications

'Data communications' has a much wider meaning than data transmission and embraces not just the electrical transmission but many other factors involved in controlling, checking and handling the movement of information in a communications-based computer system.

---

[1] Data is in fact the plural form of the noun datum. However, with common business usage datum has fallen into disuse and data has come to represent both singular and plural forms.

Data Communications Codes

The power of digital electronic computers lies in their ability to do simple tasks at very high speed. To help computers achieve high processing speeds, data is fed into computers in a logical and simplified form using binary digits. A binary digit or BIT can be defined as 'the amount of information derived from the knowledge of two equiprobables' and can be represented mathematically by a 1 or 0 or electrically by two differing conditions +ve or —ve, on or off.[1]

Computer systems' use of binary notation has required coding systems to be developed to convert alpha and numeric characters (letters and numbers) into binary notation. In this way it is possible to convert information and data which is easily recognised by humans to a form acceptable by computers. To express numeric information only four binary digits are required; and to represent alpha (letter) a further two bits must be used. A coding system that will give a full numeric and alpha character set is the Binary Coded Decimal (BCD) system with 36 characters. The structure of this system is presented in detail at Appendix 2.

An extended character set is usually required for data communications. In addition to the need to communicate letters, figures, punctuation marks, etc, a considerable number of control characters may be required. The control characters control the transmission of data, manipulate the format of a message, separate information and switch on or off devices which are connected to the communications line.

The Extended Binary Coded Decimal Interchange Code (EBCDIC) is an extension of BCD code and uses eight bits instead of six. This code is useful where an application calls for a large number of different characters. Although there are only 109 assigned meanings, there are 256 (2^8) possible combinations. The code is used mainly to transmit the eight bit bytes[2] of some computers and obviates the need for the code conversion which is often necessary between the transmission code and the code used by the computer.

International Alphabet No 5

Because of the proliferation of data transmission codes throughout the world, serious attempts have been made to standardise the codes used. The International Telegraph and Telephone Consultative Committee (CCITT), the International Standards Organisation (ISO) and national bodies have given much thought to a problem which becomes increasingly serious as the need

---

[1] For those unfamiliar with binary notation, an explanation is given in Appendix 1.

[2] A byte is 'a group of consecutive binary digits operated on as a unit by a computer'. Although the eight-bit byte is most common, the number of bits in a byte may vary between computers of different manufacturers.

grows to communicate between the data terminals of different manufacturers and between different countries.

The International Alphabet No 5 (IA 5) has been developed to satisfy the need for a standard code which will allow both sophisticated telegraphic and data communication. The new alphabet originated from a proposed American Standard Code for Information Interchange (ASCII) put forward by the American Standards Association (now the American National Standards Association) in 1962. This was developed by the CCITT and the ISO and in April 1966 the present alphabet was agreed. This was ratified by the ISO in June 1968 and at the CCITT IVth Plenary Assembly at Mar del Plata in October 1968.

Standardisation too early can adversely affect progress by impeding the introduction of new and better ideas. This argument is recognised by CCITT and ISO and the IA 5 code allows for a certain amount of flexibility enabling users to 'escape' from the normal conventions of the code by the use of special characters. Examples of the control characters used in IA 5 code are given in Appendix 3.

Telegraph codes

A number of computer-based data communications systems still make use of the long established telegraph codes. In telegraphy, the need to transmit plain language text predominates and fewer characters are needed than in data communications. Separate characters for all decimal figures and letters of the alphabet (though not necessarily capital letters and small letters) must be available, which gives a required minimum of 36 characters. Although punctuation marks, 'space', etc, could be indicated in words or combinations of these characters, this would be cumbersome and tedious for both the operator and the reader. Separate characters are therefore provided in practice for these and other purposes. Figure 1.3 shows the keyboard of a modern teleprinter, which provides for the entry of 58 different characters. The code, or alphabet, used is the five bit International Alphabet No 2 (IA 2) shown in Appendix 4 which has been widely employed for telegraphy throughout the world since it was ratified by the International Telecommunications Union (ITU) in 1932.

The number of different characters which can be derived from a code having two different states is normally given by 2^n where n is the number of different units in the code; a five unit code would therefore give 2^5 or 32 characters. However, IA 2 uses two 'shift' characters to extend the capacity of the code. The depression of a 'figures' key results in a unique character being reproduced which when transmitted informs the receiver that the characters which follow are to be interpreted as 'figures' or other 'secondary' characters.

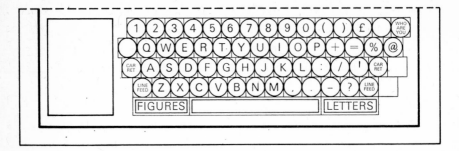

Figure 1.3   The keyboard of a modern teleprinter

Similarly 'letters' indicates that the following characters are to be letters or other 'primary' characters. In this way IA 2 offers 52 graphical (ie printable), two shift, three functional and one unallocated characters.

Efficiency of codes

The efficiency of a two condition code can be expressed by the formula:

$$E = \frac{\log_2 N}{M}$$

where   E = the efficiency of the code
         N = the number of characters or symbols required
         M = the number of bits in the code

Let us assume that in a particular application 64 different characters are required and a seven bit code is to be used. Applying the formula we have:

$$E = \frac{6}{7} = 86 \text{ per cent.}$$

If an eight bit code were to be used then the efficiency would be 6/8 or 75 per cent.

Examined in this way, the telegraph codes such as IA 2 which employ 'letter shift' and 'figure shift' characters to extend the character set seem to be extremely efficient. IA 2 is only a five unit code yet 55 different characters are available to the user. Assuming that all these characters are required this gives a coding efficiency of approximately 116 per cent.

There would appear to be scope for more development in the use of five unit codes with two or more shifts for data communications. This is not only an efficient way of encoding information as we have seen but would allow many users to utilise the relatively inexpensive terminals and facilities of the Telex network. There are, however, disadvantages in using 'shift' systems to gain encoding efficiency. If, for example, 'letter shift' and 'figure shift' were to be used for sending messages comprising a mixture of alpha and numeric information there could be a very high redundancy in the number of shift characters which would need to be sent. This could lead to a reduction in overall efficiency rather than a gain.

It would seem, therefore, that if shifts are used in the future for data transmission they will not be 'letter' or 'figure' shift but instead will be determined by consideration of the statistical probability of the occurrence of individual characters and arranging these into optimum groups. For keyboard terminals the need to change from one group to another could be a function of the terminal rather than an additional job for the operator. There is a further important factor to be considered when using shift codes which affects terminal design. Because the significance of a character or group of characters depends on a preceding shift character, that shift must somehow be stored at the receive terminal if the data is to be interpreted correctly.

Coding by statistical probability

As the amount of information transmitted continues to grow, there is likely to be an increasing amount of attention paid to reducing transmission costs by using more efficient coding methods. The development of more efficient coding for data communications is likely to be accelerated by the pressure to reduce the escalating costs involved in storing and controlling the vast and ever increasing quantities of information held on computer files.

The most promising area of development for both the file storage and data transmission codes of the future lies in codes designed according to simple statistical principles. This involves first of all deciding the character set required and then calculating the statistical probability of each character occurring. Each character is then coded into a unique combination of binary digits, the characters most likely to occur having the lowest number of bits and those least likely to occur having the highest number of bits. There are, however, synchronisation problems to be overcome before such codes with different length characters can be used for data communications.

The Nature of Data Transmission

Having organised the data into binary codes, we can now consider the problems of representing the two binary conditions of a data transmission code by suitable signals for remote transmission over communication lines. For over a hundred and thirty years, encoded information has been transmitted by simple two state signals and it is to electrical telegraphy we can most usefully turn to learn more of the nature of data transmission.

Principles of transmission

Modern telegraphy involves the use of teleprinter machines connected by land lines and/or radio systems; plate 1.1 shows a typical teleprinter for use on Telex and private telegraph circuits.

The basic functions of a transmitting teleprinter are to provide a simple means for entering information, to arrange this information into a suitable form for transmission and provide the necessary signals for onward transmission. A receiving teleprinter must be capable of responding to incoming signals and to assemble these into a printed 'receive copy' of the transmitted message.

Plate 1.1   Telegraph Teleprinter No 15

The method of entering information on a teleprinter is normally a keyboard. The basic unit of information entered is a 'character' and although numerous telegraph codes exist the most commonly used is the IA 2 (*see* Appendix 4). To arrange information entered by the keyboard shown in plate 1.1 into a form suitable for transmission, the depression of a key results in the conversion of a character into a code comprising a combination of five separate units. Each unit represents one of two possible conditions termed 'mark' or 'space', these are equivalent to the binary symbols '1' and '0' respectively.

The code must be converted into electrical signals in order to be transmitted over a line. In practice, telegraph signals are transmitted 'serially' or one element at a time. Also, because a disconnection can provide a false signal if 'space' is represented by no current flow, the 'mark' and 'space' conditions are indicated by current flowing in different directions.

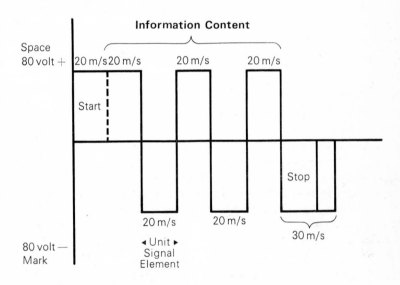

Figure 1.4   Signals transmitted to line from teleprinter

The teleprinter signals transmitted to line when the R or 4 key is depressed are shown in figure 1.4. The signals transmitted are 'digital', ie they are transmitted at pre-determined discrete levels; in this case 80 volt positive or negative – the polarity or direction of the current flow depending on whether a 'mark' or a 'space' condition is to be transmitted.

Synchronisation
When two teleprinters (or any other kind of terminal) are connected together some method of synchronisation must be employed to keep the receiver in step with the transmitter and enable communication between them. 'Asyn-

chronous' terminals such as teleprinters employ start and stop signals with opposite polarities, so that the beginning of each character can be clearly distinguished by the receiver. Synchronisation during the character is dependent on timing derived from the gearing of electric motors running at the same speed at both the transmitter and receiver. The timing starts when a transition from 'stop' to 'start' indicates the beginning of a character and stops at the end of each character. This and other methods of synchronisation are discussed more fully in Chapter 4.

Data transmission rates

There are a number of different ways in which the rate of transmission can legitimately be expressed; 'modulation rate', 'data signalling rate' and 'data (or information) transfer rate'. A great deal of confusion can be caused by the misuse of these terms and they are explained separately below.

Modulation rate

This is a term used by the communications engineer to describe the performance of a circuit in terms of the rate at which changes in the condition of the circuit can be made in a given time. More precisely it is the reciprocal of the duration of the unit signal element. The unit used in expressing modulation rate is the *'baud'* which is equal to one unit signal element per second. For example, in figure 1.5 each unit signal element is 20 ms in duration. The modulation rate is therefore:

$$\frac{1}{0.020} = 50 \text{ baud}$$

It should be noted that the expression of modulation rate in bauds does not necessarily indicate the rate at which data is transmitted.

Data signalling rate

The data signalling rate is used to express the rate at which information can be transmitted.

It is expressed in bits per second (bit/s) and for serial transmission it is defined as:

$$\left(\frac{1}{T}\right) \log_2 n$$

where T = the duration of the unit signal element in seconds and n = the number of signalling conditions.

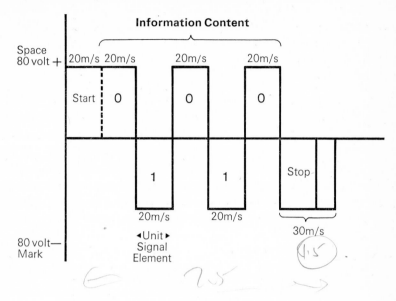

Figure 1.5 Data signalling using two voltage levels

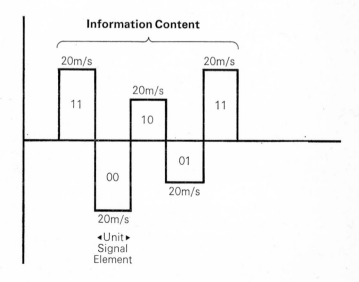

Figure 1.6 Data signalling using four voltage values

Again referring to figure 1.5 the data signalling rate would be:

$$\left(\frac{1}{0.020}\right) \times 1 = 50 \text{ bit/s}$$

It would, however, be wrong to conclude from this that a baud is the same as 1 bit/s for if more than two signalling states (multi-state signalling) were used we would have completely different answers.

Multi-state signalling can be explained by using a simple analogy.

Suppose the following data has to be passed between two persons in the same room without speaking or using written communication: 100001011001. There are, of course, many ways in which this might be achieved using two 'signal states' eg a white flag could be waved to represent binary '1' and a red flag for binary '0'.

However, if four different coloured flags were to be used, say white, red, green and yellow, further possibilities would be available. There are only four different ways of combining two binary digits 00, 01, 10 and 11, therefore the white flag could be used to represent 00, the red 01, and green 10 and the yellow 11. Thus in the example, the data 100001011001 could be sent using flags in the following order: green, white, red, red, green, red. It will be seen that with this 'four state signalling', the number of signals necessary to transmit the information is only half that necessary with two state signalling. Eight different coloured flags could be used to convey three bits of information at a time (there are eight different ways of combining three binary digits) sixteen flags for four bits and so on. Theoretically an increase in the number of flags used should result in more information being transferred with the same number of signals. There is, however, an obvious problem with coding and decoding which progressively increases; there are also technical problems which increase with the number of different states employed when multi-state electrical signalling is employed for data transmission and these are discussed later in Chapter 4.

Figure 1.6 shows a simple four state signalling system, each 20 ms unit signal element representing two binary digits. The data signalling rate would therefore be:

$$\left(\frac{1}{0.020}\right) \log_2 4 = 50 \times 2 \text{ or } 100 \text{ bit/s}$$

Note that the modulation rate is still 1/0.020 or 50 bauds.

Although serial transmission is most common in telegraphy and data transmission, parallel transmission is sometimes used, complete characters rather than separate bits being transmitted at the same time. If the simple hypothetical example in figure 1.7 is considered, it will be seen that the data signalling rate in bit/s transmitted will be a summation of the bits transmitted on each transmission path or 'channel'.[3]

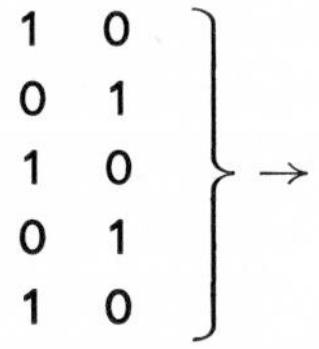

$$
\left.\begin{array}{cc}
1 & 0 \\
0 & 1 \\
1 & 0 \\
0 & 1 \\
1 & 0
\end{array}\right\} \rightarrow
$$

Figure 1.7 Serial transmission

The data signalling rate in a parallel system can therefore be expressed by:

$$
\sum_{i=1}^{i=M} \frac{1}{T_i} \log_2 N_i
$$

where M is the number of parallel channels

T_i is the duration of the unit signal element in the ith channel in seconds

and N_i is the number of signalling conditions of the modulation in the ith channel.

If in figure 1.7, there were only two signalling conditions for each of the five channels and if the duration of each unit signal element were again 20 ms we would have:

$$
\frac{1}{0.020} + \frac{1}{0.020} + \frac{1}{0.020} + \frac{1}{0.020} + \frac{1}{0.020} = 250 \text{ bit/s}
$$

---

[3] In figure 1.7 a separate wire is provided for each 'channel' but as will be seen later this is not usually the case over land lines.

Data (or information) transfer rate

Unlike data signalling rate which is used to describe the rate at which data is transmitted, 'data transfer rate' describes the rate at which data actually arrives after transmission. It is defined by CCITT as 'the average number of bits, characters or blocks per unit time passing between corresponding equipments in a data transmission system. It is expressed in terms of bits, characters or blocks per second, minute or hour'.

Frequently the corresponding equipments referred to in this definition are a 'data source' and a 'data sink'. Consider the example of an automatic paper tape transmission between two teleprinters, A and B. For the purposes of this

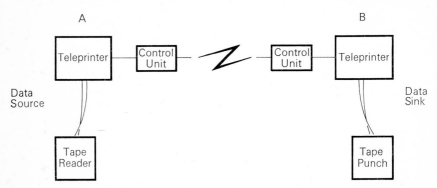

Figure 1.8   Automatic tape transmission

example, we will regard the tape reader at A as the data source and the tape punch at B as the data sink. We know from an earlier example that the data signalling rate is 50 bit/s but bits are not received at the same rate at the data sink. Assuming continuous error-free transmission 400 five unit characters would be received at the tape punch in one minute a total of 2000 bits and an average of $33\frac{1}{3}$ bit/s. The difference is accounted for by the $2\frac{1}{2}$ unit signal elements used for start/stop during transmission but which are of no use later; one third of the signals transmitted are therefore redundant.

In this simple example we could define data transfer rate as:

$$DTR = \frac{N}{T}$$

where   DTR = the data transfer rate in bit/s

          N   = the number of information bits accepted by the data sink

and   T   = the time required (in seconds) to transmit N bits.

However, we will see later (*see* Chapter 3) that the calculation of information transfer rate is not usually as simple as this and will depend upon the error rate on a particular transmission, the type of error control and line control employed and not only the number of bits but the number of complete characters which are redundant.

Although data transfer rate is a much more accurate way of describing the movement of usable information in a data communications system than any other, it cannot be stated without calculation based on knowledge of a particular system. A line or a piece of equipment cannot therefore be said to have a data transfer rate of a certain number of bits per second. For this reason, bit/s in this book will be used to indicate data signalling rate unless stated otherwise.

2 Telephone and Telex Systems

Although, increasingly, special data transmission networks are being introduced to cater for the growth in data communications, the computer user will probably always be dependent to some extent upon the existing communications networks which were set up to carry telephone and telegraph traffic. This chapter provides a general view of the characteristics of these existing networks which are of importance to the designer of a data communications system. Some additional basic material is provided for those readers who have little knowledge of telecommunications; readers who are more knowledgeable are encouraged to move on to the next section of interest.

While the needs of data communications may appear to be quite compatible with the characteristics of the telegraph system, the limitations on codes and modulation rates necessitate using the telephone system to transmit data at rates above 110 bit/s. The nature of the digital signals originating from data terminals is as foreign to the telephone system as the human voice is to the computer. Data must therefore be disguised to 'look like' speech and the ways of achieving this are discussed in Chapter 4. In this chapter the communications networks are discussed in the context for which they were designed (voice or printed information).

To clarify the discussion, many examples are given which are all drawn from current UK practice. In other countries the qualities (and sometimes the terminology) may be different, but the principles remain the same.

21

The complexity of the apparatus and transmission techniques used in tele-communications today tends to obscure the fact that the primary task of any telephone system is simply to carry intelligible sound far beyond its natural limit of audibility. An examination of the nature of sound itself is, therefore, a suitable starting point for an introduction to telephony.

Sound

Sound is the physical disturbance of air (or some other medium) which when received by the ear can be transmitted to the brain by the nervous system. Sound is produced by vibrations which cause compression and rarefaction of the air. The air vibrates with the sound source and the diaphragm of the ear will, if it is within range, vibrate in sympathy. The variations of air pressure which produce sound can be plotted graphically against time as shown in figure 2.1.

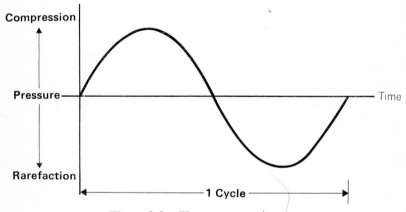

Figure 2.1   The pure sound wave

In this example the wave form is sinusoidal or 'pure'. Only one complete variation between compression and rarefaction is shown; this is termed a 'cycle'.

Pitch (frequency)

In music, notes are often referred to as being 'high' or 'low'. Perhaps this is because of the position of the notes on a musical scale or the tendency of some tenors to 'reach' for a note by standing on their toes! The fact is that so-called 'high' notes have a greater number of cycles in a given time than do 'low' notes. Middle 'C' at concert pitch for example has a frequency of 270 cycles per second (270 Hertz), while the C above middle 'C' has a frequency of 540 Hertz (Hz). The relationship between pitch and wavelength can be best illustrated by an example. If in figure 2.1 the cycle shown took 0.001 of a second to complete and were to be continually repeated, a note of 1000 cycles per second (1000 Hz) would be produced. If this took place at normal room temperature, the velocity of sound would be 340 metres/s; the 'length' of each cycle would therefore be 340/1000 or 0.34 metres; the 'wavelength' of a 1000 Hz note therefore would be 0.34 metres through air at room temperature.

Volume

Volume or loudness is determined by the 'amplitude' of the waveform or the height of the peaks of compression and rarefaction. In figure 2.2, the two soundwaves have the same frequency or pitch but (B) has a greater volume than (A).

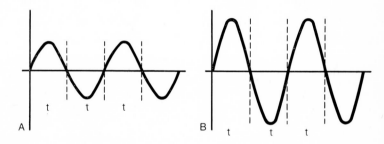

Figure 2.2   Frequency with two levels of amplitude

Tone

A person who is tone deaf might have difficulty in hearing or reproducing correct pitch. This is a fairly common malady which in no way affects the afflicted person's ability to speak or sing. Indeed tone deaf people are usually blissfully unaware of any problem and seem gifted with painfully robust voices. In contrast, the vast majority of people are able to distinguish between the characteristic sounds of say a dinner gong and a violin, or a male and female voice. This ability to tell the difference between 'tones' is of more fundamental importance to human beings for it is only in doing so that we are able to communicate.

Differences in the quality of sound are produced by variations in the funda-mental waveform (the pitch). These variations are produced by the introduction of additional frequencies known as 'harmonics' or 'overtones'. For example, if a middle 'C' is produced by a piano, the fundamental frequency is caused by the middle 'C' string vibrating 270 times a second. However, the outer edges of the string, the frame and wooden components also vibrate at different frequencies to produce harmonics providing the characteristic tone, not only of the type of instrument, but of the particular piano being played.

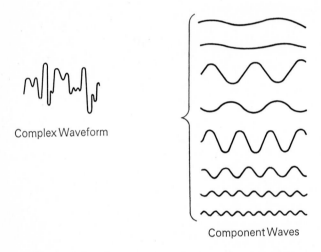

Complex Waveform

Component Waves

Figure 2.3   Components of a complex waveform

Intelligibility

With speech communications, we are primarily concerned with intelligibility. Intelligibility can be defined as 'a percentage of simple ideas correctly received over the system used for transmitting or reproducing speech'. There are problems in measuring intelligibility; this is due to the fact that the human brain has an error correction capability and, although we may miss sections from words or sentences in a telephone conversation, our brains have the ability to fill in some of the gaps and interpret the meaning. Let us assume that the following sentence is spoken during a telephone conversation – 'Now is Tom foot all goot men toot compt taid party'. This sentence would probably be corrected by the listener without too much difficulty and perhaps unconsciously into the familiar sentence – 'Now is the time for all good men to come to the aid of the party'. Many interesting tests have been made using 'logatoms' which are specially constructed sentences using words or syllables which contain no information whatsoever but are extremely useful in measuring intelligibility.

The intelligibility of the human voice is contained within the harmonics produced; most of the intelligence in human speech occurs from between 125 and 2000 Hz – a 'bandwidth' of about 2000 Hz. The CCITT recommend a circuit responding to frequencies between 300 Hz and 3400 Hz as being adequate for the purposes of telephony, giving a high degree of speech intelligibility.

The Telephone Instrument

At this point we can make the transition from the acoustic world of man to the electronic world of telecommunications by introducing the telephone instrument itself. This consists of two 'transducers' which convert the air pressure waves of sound to electrical impulses (the transmitter) and vice versa (the receiver). Typically, the transmitter comprises a diaphragm which vibrates in sympathy with the sound waves and causes variations in mechanical pressure on carbon granules contained in a capsule. These pressure variations cause changes of electrical resistance and the production of electrical signals which are an analogue of the sound waveforms.

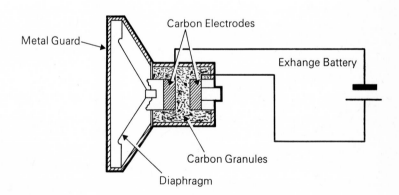

Figure 2.4   Telephone transmitter

In reverse, variations in electrical current in a line are passed through small magnetic coils in the telephone receiver which vary the magnetic attraction of a diaphragm. This vibrates in response, generating pressure waves in the air which are a sound analogue of the electrical waveform.

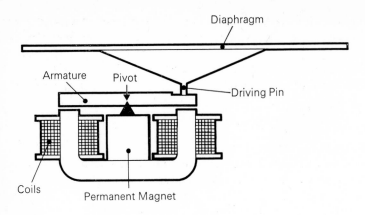

Figure 2.5   Telephone receiver

Telephone Local Line Distribution

In the UK, there are over 12 million telephone customers connected to over 6000 telephone exchanges or switching points. In the early days of the UK telephone system, the pairs of wires needed for each customer were provided by overhead wires carried on telegraph poles and connected to derricks on the roof of the exchange building (*see* plate 2.1).

Later, cables were carried by the same poles – each cable serving a number of customers connected at a 'distribution point'.

Today the most common method of connecting a customer to a telephone exchange is shown in figure 2.6.

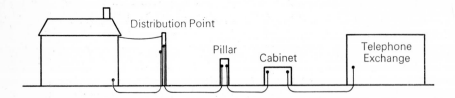

Figure 2.6   Telephone connection to exchange

The telephone exchange location is carefully selected to minimise the cost of cabling and to ensure that there are no disproportionately long lines. The exchange area is divided up into a number of 'cabinet' areas, each cabinet

Plate 2.1 Derrick on Bank Exchange, London (late 19th century)

having a maximum capacity of 800 pairs of wires. A cabinet serves a number of pillars, each with up to 200 pairs of wires, and these in turn have a number of distribution points connected to them. Each distribution point normally serves up to fifteen customers but this can be increased if shared service customers are connected.

Plate 2.2 shows the typical overhead distribution points, pillars and cabinets used in the UK. Figure 2.7 shows the distribution of cables within a telephone exchange area.

Distributing local lines in the way described has a number of advantages apart from the economic provision of lines and cables. Fault location is

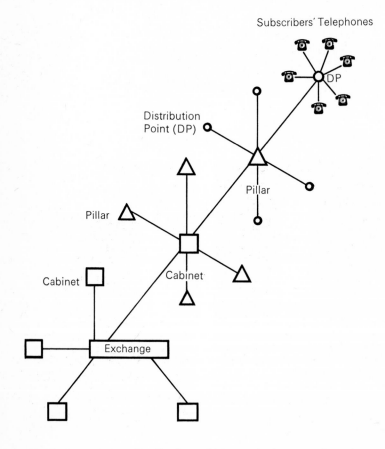

Figure 2.7   Cable distribution within a telephone exchange area

Plate 2.2a   Typical distribution pole

Plate 2.2b   PO Pillar   **Plate 2.2c**   PO Cabinet

simplified by using a cabinet and pillar system rather than a number of underground cable joints. The system is flexible in that spare line capacity can be more simply diverted to those locations in a telephone area where it is most needed. If a fault does occur in an underground cable, say between a cabinet and a pillar, a spare pair of wires can be allocated quickly by simple wire strapping. The faulty pair of wires in the cable can then be repaired later when it is convenient and economic.

It is becoming increasingly common to connect a customer's premises by an underground feed rather than overhead wires. Although this is more costly to provide, the fault liability of the 'local end' is reduced considerably. Many large business premises have internal distribution points or even internal pillars within their own premises.

Cable Pressurisations

Water or moisture in an underground cable can cause a major disruption in service to a large number of customers.

A defective sheath may not cause a fault for a considerable period of time under dry conditions, but will rapidly cause a cable breakdown under wet or damp conditions. One very effective way of overcoming this problem is to pressurise the cables by pumping in dry air. Sheath faults can then be identified by a loss of pressure and the air pressure in the cable will keep out the moisture until the sheath is repaired. The British Post Office have been using gas pressurisation since 1953. At first only the main trunk cables (carrying 'trunk' circuits) and those between exchanges carrying junction circuits were pressurised but since 1960 the pressurisation scheme was extended to those local cables between exchanges and cabinets. By 1974, some 96.4 per cent of trunk and junction circuits were pressurised. In the local network, pressurisation is complete at all exchanges over 2000 lines and of exchanges with over 500 lines some 75 per cent of the cables are pressurised between the exchanges and the cabinet.

Gas pressurisation is proving extremely effective, in 1963-4 the number of faults on trunk cables per 100 kilometres was 3.8 and 6.3 on junction cables. In 1974 those figures were 0.7 and 1.8 respectively.

Automatic Telephone Switching Systems

The basic requirements of an automatic system are:

– Apparatus must be provided at the subscriber's instrument to enable him to signal his requirements.

– Apparatus must be provided at the exchange to respond to these signals and to select the distant connection required.

– A signal (ringing current) must be applied to the called instrument to ring the subscriber's bell.

– When the called subscriber answers, the ringing current must be disconnected, a circuit completed for conversation, and the calling subscriber's meter operated so that a charge may be raised for the call.

– The automatic apparatus required for the speech path must be held in position during the setting-up period and throughout the period of conversation.

– An engaged line must be guarded against intrusion to prevent 'double connections'.

– At the end of the call, the automatic apparatus must be released in order that it may be used by other subscribers.

In addition to these requirements, it will be desirable to indicate to the caller the progress of the call. This is accomplished by means of distinctive 'tones' which are applied to the line under the following conditions:

– When the automatic switches are ready for the subscriber to dial (dialling tone).

– When the called subscriber is being rung (ringing tone).

– If the called subscriber's line is engaged (engaged tone).

– If the called subscriber's line is unobtainable (number unobtainable or NU tone).

– If the equipment is engaged as distinct from called number engaged (equipment engaged tone).

The telephone dial

The telephone dial is a signalling device which simply makes and breaks the line circuit and sends pulses of direct current to the exchange. Figure 2.8 shows the simplified make/break action of a telephone dial.

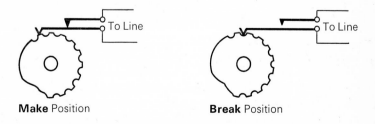

Make Position   **Break** Position

Figure 2.8   Transmission of dialled pulses

If, say, the digit 3 is dialled the return action of the dial will cause three pulses of direct current at a rate of 10 pulses per second to be transmitted; no pulses are sent during the forward action of the dial. The signalling is 'anisochronous', ie the make and break signals have different durations – $33\frac{1}{3}$ millisecond make and $66\frac{2}{3}$ millisecond break. There must be a delay between the series of pulses (pulse trains) so that the switching equipment at the exchanges is given time to operate. This 'inter train pause' (of some 700 milliseconds) is made up of the time it takes for the user to select the next digit and rotate the dial and also an inbuilt or 'lost motion' period in the dial mechanism.

Exchange Apparatus

The backbone of the telephone system in the UK, like many other countries, is still based upon electro-mechanical apparatus. The 'Strowger' electro-mechanical switch has the unusual distinction of being invented by a Kansas undertaker in 1889, and because of its simplicity and low cost has until recent years been the main element of most telephone systems.

It has, however, been recognised for many years that the Strowger 'step by step' telephone systems have reached the limit of their technological development. Strowger's main limitations are slowness, limited facilities, inflexibility, high cost of maintenance and the tendency to introduce noise into the telephone system.

The two-motion switch is the basic unit of the Strowger system

The two-motion selector shown in plate 2.3 is a typical 'group' or intermediate selector. It responds to dialled pulses by stepping in a vertical direction and automatically hunts horizontally over a number of contacts to select a free outlet to the next switching stage. Figure 2.9 shows one bank of a simple two-motion selector which consists of ten semi-circular rows or 'levels' each with ten contacts or 'outlets' giving a total of 100 outlets.

Two wires are required for the transmission path and each bank consists of double contacts separated by insulation. In practice, at least two banks and 'wipers' are provided, one set being for the testing of outlets for 'busy' conductors and for guarding against intrusion on an established call. A third bank of ten contacts is provided which doubles the number of outlets from 100 to 200.

Strowger Systems

Two types of Strowger system are used, known in the UK as 'Non-director' and 'Director'.

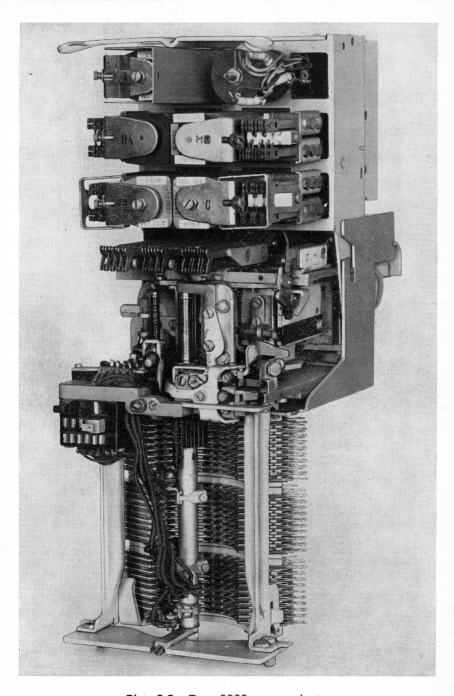

Plate 2.3 Type 2000 group selector

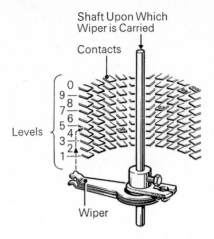

Figure 2.9   Two-motion selector (Strowger)

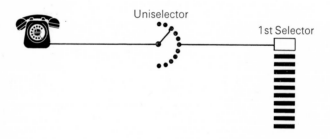

Figure 2.10   Seizure of 1st selector (Dial Tone Returned)

Non-director systems

Non-director systems employ switching which responds directly to the digits dialled by a caller. This can best be illustrated by a simple example. Consider a caller dialling another number on his own telephone exchange 45426.

When the caller lifts his telephone, a simple switch (typically a uniselector) hunts automatically for a free 1st selector which on being seized returns dialling tone to the caller (*see* figure 2.10). On receipt of the first dialled digit,

(4) the 1st selector, which is a two-motion switch, steps vertically to level 4 and hunts automatically in a horizontal rotary action for a 2nd selector (*see* figure 2.11). This responds to the next digit dialled (5) in the same way and seizes a free 3rd selector which accepts the third digit and seizes a final selector. The final selector is the last link in the step by step chain of switches. Unlike the group selectors, which precede it, the final selector does not hunt automatically but steps both vertically and horizontally in response to the last pair of dialled digits (26). In the example the 6th contact of level 2 is connected to the called customer (45426) and, if this is free, the final selector will apply ringing current to the called party's line to ring the bell and return a ringing tone to the caller.

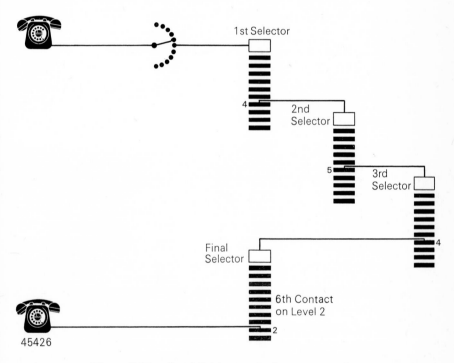

Figure 2.11   Establishing a telephone connection

A number of exchanges in a non-director area can be linked together to have a common or 'linked numbering scheme'. Such arrangements are common when there is a strong community of interest between the areas served by the exchanges. Figure 2.12 shows a simple scheme with a 'main' exchange and one satellite exchange having a common four digit linked numbering scheme.

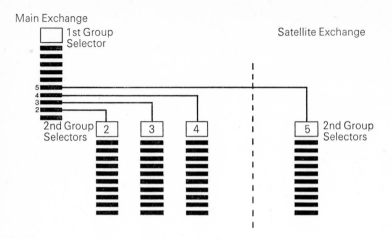

Figure 2.12   Satellite exchange arrangement

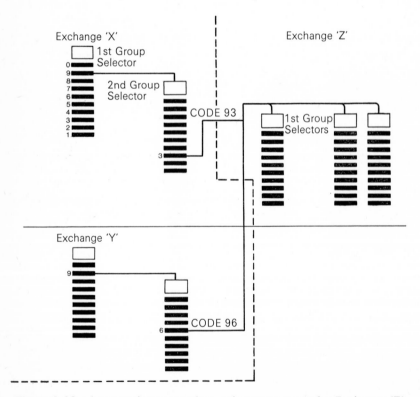

Figure 2.13   Inter-exchange routing code arrangement for Exchange 'Z'

In this example, the whole area actually covered by two exchanges would appear to be served by only one. All customers' numbers on satellite 'A' would begin with 5 and numbers on the main exchange with 2, 3 or 4. Special arrangements are necessary for one number on a satellite to call another number on the same satellite; these usually employ equipment which can discriminate between the type of call being made ensuring that each connection is made in the most efficient way possible.

In order to obtain other exchanges outside a linked numbering scheme, it is necessary to dial special codes. It will be seen from figure 2.13 that the code dialled for a particular exchange (Z) will depend on the routing digits required by the originating exchanges (X and Y).

Director systems

The high telephone density of very large cities presents a number of switching problems. In London, for example, there are over 80 exchanges with up to 10,000 lines each within a five mile radius from the centre. The majority of calls between customers in the London area pass over 'junction' routes between exchanges. In these circumstances, it is necessary to simplify the dialling arrangements between exchanges and ideally all customers within the system should dial the same digits to reach a particular number. It is also vital that the system should be flexible. It should allow for the changes in junction routings – which become necessary when communication patterns change or junction failures occur – without seriously disrupting the system.

The non-director system does not supply an efficient answer to the problems of providing simplified dialling and increased flexibility which are posed in very large cities. A different system, the 'director system' therefore needs to be used.

Figure 2.14 shows a number of exchanges linked by a 'tandem' exchange (T). A tandem exchange has no telephone numbers and its sole purpose is to provide an intermediate switching point for connections between other exchanges.

A call from exchange A to exchange E requires four routing digits – 69 to reach the tandem exchange T and 47 to step the tandem switches to select a junction to E. Similarly a call from B to E requires the routing digits 72 47. Although every exchange requires different routing digits to reach the objective exchange in a director system, the customers dial the same three digit code (628 in this example). This requires 'translation' from the digits actually dialled and those which are necessary to route the call. The equipment which performs this function is called a director and gives the system its name.

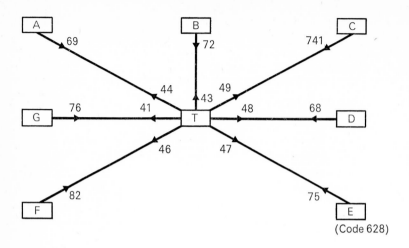

NB In practice direct routes are provided between exchanges where this is economic.

Tandem Routes ➤——◀

Figure 2.14   A simplified 'director' area with one tandem

Figure 2.15 shows the basic elements of a director exchange. Returning to the previous example, let us assume that the diagram represents exchange 'A' and a customer on this exchange calls a number on exchange 'E' – 628 7733. On receiving dialling tone (from the 'A' digit selector) the customer dials and the first digit (6) operates the 'A' digit selector vertically, which then hunts horizontally to find a free director. The director identifies the exchange required from the next two digits (28) and translates these into a maximum of 6 routing digits; in this case only 4 are required (6947). The numerical digits dialled (7733) are stored in the director unchanged and the digits 6947 7733 are sent from the director in pulse form at 10 pulses per second. The first code selector responds to the digit 6 and selects a second code selector which steps to level 9 and selects a route to the tandem exchange. Two-motion switches in the tandem exchange step to levels 4 and 7 respectively and select a junction to the objective exchange 'E' which accepts the numerical digits and connects the call. The 'A' digit selector and the director release when the last pulse has been sent out.

Changes in routing can be arranged fairly simply by changing the strapping on the translation field (*see* figure 2.15).

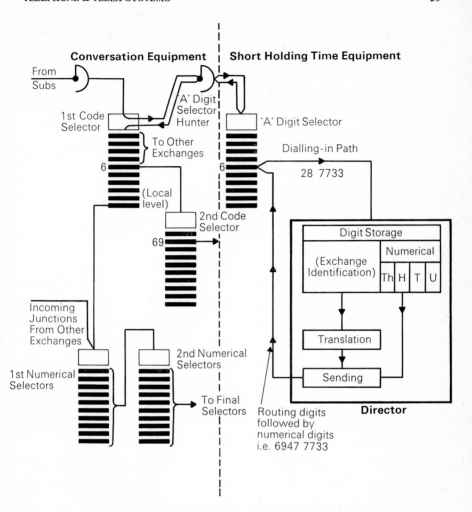

Figure 2.15   Basic elements of director exchange

Crossbar Exchanges

The Crossbar system also employs electro-mechanical technology; the first patent being filed in the US in 1916. Much of the subsequent development work was done in Sweden where the first Crossbar exchange opened in 1926. Crossbar systems are capable of further development and are superior to Strowger in many respects. Although it is recognised that all telephone exchanges will eventually be electronic, the production of electronic equipment will not be sufficient to meet the vast expansion of the UK telephone services over the next few years. Crossbar equipment is, therefore, being used as an intermediate technology for some new exchanges and for switching within the trunk networks.

Principles of operation of a Crossbar exchange

Crossbar is different to Strowger both in the equipment used and the method of operation. There are no uniselectors or two-motion selectors and the equipment does not operate step by step in response to dial pulses.

Figure 2.16 shows the simplified elements in an 'own exchange' call on a Crossbar exchange. The sequence of operation is as follows:

– When a caller lifts his receiver his line is automatically connected to a transmission relay group (TRG) which seizes a free register; dial tone is then returned to the caller.

– When the caller dials, the digits are stored in the register until the complete number has been received.

– The required number is then tested by the line marker and, if free, a connection is then established from the transmission relay group via the switching stages in the router and distributor to the required number.

– The register and line marker are then released.

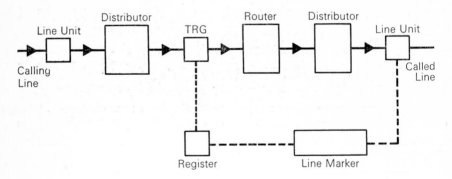

Figure 2.16 Elements of an 'own' exchange call on a Crossbar exchange

The distributors and router do not operate in response to the dial. Connections are established by control circuits. The terminal points are marked, all the possible paths between the two points are examined and if one is available it is selected. Figure 2.17 shows the switching arrangements for the Crossbar TXK1 exchange manufactured by Plessey.

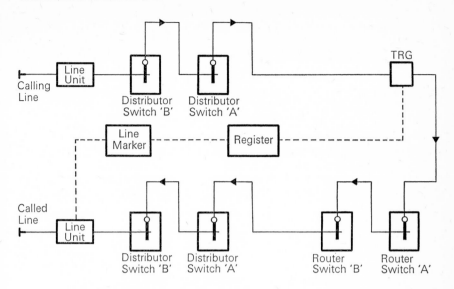

Figue 2.17   Switching arrangements of a TXK1 exchange

Plate 2.4   A Crossbar switch

Plate 2.4 shows a typical Crossbar switch.

It will be seen that at the top of the switch there are a number of electro-magnets; these are known as 'bridge magnets'. Another group of magnets, the 'select' magnets can be seen at the ends of the switch. The whole switch forms a matrix of relay contacts with 10 inlets and 28 outlets. To connect any inlet to any outlet requires the operation of the bridge and select magnets which give the required co-ordinates in the matrix.

Electronic Exchanges

Electronic exchanges have a number of advantages over their electro-mechanical predecessors. Although more expensive initially, they should eventually become cheaper to produce. The equipment is cheaper to maintain, more reliable, faster in operation and enables provision of new facilities and services at little extra cost.

Electronic exchanges can be designed using two fundamentally different techniques. These are known as space division (SD) and time division (TD).

In space division systems, a separate physical path is maintained for each speech conversation; both Strowger and Crossbar systems are therefore in this category.

Time division systems do not require a separate physical path, each con-versation being converted into digital pulses and interleaved with other conversations, using time division multiplexing (TDM) techniques, into a single digital stream. Pulse code modulation (PCM) described in Chapter 4 employs this principle.

The electronic exchanges in use today in the UK use space division techniques. More properly they should be described as semi-electronic, for a fundamental component which they use (the reed relay) is in fact a sophisticated electro-mechanical device.

The reed relay contact unit

Plate 2.5 shows the construction of a typical reed contact unit.

The unit shown has a 'make' action which brings the two gold plated contacts together in the operated position. The tensioned magnetic alloy reeds are sealed in a glass tube filled with nitrogen at atmospheric pressure. The two reeds overlap slightly and are separated by a few thousandths of an inch, the contact points being gold plated to reduce contact resistance and prolong the contact life.

The contact units are mounted within magnetic coils (*see* plate 2.5). When a current is passed through the coil a magnetic field is set up along the axis of the reeds causing the free ends to be attracted and the contact to be made.

Disconnection of the current causes the reed contacts to separate and break the circuit. The switching time of a reed relay is in the order of one milli-second. Reed relays are used in the switching network crosspoints which are a fundamental feature of space division electronic exchanges.

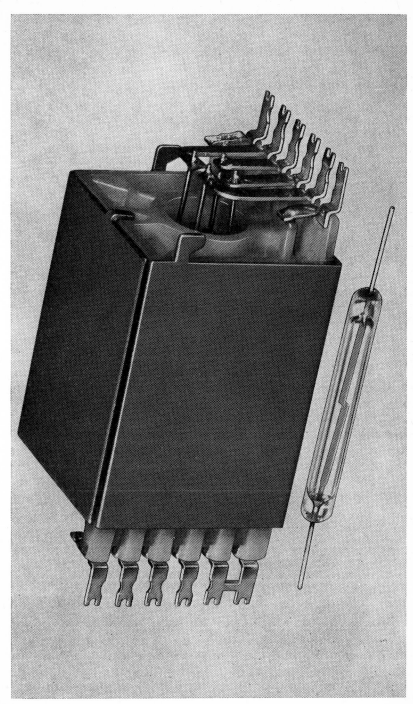

Plate 2.5 Contact units mounted in magnetic coils

In the simple example in figure 2.18, either one of two inlets can be connected
to either one of two outlets. For example, if relay 'A' is operated, its two reed
relay contacts will link the positive and negative wires of inlet 1 and outlet 1
(in practice a fourth wire P is provided). Connections between inlets and
outlets are referred to as crosspoints.

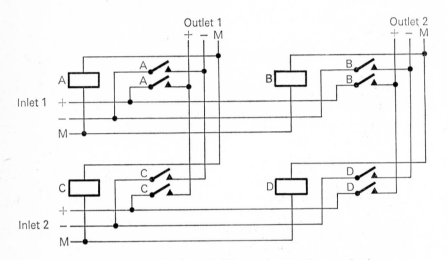

Figure 2.18   A simple switching network using reed relays

Call control
The methods used to set up a path through the switching network to establish
a connection vary according to the type of exchange. There are, however, two
main principles of operation, these are 'stored program control' and 'marker
control with end-to-end selection'.

Stored program control
With this type of control, the functions of the control equipment are similar
to that of a computer. All terminations on the exchange are interrogated
(scanned) at frequent intervals, usually fractions of a second, and data on the
state of the termination is passed to the common control equipment. Here it is
processed and associated with data on services required by the termination
or a demand for a connection to it. Having processed the data and determined
the requirement, the control then examines the state of the switching network
and, if a path is available, performs the required switching operations. Special
requirements relating to connections and services are programmed into the
equipment and may be altered as required. The range of services that can be
provided by this type of control is dependent upon the capacity of the
program and in some circumstances the availability of peripheral units.

Marker control with end-to-end selection

Stored program control is expensive to provide in small units and is profitable only when the exchange is sufficiently large for the cost to be spread over a comparatively large number of connections. Its use is, therefore, confined to the larger electronic exchanges. For smaller electronic exchanges and units of electronic equipment, it has been necessary to employ a simpler means of control and 'marker control with end-to-end selection' is used.

This method involves assessing, for each call, the location of the two terminal points in the exchange switching network, marking them electrically, and then by means of control equipment associated with the network, selecting and switching a path through it. Common control units are comparatively small and have only a limited capacity for program variations.

Although control flexibility varies from one exchange to another, all types provide complete numbering flexibility within electronic units and considerable flexibility in providing standard facilities.

The Subscriber Trunk Dialling (STD) System

STD provides customers on the telephone network with facilities to dial trunk calls automatically without the assistance of an operator. From the users' viewpoint it extends the facilities of director systems to a national level.

Each customer has a national number comprising 8, 9 or 10 digits. The first digit of a national number is always 0 and is used to route the call from the local exchange to special equipment called a 'register translator' at a 'Group Switching Centre' (GSC). This equipment accepts the remaining digits dialled, translates the information received into the routing digits necessary to connect the call and provides charging information when the call is satisfactorily established as shown in figure 2.19.

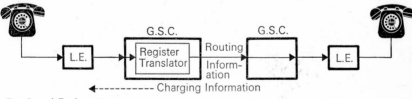

L.E. — Local Exchange
G.S.C. — Group Switching Centre

Figure 2.19   Basic elements of a STD call

Translation of the dialled information is necessary because the routing of a call will vary according to the place from which it is originated. However, the same national number for a customer is dialled from any exchange in the country with STD facilities. The register translator must, therefore, identify the number required from the digits dialled and translate or change these in order to route the call. Figure 2.20 shows the simplified elements of a register translator.

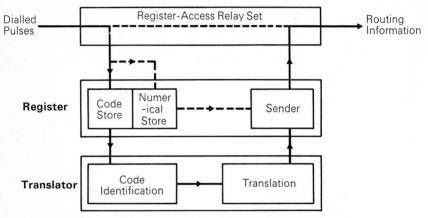

Figure 2.20   Principle of the register translator

A number of different designs of register translator are in use and plate 2.6 shows one type which uses magnetic drum equipment. These have a capacity of 1450 translations.

Plate 2.6   Magnetic drum – GRACE (Group Routing and Automatic Charging Equipment)

The STD network

The STD routing and transmission plan used in the UK is shown in figure 2.21.

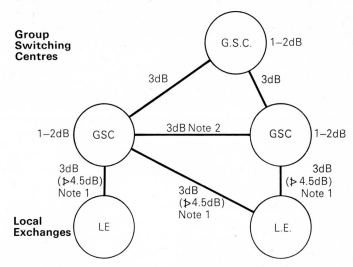

Note 1: Limits in brackets refer to unamplified circuits
Note 2: This limit may rise to 7·5dB on circuits carrying terminal traffic only
Note 3: Switching loss at terminal local exchange is included in allowance for
        subscriber's line and instrument

Figure 2.21   STD routing and transmission plan (2-wire switched)

There are some 360 Group Switching Centres (GSCs) in the trunk network. Transmission losses prevent more than two GSCs being connected in tandem (series) on an STD call. The worst connection between local exchanges from a transmission planning point of view is shown in figure 2.22.

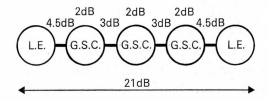

Figure 2.22   Extreme connection between Local Exchanges (L.E.)

The figures shown are nominal planning values at the test frequency of 800 Hz and in practice figures are likely to be better or slightly worse than this. The losses shown at the GSCs are due to the fact that, although the circuits between GSCs are four-wire the switches used in GSCs can only switch two wires. This necessitates four-wire, to two-wire conversion and vice versa and the hybrid transformers used for this conversion introduce losses of between 1 and $1\frac{1}{2}$ dB.

STD dialling limitations

In 1974 98 per cent of telephone customers in the UK had STD facilities. Although this is a great step forward to a fully automated inland telephone network, many of these customers cannot yet be given the full dialling facilities they need. The reason for this is that the provision of group switching centres with their special equipment and the implementation of an STD network are only the first stage in the Post Office plan to fully automate the system. At present dialling access may be restricted for any one or all of the following reasons:

- No call can be made which requires more than two GSCs in tandem.
- Some types of register translators (used in non-director areas) can only provide five or six translated routing digits. This is insufficient to route some calls.
- Such types of register translators can only provide 300 translations whereas over 700 translations are required to route calls to every part of the country.

A great deal of work is done continuously in providing dialling access to where it is most needed and only a small percentage of trunk calls cannot be dialled by customers with STD access.

The transit network

The transit network is a superimposed network designed primarily to overcome the dialling limitations described above. The network is being gradually expanded and by 1978 will allow any customer to dial any other customer in the UK.

This new network is designed to incorporate:

- Improved transmission standards.
- Transit registers to overcome the limitation of register translators.
- Faster signalling and switching to reduce call set up times.
- Automatic alternative routing of calls.

The transit network will therefore provide better overall performance on the long distance calls which must be provided over multiple links.

Local exchanges will continue to be directly connected to GSCs and the majority of trunk calls will still be two-wire switched and carried over direct

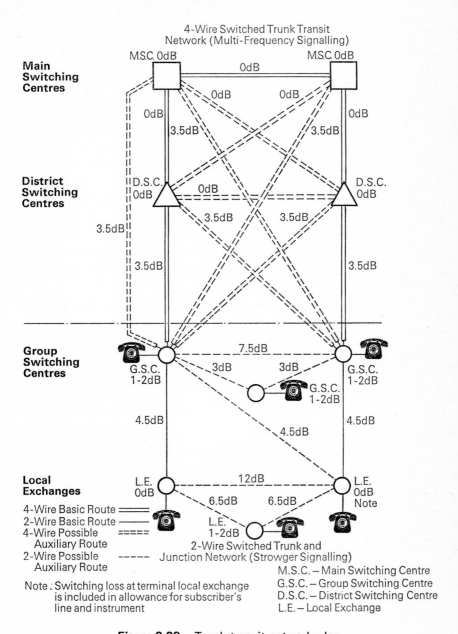

Main Switching Centres

4-Wire Switched Trunk Transit Network (Multi-Frequency Signalling)

M.S.C. 0dB   0dB   M.S.C. 0dB

0dB   0dB   0dB   0dB

0dB

3.5dB   3.5dB

District Switching Centres

D.S.C. 0dB   0dB   D.S.C. 0dB

3.5dB   3.5dB   3.5dB

3.5dB   3.5dB

Group Switching Centres

7.5dB

G.S.C. 1-2dB   3dB   3dB   G.S.C. 1-2dB

G.S.C. 1-2dB

4.5dB   4.5dB   4.5dB

Local Exchanges

L.E. 0dB   12dB   L.E. 0dB Note

4-Wire Basic Route
2-Wire Basic Route
4-Wire Possible Auxiliary Route
2-Wire Possible Auxiliary Route

6.5dB   6.5dB

L.E. 1-2dB

2-Wire Switched Trunk and Junction Network (Strowger Signalling)

Note: Switching loss at terminal local exchange is included in allowance for subscriber's line and instrument

M.S.C. — Main Switching Centre
G.S.C. — Group Switching Centre
D.S.C. — District Switching Centre
L.E. — Local Exchange

Figure 2.23 Trunk transit network plan

circuits between GSCs. However, new 'transit' exchanges with four-wire switching and additional translation facilities are being provided, together with a separate network of trunk circuits. The trunk transit network plan is shown in figure 2.23.

The four-wire switching obviates two-wire/four-wire conversion and there are therefore no switching losses introduced at the transit switching centres. A call routed over the completed UK national network will have a design maximum overall loss between different local exchanges of 16dB (LE-GSC-DSC-MSC-MSC-DSC-GSC-LE), plus the switching loss of 1-2dB at each GSC.

Transit signalling and switching

One of the problems with multi-link calls is the call set up time. If this is too high, customers will assume that there is a fault condition and prematurely release the call. Call set up time can be defined as the total time necessary to connect the call but the important factor is the waiting time after the last digit is dialled and a tone (ring tone, engaged tone, number unobtainable tone) being received from the network.

The signalling systems in general use today are designed to operate Strowger step by step switches and therefore dial pulses or their voice frequency equivalent are transmitted one at a time to line at a rate of ten pulses per second.

The transit network employs faster parallel signalling between registers using a combination of two frequencies out of six. Applying the permutation formulae:

$$\frac{M!}{n!\,(M-n)!} \quad (M = \text{total number of states}: n = \text{required number of states})$$

this gives $\dfrac{6!}{2!\,(6-2)!}$ or 15 different signal combinations

These are used in a forward direction for the decimal digits, to describe the class of service (coin box customer, general customer and operator) and one group of two frequencies is used to send a 'prefix' signal. In the reverse direction, a separate group of frequencies is used to return signals such as 'number received' or 'congestion'. Crossbar equipment is used to give faster switching than would be possible by using Strowger.

Although the inter-communication between registers will be in parallel form the seizure, release, and supervisory functions of the line will normally use a more conventional sequential single frequency signalling system.

STD charging principles

There are over 6000 telephone exchanges in the UK and to arrange separate charging on a point to point basis would have proved both complex and costly. Since 1958, the country has been divided up into some 630 charging groups; although the average group area is roughly 150 square miles, this varies considerably depending on telephone density and geographic considerations.

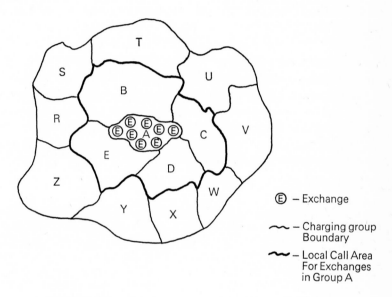

Figure 2.24   Charge group arrangement for Area A

A typical charge group is shown in figure 2.24. Calls within the charge group and normally calls to adjacent charge groups are termed 'local calls' and are given the longest time for a unit fee. Trunk calls, ie those outside the local call area, are charged according to the distance between the two charge group measuring points, although over 56 kms the cost is independent of distance. Figure 2.25 shows a typical distribution of calls in a telephone exchange. Generally there is a peak period between 9.30 a.m. and 11.30 a.m. and a lesser peak in the afternoon.

This pattern is reflected in the call charges. The peak period 9.0 a.m. to 1.00 p.m. attracts the highest rate, the 'standard' rate is 8.0 a.m. to 9.0 a.m. and 1.00 p.m. to 6.0 p.m. while the 'cheap' rate is 6.0 p.m.-8.0 a.m. and all day Saturday and Sunday. Substantial savings may be made by both speech and

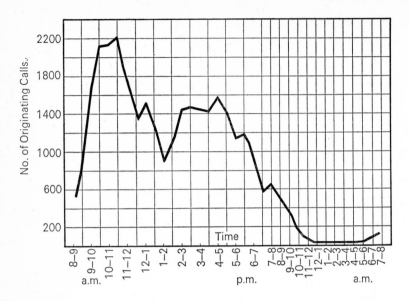

Figure 2.25   Typical 24-hour distribution of calls in a 3600 line exchange

data customers in using the cheap period, where charges can be as little as 20 per cent of those made during the peak period. A special 'Midnight Line' facility is offered which allows unlimited inland calls to be made between 12.0 midnight and 6.0 a.m.

The Telex Service

The Telex service is a switched telegraph system which has its own exchanges and uses teleprinters instead of telephones. In 1974, there were 49,000 Telex customers in the UK and the service is growing at a rate of 12 per cent per annum.

The service is designed to offer a means whereby printed messages can be sent quickly and economically between any Telex customers within and between most countries in the world.

The speed of Telex

The design speed of Telex is geared to the typing speed of a teleprinter operator. This varies but is unlikely to exceed the maximum speed of the service; this is normally expressed as either $66\frac{2}{3}$ words per minute (where a word equals five characters plus a space) or as 400 characters per minute. Each character comprises five units of information (in IA 2 code), but in order to transmit this information each character must be preceded by a start signal and a stop signal, the latter being one and a half times the duration of the other signals (see Chapter 1). At 400 characters per minute the maximum modulation rate required of the circuits employed by Telex must therefore be:

$$\frac{400 \times 7.5}{60} = 50 \text{ baud}$$

The use of Telex

Telex can be used:

— In a conversational mode between teleprinter terminals; this is particularly useful on international calls to foreign countries where the printed word may be easier to translate than the spoken word.

— The transmission or reception of messages where a reply is not expected at once. In this mode, the Telex system is effectively a speedier postal service.

— For 'Broadcast' of messages. Using the UK Post Office 'Multelex' service a message may be 'broadcast' to a number of points by the transmission of one message. Alternatively a message may be stored on punched paper tape and by separately dialling the required Telex stations the message can be sent to a number of stations consecutively.

— As a 'receive only' terminal in circumstances where it is important only to receive up-to-date information.

— For the transmission or reception of messages in a prescribed format. 'Sprocket feed' facilities can be provided for use with specially designed stationery.

The use of Telex for Data Communication

A major advantage of using Telex for data transmission is the fact that most large businesses use Telex anyway for message traffic; there is, therefore, no additional annual rental, the only charge being for the additional time used on the system. However, although the Telex system is wholly suited for some types of low volume data communication, there can be problems. The IA 2 code, which is normally used, employs two 'shifts' to derive both letters and figures and, although this is efficient for ordinary administrative message transmission, a data message may contain a large number of contiguous letters and figures. In these cases a great deal of transmission time may be absorbed in sending 'shift' characters. This can be abbreviated to some extent by using other more suitable codes, but for many applications the main drawback is the relative slowness of the system. Using Telex for an unsuitable data communications application may not only result in inefficient data communications, but have an adverse effect on the efficiency of the existing message traffic.

(Chapter 11 describes the Datel 100 service and the facilities that can be offered on the Telex system for low speed data transmission.)

3 Communicating Information

As you read these lines, you are forming part of an information system; the author being the message source (transmitter), the publication the message medium and yourself the receiver. This is an example of a 'simplex' system, communication being in one direction only. In a telephone conversation, people do not generally speak at once but exchange roles as transmitter and receiver maintaining a check on understanding and accuracy of the messages they are each receiving. This type of information system where messages are transmitted in both directions but not at the same time is termed 'half-duplex' and again we find the three essential parts of an information system – a message source, a message medium (the telephone line) and a receiver. A great deal of information can, of course, be exchanged in both directions at the same time by two people gazing into one another's eyes. In their attempts to describe this simultaneous transmission of messages, poets have surprisingly failed to recognise that this is simply a 'duplex' information system.

It is only recently that communication itself has been studied; man throughout the ages having concentrated on the methods of communicating. The work done in this comparatively new study of communication theory has provided a better understanding of the factors which limit the rate at which information can be transferred. To the communication theorist, information is 'any organised signal'. This, of course, pre-supposes that these organised signals have some meaning which is understandable to a receiver. In speech conversation within a room, information in this sense would consist of the complex sound waves 'organised' by the vocal chords, pharynx, and tongue of the speaker (transmitter) being transmitted via the medium of air to the listener (receiver). Information on a telephone circuit may consist of a series of tones, a group of tones, direct current pulses or any other signals which are organised. Collectively, the information comprises the message. Noise also has a precise meaning in communication theory and can be defined as 'any signal which interferes with the message being sent'. Music, no matter how beautiful, could therefore be regarded as noise by two people wishing to talk to one another during a concert.

Gardeners are well aware of the fact that man's view of orderliness does not coincide with that of nature. Reversion to nature is not a problem exclusive to gardeners, however, and all man's attempts to impose his own version of order are opposed by nature's. This strong natural force is evident in the oxidisation of metals and is most familiar in the form of rust. This force is at work on telecommunications channels in opposition to organised signals (information) producing weakening and distortion of the signals. It also manifests itself in the background noise which can sometimes be heard as a hiss on telephone or radio channels. This type of 'white noise' (or gaussian noise) is inevitable on telecommunications channels, being produced by a natural movement of electrons which varies with temperature. The term 'white noise' is used because just as white light contains all the colours in the spectrum, white noise is purely random and can be of any frequency. Impulsive noise is also a serious problem in the transfer of information on telecommunications links. This can often be heard as clicks in a telephone conversation and is less of a natural phenomenon, being produced as a result of interference from other telephone circuits. Whether either type of noise interferes significantly with the information is obviously connected with the power of the organised signal relative to the power of the noise and to the sensitivity of the apparatus receiving the signal.

Before considering the practical limitations of a communications channel to carry information, it is useful to exclude the noise factor and examine the purely theoretical maximum capacity. This immediately brings in the problem of bandwidth. With speech conversation, we have seen (see Chapter 2) that, as the main problem is conveying intelligibility, it is necessary to provide telephone channels, of adequate bandwidth. The rate at which analogue speech information is transmitted is not usually constrained by the telephone channel but by the natural rate of the conversation.

Bandwidth is also a constraint on the rate at which digital information can be transmitted. This can perhaps be seen more clearly if we examine the capacity of the human ear, with a maximum bandwidth of 20,000 Hz, to accept digital information. We often receive what might loosely be described as digital signals and an example of this can be heard whenever we sit in a

railway compartment. The typical two state di di di dum sound rises with
the speed of the train. The pitch of this sound continues to rise with speed
and if the train were to travel fast enough the frequency of the signal would
rise to a point where we could no longer hear it. The relationship between the
rate at which information can be transmitted and bandwidth can perhaps
be seen more clearly if we examine a telegraph type signal ignoring for
convenience the usual start/stop elements. We can see from figure 3.1 that

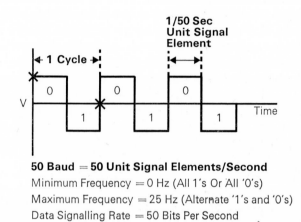

50 Baud = 50 Unit Signal Elements/Second
Minimum Frequency = 0 Hz (All 1's Or All '0's)
Maximum Frequency = 25 Hz (Alternate '1's and '0's)
Data Signalling Rate = 50 Bits Per Second

Figure 3.1   Relationship between bandwidth and information rate

this 50 baud signal would carry 50 bits per second of information. However,
it is also apparent that the fundamental frequency produced by sending this
information would vary between 0 Hz (when all ones or zeros were transmitted) to a maximum of 25 Hz if alternative zeros and ones were transmitted. One bit of information is therefore represented in each half cycle of
the 25 Hz square waveform. Nyquist[1] showed that, in a channel without
noise, a signal with no frequencies greater than W could carry 2W voltage
values. This means that in the idealised situation of a noiseless channel and
using only two voltage values serially (to represent binary '0' and '1') the
maximum theoretical capacity of the channel C would be 2W, where W is
the bandwidth of the channel.

---

[1] Nyquist, H. 'Certain Factors Affecting Telegraph Speed' (1924) and 'Certain Topics in
Telegraph Transmission Theory' (1928). Trans. AIEE.

If more than 2 voltage levels were used, the maximum frequency would be unchanged. Figure 3.2 shows a system employing four states.

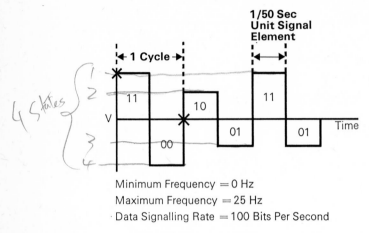

Minimum Frequency = 0 Hz
Maximum Frequency = 25 Hz
Data Signalling Rate = 100 Bits Per Second

Figure 3.2   Signalling using 4 levels

In this example, we again have fundamental frequencies which may vary between 0 Hz and 25 Hz (varying over a 25 Hz bandwidth), but two bits of information can be derived from each half cycle.

We can, therefore, extend the theoretical channel capacity in the absence of white noise to include provision for multi-state signalling:

$$C = 2W \log_2 L$$

where C = the channel capacity in bit/s
         W = the bandwidth
and L = the number of states.

Eg: bandwidth $(W) = 2000$ Hz
    number of states $(L) = 8$, then
    $C = (2 \times 2000) \times (\log_2 8)$
       $= 4000 \times 3 = 12,000$ bit/s

It would seem from this that channel capacity could be increased *ad infinitum* by increasing the number of signalling levels. Unfortunately, this is not true in practice; although these formulae are useful in showing the relationship between bandwidth, signalling levels and channel capacity, there are very real snags:

    – There are no telecommunications channels which are completely free of white noise or other disturbances — PCM channels come closest to this ideal situation;

– The number of states that can be used is limited by the power available to transmit the signals, the problems of encoding and decoding and the sensitivity of the receiver to interpret the different signalling levels.

There are three main factors which determine the amount of information which can be transmitted on a channel:

(i) the bandwidth available;

(ii) the power level of the signal;

(iii) the power level of the noise present on the channel.

The work of Claude E Shannon[2] is of fundamental importance in proving mathematically that a communications channel has a finite capacity. The Shannon/Hartley law is now recognised as representing the theoretical maximum capacity of a channel in the presence of white noise and is given by:

$$C = W \log_2 \left(1 + \frac{N}{S}\right)$$

where C = channel capacity
        W = bandwidth

$\dfrac{S}{N}$ = signal to noise ratio

NOTE: It is important to remember that the noise referred to here is 'white noise'. Other forms of disturbance, which are present in practice, include 'impulse noise', or noise peaks which are critical in determining the error performance of a channel.

Applying this formula to a fairly good quality speech channel with a bandwidth of 3000 Hz and a signal to noise ratio of —30 dB we have:

$$C = 3000 \log_2 \left(1 + \frac{1000}{1}\right)$$

$C = 30,000 \text{ bit/s}$

This is very much more than could be achieved in practice with a circuit of this kind. The actual rates achieved are not solely dependent on the channel but on the modems used. It is most unlikely that modems could be designed economically to approach anywhere near the theoretical maximum capacity

---

[2] 'Mathematical Theory of Communication', Bell Systems Technical Journal (July and October 1948).

of channels. In most commercial applications, where there is a requirement to transmit and receive large quantities of data, the cost per bit transmitted is still of primary importance. As the rate of transmission over analogue transmission media increases the encoding and decoding of the information grows more complex and the sensitivity of the modems has to be improved. This not only inevitably increases the cost of the modems but may adversely affect their reliability. It seems unlikely that rates better than 10,000 bit/s will prove to be economic over telephone channels in the foreseeable future.

It is obvious that rates can be improved by increasing the bandwidth and the Post Office Datel 48K service offers rates at 40.8, 48 and 50 kilobits per second on wider bandwidth channels (*see* Chapter 11). It will also be apparent that a reduction in the level of noise on the circuit will give a better performance. Unfortunately, the noise level cannot be improved economically beyond the published specification of the circuit; the power of the signal must also be kept within clearly defined limits to avoid interference with other users on the telephone system.

4 Transmission and Modulation Systems

The Transmission Response of Telephone Circuits

The electrical signals originating from the telephone are weakened (or attenuated) as they are transmitted along circuits, following the law of geometric progressions, ie there is a uniform percentage loss. Other losses are introduced by the telephone instruments themselves, switchboard connections, automatic equipment, etc. The communications engineer needs to know the loss of power introduced by every component and every section in the complete circuit in order to arrive at the total 'insertion loss' or 'overall loss'. The insertion loss of a circuit is the end to end loss measured using a test frequency of 800 Hz. Although it would be possible to represent the loss of each section or component in a circuit by a ratio of the power sent to the power received, the loss overall could only then be determined by complicated and time consuming multiplications. In practice, the logarithms of ratios are used so that the aggregate effect of a series of items may be arrived at by simply adding them together.

The loss or gain in a circuit, or section of a circuit, can be given by:

$$N = \log_{10} \frac{P1}{P2} \text{ Bels,}$$

where: N = the number of Bels,
$P1$ = the power sent, and
$P2$ = the power received.

61

In practice, the Bel is an inconveniently large unit and the decibel (dB) or one tenth of a Bel is used so that loss or gain (in decibels) equals:

$$10 \log_{10} \frac{P1}{P2}$$

If the received power (P2) is greater than the power sent (P1), as for example when an amplifier is used, then the logarithm of P1 over P2 will be negative; if P1 is greater than P2 the logarithm will be positive. If the received power measured on a circuit was only a thousandth of the power sent then:

$$10 \log_{10} \frac{P1}{P2} = 10 \log_{10} \frac{1000}{1} = +30 \, dB$$

There are always losses in telephony and a 'zero loss' circuit is one in which the gains from amplifiers in the circuit are adjusted exactly to counter balance losses due to the line and apparatus.

The decibel is not an absolute unit, but is the logarithmic expression of a ratio. It can be used, as we have seen, to describe overall loss in terms of the ratio between the power sent and the power received in a circuit; similarly, it can be used to express the ratio between the signal and the noise on a line – there must, however, always be some reference level.

Table 4.1 shows power ratios corresponding to various decibel losses:

dB	Power Ratios (power sent to power received)	dB	Power Ratios (power sent to power received)
+3	2:1	+23	200:1
+6	4:1	+26	400:1
+9	8:1	+29	800:1
+10	10:1	+30	1000:1
+13	20:1	+33	2000:1
+16	40:1	+36	4000:1
+19	80:1	+39	8000:1
+20	100:1	+40	10000:1

Table 4.1

Frequency response

The ability of a particular telephone circuit to 'carry' or respond to different frequencies is referred to as its 'frequency response'.

Higher frequencies will generally be attenuated to a greater extent than lower frequencies. Figure 4.1 shows the attenuation introduced at various frequencies by a type of 0.9mm paper covered cable, commonly used in the UK (0.9mm refers to the diameter of each copper conductor).

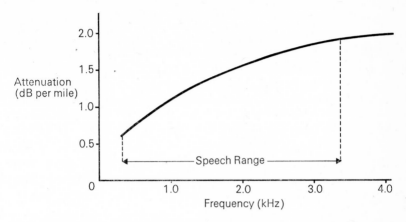

Figure 4.1   Attenuation/Frequency curve – 0.9mm cable

In considering the transmission of a complex speech type waveform, it will be apparent that over long distances the higher frequencies will be very much more attenuated than the lower frequencies, and if this effect is severe, intelligibility will suffer. Some examples of the limiting distances over which speech can be transmitted using ordinary two-wire circuits in cables are given in table 4.2.

Diameter in millimetres of Copper Conductor	Limiting distance for satisfactory speech
0.63 mm	9.5 km
0.9 mm	14.5 km
1.27 mm	20.0 km

Table 4.2

Loading

The power of a signal at any point in a circuit expressed in milliwatts (mW) can be calculated by multiplying the voltage and the current.[1]

Power (mW) = Voltage × Current × 1000

---

[1] In an AC waveform, the values of current and voltage are constantly varying. Although peak values are shown for simplicity in figures, the effective or 'RMS' value is normally used. This is defined as the square root of the mean (average) value of the square of the instantaneous values taken over one complete cycle.

With a 'pure' or sinusoidal waveform, the RMS value is 0.707 times the peak value. For example, an AC wave with a peak value of 325V has an RMS value of 230V.

This is best illustrated using a simple AC waveform as shown in figure 4.2. When the voltage is at its peak the current is also at its highest giving maximum power. In these circumstances the circuit is said to be 'resonant'.

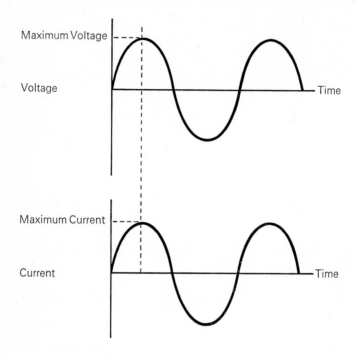

Figure 4.2 'Resonant' circuit

In telephone cables and on overhead routes, telephone wires run over long distances in close proximity. The effect of this is that a circuit becomes capable of storing electrical energy and is said to have 'capacitance'. Although it is unwanted in these circumstances, capacitance can be a valuable property and 'capacitors' are especially designed and constructed to have a wide variety of uses. For example, because capacitors can be charged, store electrical energy for long periods and discharge very quickly when required, they are used in flash photography, the 'flash' being provided by the rapid discharge of a capacitor. These properties of a capacitor are highly un-desirable when they occur uninvited on a telephone circuit. The line itself becomes a capacitor which can store and discharge electrical energy. This means that the current flowing at any time in a circuit with capacitance is to some extent independent of the electro-motive force (the voltage) applied. In these circumstances, the current and the voltage become out of phase and the current is said to 'lead on the voltage' as shown in figure 4.3. It follows that at any instant the product of the voltage and the current is less than maximum which results in a loss of power.

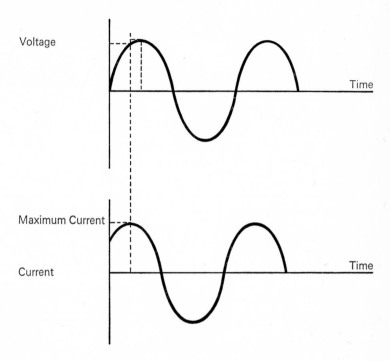

Figure 4.3   Circuit with capacitance

An opposite effect to capacitance is present in circuits which have coils of wire such as relays or electric motors. Whenever the current value changes in a coil, self-induction occurs causing an electro-motive force or 'back EMF' to oppose the flow of current. When alternating current or fluctuating direct current flows in a circuit with inductance, the current is always in a state of change and the build-up of current is slowed so that it 'lags on the voltage' as shown in figure 4.4.

In telephony, inductance is often added to counteract the effect of capacitance and so reduce the power loss in a circuit; this activity is known as 'loading'. In practice, loading is normally effected by induction coils housed in iron cases, either buried direct in the ground or located in manholes at appropriate distances along the cable route. 'Loading pots' can also be used with aerial cables and are then fitted on telephone poles. Distance between successive loading pots varies from 200 metres to about 2 km.

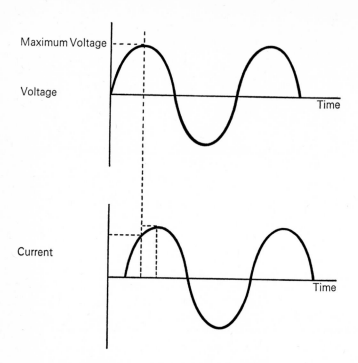

Figure 4.4   Circuit with inductance

With maximum loading, the limiting distance for satisfactory speech transmission can be increased to the figures given in table 4.3.

	Limiting Distance for Satisfactory Speech	
	Unloaded	Loaded
0.63 mm conductors	9.5 km	35 km
0.9 mm conductors	14.5 km	67 km
1.27 mm conductors	20.0 km	112 km

Table 4.3

Although loading serves to counteract the power losses due to unwanted capacitance in a circuit, it has also an adverse effect on the 'bandwidth', or range of frequencies which the circuit can effectively carry. The frequency response of a circuit loaded in this way is illustrated in figure 4.5 and it will be seen that there is a sharp 'cut-off' beyond which frequencies cannot be carried.

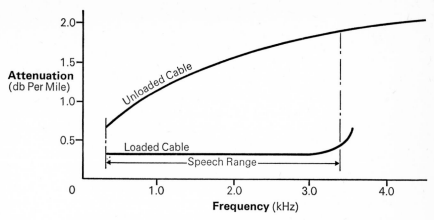

Figure 4.5 Loaded circuit (frequency response)

Filters

Artificial circuits can be designed (comprising in their simplest forms inductance and capacitance) which have a 'cut-off' at any frequency desired. Exact values can be calculated mathematically and modern design techniques are producing filters which have a sharper 'cut-off' than their predecessors. Figure 4.6 shows a 'low pass' filter which allows all frequencies below the

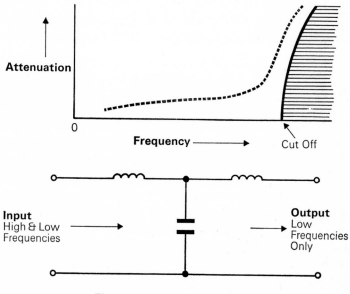

Figure 4.6 Low pass filter

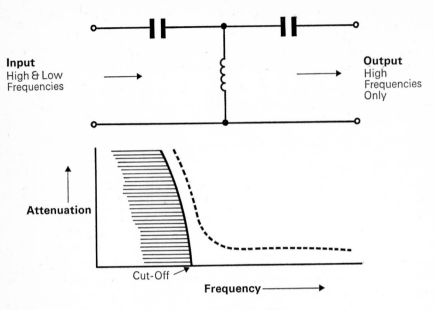

Figure 4.7   High pass filter

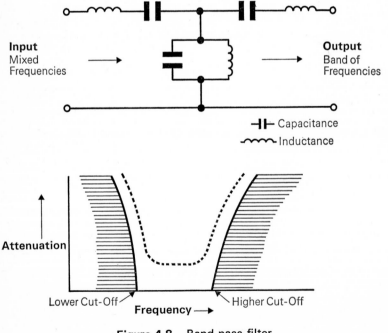

Figure 4.8   Band pass filter

cut-off to pass almost without attenuation whilst blocking all frequencies above the cut-off.

Figure 4.7 shows a high pass filter which allows the higher frequencies to be passed whilst greatly attenuating lower frequencies.

A band pass filter, as illustrated in figure 4.8, allows a band of frequencies to pass whilst cutting off the higher frequencies above the band and the lower frequencies below the band.

Amplified Circuits
Line loading is effective only over limited distances. Where a high standard of transmission is needed over long circuits, amplifiers or 'repeaters' have to be used to raise the power to a level suitable for reception or for onward transmission over a further section of line. Since both loading and amplifiers are designed to off-set attenuation, the use of amplifiers will allow loading to be lighter; in some cases amplifier circuits can be arranged to correct for the varying frequency response of the line, thus allowing loading to be dispensed with altogether. Smaller gauge and therefore cheaper line conductors can be used when amplifiers are introduced.

Two-wire amplifiers
The thermionic valve or transistor amplifier is a one-way device and if introduced into a two-wire telephone circuit will allow speech to pass in one

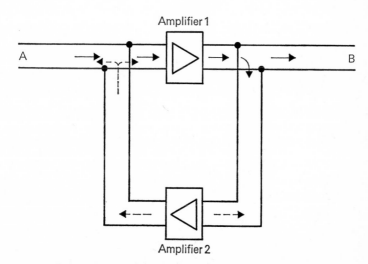

Figure 4.9 Impracticable amplifier connection

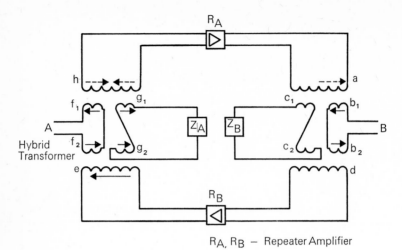

RA, RB — Repeater Amplifier
ZA, ZB — Line Balance Impedances

Figure 4.10   2-wire amplifier

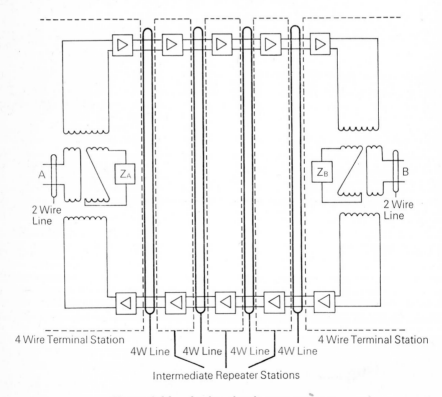

Figure 4.11   4-wire circuit arrangement

direction only. Figure 4.9 shows an impracticable amplifier arrangement which would result in 'singing' caused by each amplifier driving the other, and a more practicable arrangement is shown in figure 4.10.

By using special (hybrid) transformers, speech is possible in both directions simultaneously. However, if this kind of two-wire arrangement were to be used over long distances, speech would be unsatisfactory because:

- The two hybrid transformers used at each stage introduce additional losses of 6 dB which have to be made good by the amplifiers. This calls for the insertion of amplifiers in the line at more frequent intervals and is a costly arrangement.

- The effective operation of a chain of hybrid transformers requires very careful balancing at each stage if singing is to be avoided.

Four-wire working
Most main physical trunk (long distance) circuits consist of four wires. One pair is used for transmission in each direction. The arrangement is shown in figure 4.11.

Noise on Telephone Circuits
Any noises, whether induced from outside sources (power line, etc) or due to circuit defects (valve noise, bad joints, etc) are naturally amplified with transmitted speech. The repeater stations must, therefore, be provided near enough to each other to ensure that at the input to each amplifier the noise level in the preceding section of line is not greater than a tolerable proportion of the total power. This 'signal to noise' ratio is often the limiting factor in determining the degree of amplification which can be obtained and is extremely important when considering the transmission of data.

Echo Effect
Difficulty can arise on long circuits due to the reflection effect, or echo, which causes the speaker to hear his own words repeated back to him. Reflection occurs whenever there is a change in the electrical characteristics of a circuit, eg a two-wire circuit connected to a four-wire circuit. This echo effect is rarely a problem within a small country because of the relatively short distances involved. On very long calls, however, echoes are a serious problem, as they may seriously inhibit speech. On inter-continental circuits therefore, echo 'suppressors' are usually fitted between the 'go' and 'return' pairs permitting only one pair to transmit speech at a time. (These prevent the

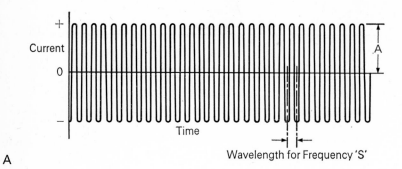

A

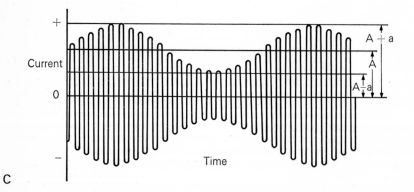

B

C

Figure 4.12   The principle of modulation

simultaneous transmission of data in both directions and if this is required then devices have to be introduced to 'disable' the echo suppressors.)

Modulation

The achievement of maximum utilisation of capacity is a problem common in business today. A similar problem exists on communication lines. We know that all the intelligence of speech can satisfactorily be contained within a nominal bandwidth of 3000 Hz. However, unloaded lines fitted with amplifiers can transmit a much greater range of frequencies than this. To use such a line over long distances for only one speech conversation is comparable to using a large motorway for one vehicle travelling in each direction.

If whilst a circuit is carrying one conversation at normal speech frequencies, another conversation is lifted into a higher band of similar width, both conversations can be carried over the same circuit. The technique to achieve this is 'modulation' which can be described as the process by which a characteristic of one wave is varied in accordance with another wave or signal. Figure 4.12 illustrates graphically the effect of a speech wave 's' modulating a 'carrier' wave 'c' when the technique of 'amplitude modulation' is used.

The typical 'envelope' shown in the lower part of the diagram is in fact a compound of three frequencies:

    c   the original 'carrier' frequency

    c+s   the sum of the 'carrier' and modulating frequency

    c − s the difference between the carrier and the modulating frequency

It is therefore more convenient to plot frequency against time graphically rather than amplitude against time, as in Part A of figure 4.13.

Part B of figure 4.13 illustrates a typical speech waveform and part C illustrates the complex waveforms after modulating the 10 kHz carrier 'C'. It will be seen that the intelligence now lies both in the upper 'side band' 10.3 to 13.4 kHz and also in the lower side band 6.6 to 9.7 kHz. It is common practice to transmit only the lower side band, the carrier being suppressed in a modulator which is of special design and the upper side band being suppressed by the use of a low pass or band pass filter; in this way power requirements are reduced and the number of channels which can be accommodated in a given frequency range is increased. At the receiving end, a locally generated carrier, of the same frequency and in the same phase relationship as the original carrier is introduced (to restore the conversation to the original speech frequencies). This technique is known as 'demodulation'. The

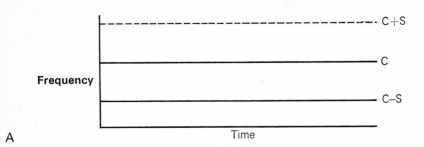

A

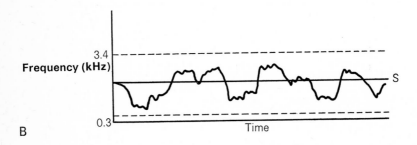

B

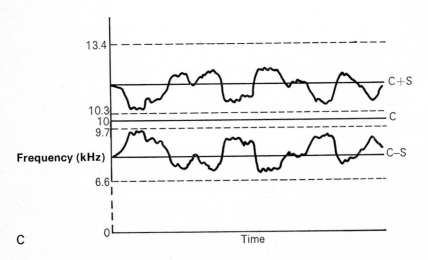

C

Figure 4.13   Modulation by speech wave

demodulator works on the same basis as the modulator in that three frequencies will be produced:

$$c \qquad = c$$
$$c+(c-s) \ = 2c-s$$
$$c-(c-s) \ = s \text{ (the original speech frequencies)}$$

The third frequency is the original speech frequency (or band of frequencies);
it may be filtered off by means of a low pass filter and amplified as required.
The principle of lower side band suppressed carrier working is shown in
figure 4.14.

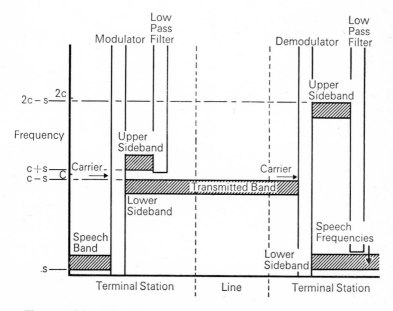

Figure 4.14   Principle of lower sideband suppressed carrier working

The technique of modulation, as described, is the basis of Frequency Division
Multiplexing (FDM) which is a system widely used to gain line economies
both in speech and data transmission.

Carrier Systems

A circuit has to be modified into a 'carrier' system in order to allow several
voice frequency calls to be carried simultaneously. A carrier system employing

carrier frequencies between 64 to 108 kHz is shown in figure 4.15; only the lower sideband is transmitted for each of the twelve speech channels which are derived. Improvements in cable design have made it possible to introduce a carrier system providing 60 channels. A 60 channel group is formed by combining five 12 channel groups (*see* figure 4.16). Each 12 channel group, after assembly in the range 60 to 108 kHz is arranged to modulate one of the carrier frequencies 420 kHz, 468 kHz, 516 kHz, 564 and 612 kHz. The lower

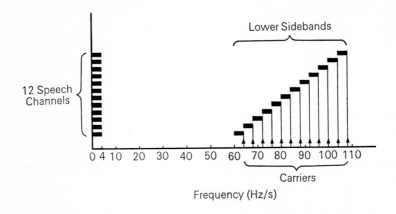

Figure 4.15   12 channel carrier system

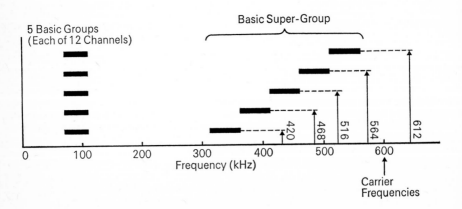

Figure 4.16   60 channel carrier system

side bands are selected in each case and when combined, occupy a frequency band 312 to 552 kHz.

This complete band termed a 'supergroup', then modulates a carrier frequency of 564 kHz and the lower side band of 12 to 252 kHz is transmitted to line.

Coaxial cables

It is theoretically possible for a carrier system to be extended to say 120 channels, employing line frequencies in higher ranges. The attenuation introduced by normal cables at these frequencies would, however, be very great and repeater station spacing would have to be much less than the 20 km required for the 60 channel system. This is not economic in practice, but fortunately it has been found possible to exploit the carrier system further by using 'coaxial' cables, which have a relatively low attenuation at high frequencies.

In a coaxial cable, the conventional pair of wires forming the conductors is replaced by a solid copper rod running concentrically in a copper tube (*see* figure 4.17). The space between the conductors should, ideally, be filled with air, but it is necessary of course, to provide 'spacers' at intervals to keep the conductor rod central in the tube.

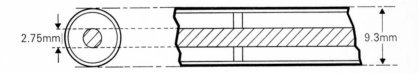

Figure 4.17   Coaxial tube (9.3mm outer, 2.75mm centre conductor)

At very high frequencies, current flow takes place mainly near the surface of the conductors and in a coaxial tube the current flow is concentrated near the inner surface of the tube and the outer surface of the rod. External high frequency influences on the cable will mainly affect the outer surface of the tube and hence interfere very little with the transmission. The comparative attenuation of carrier and coaxial cables is illustrated in figure 4.18.

By introducing several stages of modulation, current coaxial systems can now carry up to 2700 channels and microwave radio links can carry an equivalent number.

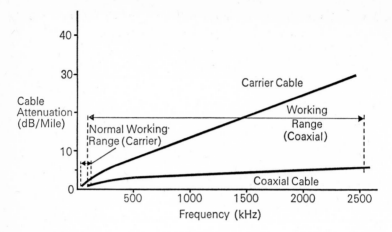

Figure 4.18   Comparative attenuation of carrier and coaxial cables

Pulse Code Modulation (PCM)

Earlier, we saw how frequency division multiplexing could be used in carrier systems to make more economic use of line plant. Although economic over long distances (trunk routes) carrier systems are less economic over the more numerous short distance circuits (junction routes). In the continuing drive for economy, transmission engineers in many countries have been engaged for many years in finding a multiplexing system suitable for short distance circuits. Pulse Code Modulation (PCM) was first invented by A H Reeves in 1938 but it is only in recent years that the invention and economic manufacture of suitable components has made the use of PCM viable and it is now used extensively. In London, it has been employed widely to provide extra telephone capacity where the laying of extra cables would have been difficult or even impossible. These circumstances occur, particularly in central London, where the ducts in which telephone cables are laid are often full to capacity. To dig up the roads of central London in order to lay extra track would be enormously expensive and would exchange one form of congestion for another.

So PCM can be used for economic multiplexing or as a useful expedient, but what is it? Basically it is a form of modulation and de-modulation which converts analogue speech into a series of coded digital pulses for transmission and on reception transforms the pulses back into speech. Although the existence of PCM systems in parts of the telephone network does not directly affect the data user, some knowledge of the principles of PCM can be useful for the student of data communications. First of all, the basic principles involved can be applied to the transmission of data from analogue terminals (usually measuring devices). Secondly, PCM can be useful in introducing the concept of time division multiplexing (TDM) (*see also* Chapter 9). Thirdly, to know a little about PCM is helpful in understanding future trends in the economics and technology of telecommunications.

Principles of PCM

The purpose of PCM is to provide an economic means of deriving a number of speech channels from one physical speech circuit. There are three stages in the progressive build-up of a PCM system.

Pulse Amplitude Modulation (PAM)

The first stage in the process is to sample an incoming analogue speech signal at specific intervals and produce a series of pulses. Figure 4.19 shows that the amplitude of these pulses is determined from the sample of the original speech waveform.

The mechanism of the human ear is such that if these pulses were to be sent to line with only a very short period of time between pulses (about one ten

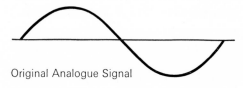

Original Analogue Signal

Pulse Samples

Impression of Samples as Indicated by Human Ear

Figure 4.19   Sampling analogue signals

thousandth of a second) then the resultant small variations would be smoothed out and be unnoticeable to the listener. The process of conveying information to line by means of samples of an analogue waveform is known as pulse amplitude modulation. The number of such pulses required is relative to the bandwidth or range of frequencies to be reproduced and can be given as:

$$n = 2W \quad \text{where } n = \text{number of pulses required in one second}$$
$$\text{and } W = \text{the bandwidth}$$

If, therefore, we wished to re-constitute reasonably faithfully an analogue signal which would vary over a frequency range of 200 Hz, we would need 400 pulses. To reproduce speech conversation 8000 PAM pulses per second are needed to give good quality speech over a bandwidth of 4000 Hz.

It should be emphasised that pulse amplitude modulation is merely the starting point in a practical system. All telephone channels are subject to noise; as this affects signal amplitude rather than frequency the PAM pulses would be subject to distortion if sent to line in this form. There would also be the problem of amplifying noise with the signal at 'repeater' or amplifying stations.

Pulse Code Modulation (PCM)

If, instead of sending pulses of varying amplitudes to line, pulses consisting of only two levels of amplitude could be sent, then, it is obvious that the noise problem could be reduced substantially. This is in fact what is achieved by using code modulation. In a PCM system, levels of amplitude are checked as described earlier. By using a number of reference levels, an amplitude sample

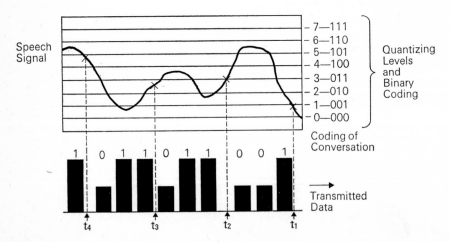

Figure 4.20   Pulse Code Modulation with eight quantizing levels

is translated into a unique binary code which describes a particular reference point. The binary coded information is sent to line using two-state pulses and on receipt of the information the decoding logic at the receiving end recognises the coded sample and reconstitutes an amplitude signal at the required level. This process is shown in simplified form in figure 4.20

Quantizing

It was said earlier that the human ear will ignore small variations in amplitude which may occur through sampling. Not only must the pulses representing each conversation be sent with small intervals of time between them but also the strength of the signal (the amplitude) must be capable of being reconstituted reasonably faithfully. Figure 4.20 shows a speech wave sampled for amplitude and then encoded using pulse code modulation. Only eight reference levels are used for simplicity, each of which can be identified by a combination of three binary digits. The process of dividing an analogue signal into digital form and re-assembling it into analogue form is known as quantization. In the example shown the 'quantizing error' resulting from using only eight reference levels would be obvious to the listener in the form of distortion of the originating voice. In practice, most pulse code modulation systems use at least 128 quantizing levels, each pulse being coded into seven binary digits.

An eighth bit is usually added to each 'character' for supervisory purposes. This means that each of the original 8000 PAM pulses is coded into eight bits and 64,000 bit/s are therefore necessary to represent one speech conversation.

Time Division Multiplexing (TDM)

By interleaving the coded 'characters' in a high speed digital data stream, it is possible to divide a physical pair of wires into a number of separate voice channels. This process is known as time division multiplexing (TDM) and is illustrated in simplified form in figure 4.21.

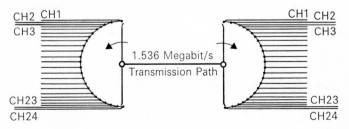

Figure 4.21 Time Division Multiplexing

A PCM system widely used by the British Post Office provides 24 channels. As 64,000 bit/s are required for each speech channel, the PCM links operate at 1.536 megabit/s in each direction. The high speed digital data is arranged in 'frames', each frame containing the coded data representing one sample from each of the 24 channels. A frame, therefore, consists of 192 binary digits and is illustrated in figure 4.22.

Sampling Frame of 192 Bits

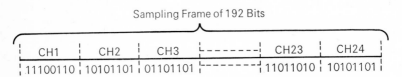

Figure 4.22   PCM data frame

The four-wire circuits employed to enable both way simultaneous conversations are two pairs of wires in standard cables with all loading removed. Special regenerative repeaters are fitted every 2 km which can detect the distorted low voltage (± 3 volts) direct current signals and reproduce them as new square wave pulses.

There are a number of advantages in using PCM for time division multiplexing. These are:

– It can be used as a short or long term expedient where the provision of extra cable capacity would be difficult or uneconomic.

– It is generally cheaper than other transmissions systems in the range 10 to 60 km.

– With the trend towards decreasing costs of the logic circuitry and large bandwidths that PCM systems give, there are clearly foreseeable long term economic benefits in using PCM systems.

– As new pulses are produced at every stage of regeneration, noise is not passed on with the signals – a big problem in amplifying analogue signals.

– It is technically possible to provide routing information preceding the digital speech information on each channel. This offers potential advantages of faster switching and greater compatibility with the exchanges of the future which employ computer technology.

Modulation Systems for Data Transmission

Sending digital data signals on an analogue system is like joining a noisy club where everybody speaks a different language and has rather unpleasant habits. To enter the club it is necessary to adopt a peculiar, complicated disguise and behave in such a way as to be inconspicuous to the vast majority of members. This analogy fairly describes the somewhat uncomfortable situation facing the data communications user on a speech system. The obvious question is 'why join?'. The answer is that the rate at which data can be transmitted is to a great extent dependent on the bandwidth of the transmission medium employed. The wider bandwidth analogue telephone channels have a greater potential for carrying higher data rates than the lower bandwidth digital telegraph channels. However, in order to utilise the telephone network for data transmission some means must be found of converting the digital data signals into a form suitable for transmission over circuits primarily designed for speech.

Let us take a simple example involving the transmission of punched paper tape information between a terminal in Coventry (A) and a terminal in Chester (B). A call is established using the public switched network and an analogue link for speech communication is established (*see* figure 4.23).

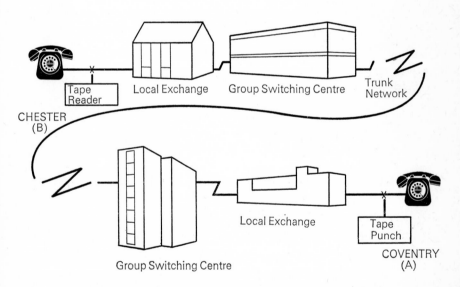

Figure 4.23   Analogue link between Coventry and Chester

Figure 4.24   Digital output signals from a punched paper tape transmitter

Let us now consider the electrical signals produced by the paper tape transmitter at A (*see* figure 4.24). The output is typical of many data terminals and consists of a series of low voltage direct current signals, the significance of which is determined by the polarity.

If we attempted to connect this device to the A end of the line, the digital signals would not be transmitted to B because:

- 'Transmission bridges' are employed in the local exchanges which prevent the passage of direct current (DC). These devices, whilst allowing the passage of alternating current (AC) or fluctuating direct current speech signals, would block the transmission of the square wave digital pulses.

- The carrier systems require the modulation of a high frequency analogue signal by a lower frequency analogue signal and no DC path is available to transmit the digital signal.

These are but two of the practical reasons why digital signals cannot be passed over an analogue network. There is also the more fundamental reason that digital and analogue signals require different amplifying techniques to overcome the problem of attenuation. Digital transmission systems employ 'regenerative repeaters' and digital signals cannot be amplified by conventional analogue repeaters.

In order to transmit data from a punched paper tape transmitter, we must somehow make the digital data signals 'look like' analogue speech signals. The process of changing the digital signals into analogue is termed modulation; the reverse process of converting back from analogue into digital is known as demodulation. The name 'modem' is given to the device which performs these functions.

There are three basic methods employed in generally available modem design, each having respective advantages and disadvantages.

Amplitude Modulation

With amplitude modulation, the amplitude (or strength) of the carrier wave is varied in sympathy with the signal to be sent. The simplest form of amplitude modulation is to represent binary '0' by using a single signal of fixed amplitude and binary '1' by switching off the signal. This method, however, whereby the absence of a signal denotes that some information is being sent, has an obvious weakness — a fault condition could be misinterpreted as data received (*see* figure 4.25).

Other forms of amplitude modulation are shown in figure 4.26 and 4.27.

A simplified example of a multi-level amplitude modulation signal using four levels of amplitude is shown in figure 4.27.

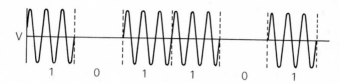

Figure 4.25   Amplitude modulation

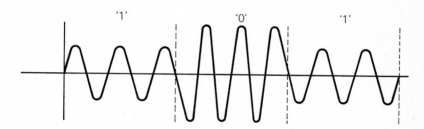

Figure 4.26   Variable amplitude modulation

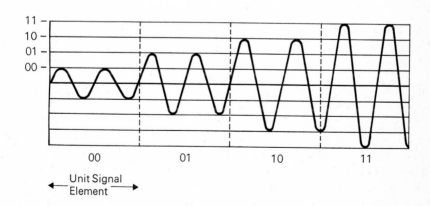

Figure 4.27   Multi-level amplitude modulation

Assuming the modulation rate of the signals in figure 4.27 to be 1000 baud (1000 unit signal elements per second), the data signalling rate would be 2000 bit/s. The data signalling rate in all multi-level systems is:

$$M\log_2 n \quad \text{where } n = \text{the number of signal states}$$
$$\text{and } M = \text{the modulation rate.}$$

As with speech telephony, the upper side band and carrier may be suppressed to reduce the bandwidth requirement and concentrate the power available on the signal containing the information. At the demodulator a detection process must convert the amplitude modulated signal back to the original form. If there is no suppression of the upper side band or carrier, this is known as 'envelope detection'.

'Synchronous detection' is used when the *carrier and upper* side band are suppressed at the modulator and involves the use of a locally produced source of carrier for demodulation, which has the same frequency and phase as that of the original. In carrier telephony, where a large number of channels are being derived from a given bandwidth, one channel may be used exclusively for sending a reference carrier from which the other carriers necessary can be reconstituted. On single circuits, this is obviously not economic. One method of obtaining the necessary reference wave is to suppress the original carrier only partially. In this way, most of the energy can be concentrated on the data signal but the reference wave can be reconstituted from the original carrier; this is termed 'coherent' detection.

Amplitude modulation is vulnerable to the common types of noise – noise tending to affect amplitude rather than frequency of signals. Improved modem design is overcoming this problem.

A number of modems have been designed using multi-level symbols where one sideband may be eliminated altogether. Other types suppress one sideband so that only a vestige of the sideband remains enabling envelope or coherent detection to be employed; these are termed VSB (vestigial sideband) modems.

Frequency Shift Keying (FSK)

The frequency of the carrier in figure 4.28 assumes one value for a '1' bit and another for an '0' bit; this is commonly known as frequency shift keying. One of the problems in using frequency modulation for data transmission is that the gap between frequencies used must be increased as the modulation rate is increased. This creates a particular problem when the public switched telephone network is used to transmit data. Different basic frequencies (usually two) are used for switching and supervising telephone calls on the

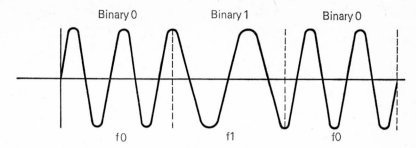

Figure 4.28   Frequency Shift Keying (FSK)

network. These frequencies must be avoided, when transmitting data, to guard against false operation or premature clearance of calls which could be caused by interference with the signalling systems. Multi-level signalling is possible using frequency modulation, but the greater the number of separate frequencies to be transmitted the greater becomes the bandwidth requirement. 'Frequency attenuation', where some frequencies are weakened more than others, also becomes a more serious problem as the number of frequencies used increases.

Phase Modulation
The principles of phase modulation can best be understood by first examining the way in which an alternating current (AC) waveform is produced using a simple generator. This is illustrated in figure 4.29.

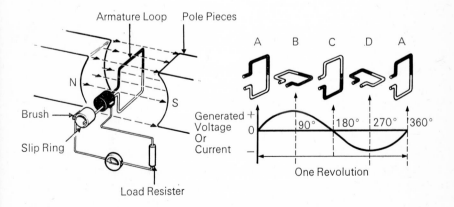

Figure 4.29   The elementary generator

Maximum current is produced when the moving armature is cutting the greatest number lines of magnetic force, ie when the armature is at 90 degrees or 270 degrees in relation to the lines of force. Minimum current is produced when the armature is parallel to the lines of force, ie is at an angle of 0 degrees or 180 degrees in relation to the line of force. One very simple way of understanding phase modulation for data transmission is to consider the outputs from two different generators each revolving at the same frequency but being 180 degrees 'out-of-step' or 'out-of-phase'. We could switch the output from each of these generators to represent binary '0' and binary '1' respectively. Let us assume that the following binary digits are to be sent using this type of simplified phase modulation:

0 1 0

The output from the generators could be shown graphically as in figure 4.30.

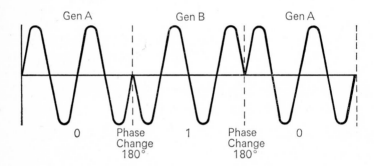

Figure 4.30   Phase inversion (2 phase modulation)

This type of modulation is often referred to as 'phase inversion' and demodulation involves the detection of the different phase relationships in order to reconstitute the original binary data.

There are two different types of phase modulation which detect the phase information contained in the data signal in two different ways. One method ascribes a meaning to each phase position so that 0 is given the meaning binary '0' and 180 binary '1'. A 'reference wave' of the same frequency as the data signal and of constant phase must be provided at the demodulator to detect the phase of the incoming data signal. This method is known as 'fixed reference phase modulation'.

The second method does not require a separate reference wave and assigns meaning not to the phase conditions themselves but to the changes in phase from a previous symbol. A change in phase might be interpreted as binary '1' if the preceding binary digit was binary '0' and vice versa. This method is known as 'differential phase modulation'.

One of the advantages of phase modulation is that multi-phase transmission can be employed which is economical in terms of the bandwidth requirements. By using four different phases, two bits of information (dibits) can be represented by one phase change, eight different phases can be represented by three bits, and so on. There are, however, technical difficulties in detecting small changes in phase and costs tend to increase disproportionately to the benefits as the number of phases used is increased. Table 4.4 shows the number of bit/s of data which could theoretically be sent using different phase states on a circuit being modulated 1200 times in one second (1200 baud).

Modulation rate	Number of phases or states	Bit/s
1200 baud	2	1200
1200 baud	4	2400
1200 baud	8	3600
1200 baud	16	4800
1200 baud	32	6000

Table 4.4

The Post Office Modem Number 7 used in the UK Datel 2400 service employs a technique of differential four phase modulation.

For modulation, serial binary data is fed to the sender coding logic (*see* figure 4.31) with timing signals from a control unit. The data is held in a two

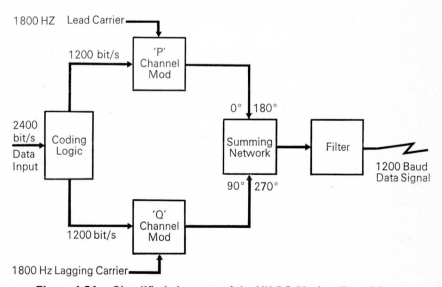

Figure 4.31   Simplified elements of the UK PO Modem 7 modulator

bit shift register so that the data can be associated in pairs (dibits). The first bit of the pair is released through to the P channel modulator and second to the Q channel modulator. These two modulators are modulated in such a way that the P channel leads with a 1800 Hz carrier that is 90 degrees ahead of the Q channel. By utilising the differences in phase, the characteristic of the bits received at the P and Q channels and the characteristics of the previous pair of bits, adjustments are made in the summing network which generates a 1200 baud, four-phase signal. The original information in binary form has been translated into a phase condition on a 1200 baud signal; the key to the information content is now in the phase condition.

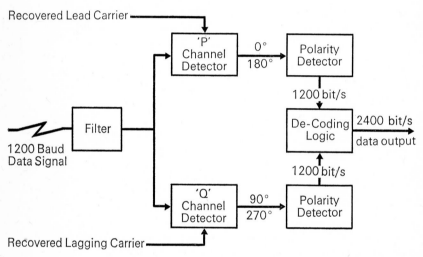

Figure 4.32   Simplified elements of the UK PO Modem 7 demodulator

At the receiving demodulator (*see* figure 4.32), the objective is to convert the incoming phase signal into the original binary condition. Essentially the process is the reverse of modulation. The previous incoming data has set the demodulator in such a way that it is possible to detect the change of the phase of the signal. The 1800 Hz carrier is recovered and the phase changes are detected by the polarity detectors which in turn generate the translation in the de-coding logic to reproduce the binary data.

In a modulation system of this type where phase changes occur, it is vital that the demodulator is continuously synchronised with the modulator. This is achieved by using electronic timing devices at the end station (derived from either the terminal or the modem) which ensure accurate timing of the transmitter signals. At the demodulator, accurate timing is achieved by maintaining synchronisation between receive timing equipment and detected phase changes of the incoming signals.

There are at present two alternative international standards for differential four-phase modulation modems on public switched telephone networks (CCITT recommendation V26). The Post Office Modem 7C, just described, uses alternative A modulation as shown in figure 4.33.

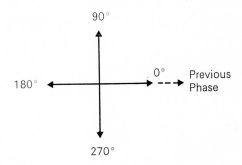

Figure 4.33   Alternative A (CCITT V26) – phase shifts of a 4-phase signal

Although the modem 7C has proved to give an extremely good performance, there is an inherent minor weakness with alternative A. If a data message contains long strings of repetitive dibits, eg 0000000 – – – 00 then the absence of phase changes can cause synchronisation problems – synchronisation relying on sampling the phase changes of the line signal. Although these problems can be largely overcome by good design, there are advantages in using the continuous phase changes of alternative B; these are shown in figure 4.34.

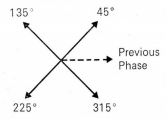

Figure 4.34   Alternative B (CCITT V26) – phase shifts of a 4-phase signal

Quadrature Amplitude Modulation (QAM)

QAM can be regarded as a combination of phase modulation and amplitude modulation. It is a technique which is being used increasingly in the range over 2400-10,000 bit/s.

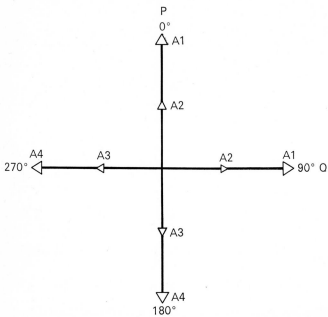

Figure 4.35   Combined phase and amplitude modulated signals in a QAM system

Figure 4.35 shows a vector diagram of a typical QAM system where two signals of the same frequency are used with a minimum phase difference of 90° (the signals are said to be in phase quadrature). Each of these signals P and Q has four possible levels of amplitude A1, A2, A3, and A4. The combination of the signals results in 16 separate symbols as shown in figure 4.36.

If, for example, the phases of the P channel and Q channels were 0° and 180° and their amplitudes A1 and A2 respectively, the resultant signal would have a phase angle and amplitude as shown in A3 of the matrix. It will be seen that there are twelve possible phase angles but only three possible levels of amplitude.

Each of the 16 different conditions can signify four bits of information and the coding method is shown in figure 4.36.

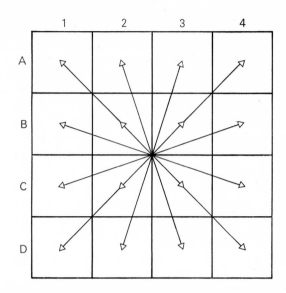

Figure 4.36 Sixteen positions resulting from a QAM system

Use of Speech Band Private Circuits and the Public Switched Telephone Network for Data Transmission

With *speech* communication between two fixed locations the choice between using the Public Switched Telephone Network (PSTN) or renting a private circuit is usually determined by purely cost considerations. The actual or estimated call charges between two points are directly compared with the cost of a private circuit, full time or part time. Although there may be a difference in convenience between these alternatives there is no difference in perform-ance – the sole measure of this being intelligibility.

In *data communications* the situation is very different. Certainly economic factors are important, but the system performance required can be the deciding factor in choosing between use of private circuits and the PSTN.

In this section we will examine those aspects of point to point private circuits and the PSTN which affect the transmission of data. Circuits with multiple connections are discussed in Chapter 9.

The Characteristics of Speech Band Private Circuits

The Post Office data transmission services are usually described in terms of performance, such as the data signalling rate, and the facilities which are offered (*see* Chapter 11). Because both modems and lines are part of a total service, it is unnecessary for customers to specify the type of private circuit required. However, in addition to these services, the Post Office supplies a range of private circuits on a 'wires only' basis to which a large number of private equipments, including modems, have been given permission to be connected. By agreement between the Post Office and suppliers, a customer will be advised by his supplier regarding the type of circuit required so that he may order it from the Post Office. This simplifies the ordering arrangements and should ensure that the line provided is to the specification required by the equipment connected to it. It is, however, the customer's responsibility to obtain the necessary information from the equipment supplier and advise the Post Office of the exact requirements. Typical information needed from a supplier is as follows:

- Whether two-wire or four-wire presentation is required.
- Whether signalling wires are required.
- The quality of the circuit required.

All manufacturers or suppliers of communications equipment are familiar with the ordering procedure and there should be no difficulty in obtaining the necessary information in the form that is needed. Nevertheless, it is useful for systems designers and others to be aware of the meaning and significance of each of the three factors listed.

Two-wire or four-wire presentation

The majority of telephone circuits over 40 km are amplified and have separate transmit and receive channels for most of their length. A '2-wire' private circuit terminated on modems is shown in simplified form in figure 4.37.

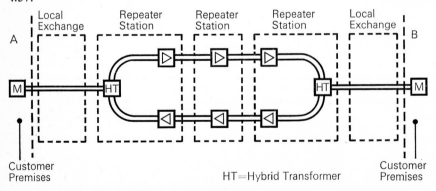

Figure 4.37   A 2-wire presented private circuit terminated on modems

The two-wire parts of the line are confined to the sections between the customer's premises and the repeater (or amplifying) stations at each end. A circuit such as this is limited by these two-wire sections. For example, if frequency shift modems were used to the CCITT Specification V23 to transmit data at 1200 bit/s, the frequencies 1300 Hz and 2100 Hz would be used for binary '1' and binary '0' respectively. Data at 1200 bit/s could not, therefore, be transmitted from A to B and B to A simultaneously because the frequencies transmitted from each end could not be distinguished from one another. Full duplex operation would, therefore, be impossible at the higher speed with this type of modem. However, it would be possible on such a circuit to use a narrow bandwidth return channel using other frequencies (say, 390 Hz and 450 Hz). Data could then be passed from A to B at the higher speed and supervisory data simultaneously returned B to A at a lower speed (say, 75 bit/s) because filtering in the modems would effectively separate the circuit into a high and a low speed channel. Similarly, if only low speed data is required in each direction modems are available which will give duplex operation over a two-wire presented private circuit. For example, modems to CCITT Recommendation V21 use the following frequencies:

Channel 1	Binary '0'	1180 Hz
	Binary '1'	980 Hz
Channel 2	Binary '0'	1850 Hz
	Binary '1'	1650 Hz

Because of the lower speed operation (up to 300 bit/s), such modems only require part of the available bandwidth for each direction of transmission. The examples quoted merely serve to illustrate the kind of limitations which exist on two-wire presented circuits used for data transmission. A very much better performance may be achieved in practice depending on the type of modem and the 'quality' of the two-wire presented circuit.

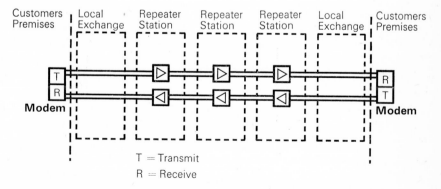

Figure 4.38 A 4-wire presented circuit terminated on modems

Figure 4.38 shows a four-wire presented circuit and it will be seen that this merely involves extending the four wires from the customer's premises at each end to the respective repeater stations.

The circuit is now divided into two completely separate channels of communication each with the same bandwidth. Modems can, therefore, be used which give full duplex facilities. For example, V23 modems at each end could provide 1200 bit/s in both directions simultaneously using frequencies 1300 Hz and 2100 Hz.

Signalling requirements

Circuits used for off-line operation are not usually used for continual communication but are manually switched in as and when required. This necessitates some method of signalling to establish communication. Commonly, a telephone is associated with the modem or terminal at each end and the operators speak before switching the circuit for data transmission. With Datel services, speech and signalling are provided at the customer's request; the most suitable method of providing these facilities being determined by the Post Office. If private equipment is used on a 'wires only' circuit, the Post Office will again provide speech and signalling facilities if required, but this may be provided by the equipment manufacturer. In the latter case, the type of signalling used will depend on the method employed by the particular equipment and may require a special circuit terminating arrangement provided by the Post Office.

Figure 4.39 illustrates a normal UK Post Office four-wire circuit terminating arrangement and figure 4.40 shows the type of arrangement which must be provided when the private equipment is using a particular type of signalling known as balanced battery.

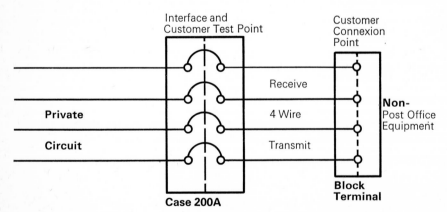

Figure 4.39   4-wire presentation to private equipment

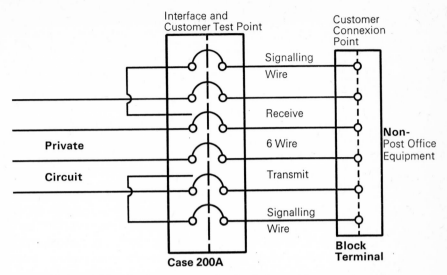

Figure 4.40   6-wire presentation for balanced battery signalling

The quality of private circuits

Describing a private circuit is a very different problem to that of describing a piece of equipment such as a computer terminal. Equipment specifications emphasise performance in language which is familiar to the computer professional. Conversely, communications authorities modestly specify the limitations of circuits in technical terms which may be difficult for the uninitiated to grasp. There are good reasons both for the apparent modesty and the technicalities. A circuit has not, in fact, got a performance which can be described. There is no such thing, for example, as a 1200 bit/s circuit, as the data signalling rates which can be achieved will depend to a great extent on the equipment which is used on the circuit. A 'wires only' private circuit can, therefore, only be described in terms of certain characteristics and these are quoted in such a way as to enable manufacturers to design equipment to make the best use of the circuit. Communication is, therefore, essentially between the initiated and accurate description demands precise technical specification.

Although circuit specifications are apparently daunting they are, in fact, not too difficult to understand, and an attempt will be made in this section to explain the key factors as simply as possible.

Insertion loss

As described earlier in this chapter, insertion loss, sometimes known as overall loss, is the loss in decibels between one end of a circuit and the other at a stipulated frequency; in the UK Post Office, the test frequency used most commonly is 800 Hz. If, therefore, a circuit were to be described as having an insertion loss of +10 dB this would express the ratio of the power of a transmitted 800 Hz signal to the power of a received 800 Hz signal in decibels.

$$10 \log_{10} \frac{\text{Power sent}}{\text{Power received}} = +10\,\text{dB}$$

	Schedule A	Schedule B	Schedule C	Schedule D
Loss/frequency response (relative to 800Hz)(dB)				
Frequency band (Hz)				
300—500	−7 to +12	−3 to +10	−2 to +7	−2 to +6
500—2000	−7 to + 8	−3 to + 6	−1 to +4	−1 to +3
2000—2600	Not specified	−3 to + 6	−1 to +4	−1 to +3
2600—2800	Not specified	−3 to +10	−1 to +4	−1 to +3
2800—3000	Not specified	−3 to +10	−2 to +7	−2 to +6
Group delay/frequency response μ secs relative to minimum				
500—600	Not specified	Not specified	Not specified	3000
600—1000	Not specified	Not specified	Not specified	1500
1000—2600	1250	1000	1000	500
2600—2800	Not specified	Not specified	Not specified	3000
Random circuit noise (dBmOp)	−42	−42	−42	−45
Impulsive noise				
No more than 18 impulsive noise counts to exceed the threshold limit in any period of 15 mins	Threshold limit −18dBmO	Threshold limit −18dBmO	Threshold limit −18dBmO	Threshold limit −21dBmO
Signal to quantizing noise level (dB)	22	22	22	22
Maximum frequency error (Hz)	2	2	2	2
Transmit to receive crosstalk attentuation. 4 wire presented circuits measured at 2000 Hz. (dB)		45	45	45
Signal to listener echo ratio (dB) 2 wire presented ccts	16	20	20	20
Variation with time of the insertion loss at 800Hz (dB)	±3	±3	±3	±3

Table 4.5   Examples of UK Post Office range of private circuits

In other words, if an 800 Hz signal was transmitted on a line with an insertion loss of $+10$ dB, the received signal would be a tenth of the power of the original signal. If two pieces of equipment are working next to one another (back to back), there will be no measurable loss between them. However, if they are separated by distance and connected by wires a loss will be inserted – hence the term.

For non-data purposes, the quality of the circuit required is often expressed only in terms of the maximum insertion loss (at 800 Hz) which can be tolerated by the private equipment to be used. In these cases, the Post Office will provide a suitable line and maintain it to this measured characteristic.

Modems, and many other types of private equipment, are usually more demanding in their requirements and their effective operation will depend on the nature of other circuit characteristics in addition to insertion loss. The communications authorities offer a range of private circuits to meet different requirements and table 4.5 gives examples of four UK Post Office ranges.[1]

Schedule D in this list is virtually the same as the CCITT Specification M102 for a high quality circuit suitable for data transmission and this Schedule will be used to explain, step by step, the meaning of each of the terms used and their significance to data transmission.

Loss/frequency response (relative to 800 Hz)
On any telephone circuit, some frequencies transmitted will be weakened (or attenuated) more than others during transmission. Loss/frequency response is a term used to describe the variation in losses which can be expected in different sections of the available bandwidth of a circuit. The figures quoted are in decibels (dB) and are relative to the insertion loss at 800 Hz. In table 4.5, the figures for Schedule D show that frequencies transmitted within the band 300-500 Hz would not vary outside the limits of 2 dB stronger and 6 dB weaker than the power of a signal at 800 Hz.

The limits can be seen more clearly in figure 4.41. This is a good quality circuit and the variation in loss is limited to 4 dB (sometimes known as 'spread') over the range 500-3000 Hz. At the extremities of the band the limit of variation is much wider (up to 8 dB).

The loss/frequency response of Schedule B is shown in figure 4.42.

A Schedule B circuit is of lower quality – and therefore lower cost – than a Schedule D circuit. If, for example, the insertion loss at 800 Hz was $+3$ dB,

---

[1] The ranges described are planned to be introduced at the end of 1975, the beginning of 1976.

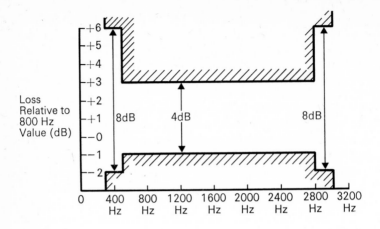

NB + Means more loss

Figure 4.41   Limits for loss/frequency characteristics of a schedule D private circuit

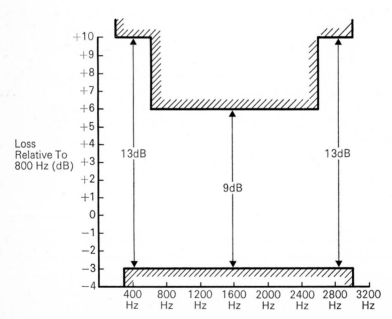

Figure 4.42   Limits for loss/frequency characteristics of schedule B private circuit

then the frequencies in the range 500 Hz to 2600 Hz could vary between +6 dB weaker and —3 dB stronger in relation to it, ie between +10 dB and 0 dB.

Loss/frequency response is not an important factor in speech transmission. Although there may be a noticeable effect in a voice sounding higher or lower due to some frequencies being attenuated more than others, this does not affect intelligibility unduly unless loading severely restricts the bandwidth available. In data transmission, the distortion introduced by a poor loss/ frequency response may impair a receive modem's ability to interpret the signals correctly. If, for example, FSK techniques are used on a circuit which severely attenuates the higher frequency (binary '0') relative to the lower frequency (binary '1') errors could be introduced. Again, in parallel transmission systems where two or more frequencies may be transmitted at once to send a character, a poor loss/frequency response may produce errors.

Generally, higher frequencies are attenuated more than lower frequencies and lines can be equalised to give a better frequency response; further improvements being gained by careful selection of line plant. However, there are technical and economic limits to what can be achieved and speech band circuits are not likely to be improved much beyond the limits of Schedule D shown.

Group delay/frequency response

Just as attenuation varies with frequency, the propagation time of a signal through a telephone channel is also dependent on frequency. The condition which causes some frequencies to be slower than others is known as delay distortion. In data transmission, information is transmitted through rapid changes in the signal state and the term group delay/frequency response refers to a time measurement of a change in a signal at different frequencies through a system.

It is the difference in delay of frequencies within a group which is important and on a circuit with limits such as those given in table 4.5, a change in the signal phase would not be delayed more than the figures shown relative to the minimum delay. The minimum delay cannot be stated because this will depend on the length of the circuit; it may also vary at different frequencies depending on the type of telephone plant used. The limits are shown graphically in figure 4.43.

The effect of delay distortion of a few milliseconds is not significant in speech telephony as the human ear is a fairly slow device which requires sounds to exist for at least a fifth of a second for them to be recognised. The effect of group delay distortion on data transmission will depend on the transmission

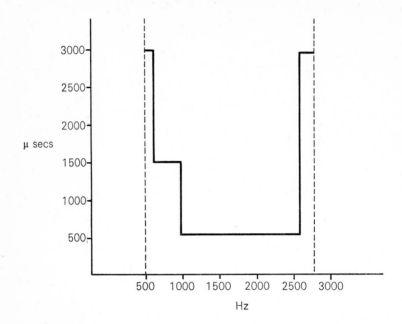

Figure 4.43   Group delay/frequency limits of schedule D circuits

techniques used. When parallel transmission is employed, the effect of the different frequencies, which make up a character, arriving at different times can obviously create problems. More serious is the effect on higher speed modems which rely on the selection of one of a number of conditions of the line signal for efficient operation.

The main reason for group delay distortion is the presence of filters in a telephone channel. The bandpass filters, for example, which are used in carrier telephony for multiplexing, increase the delay at the upper and lower frequency extremities of each channel. The use of loading on long junction routes effectively creates a low pass filter which increases the delay of the higher frequencies.

Equalisation for group delay on private circuits is not a simple matter. Delay equalisers are used when necessary, which in effect slow down the faster frequencies and so reduce the difference in delay; the slight increase in total propagation delay which results from this is not important. However, the main aim in providing circuits to the high quality demanded by Schedule D is to reduce group delay distortion by careful selection of line plant.

Random circuit noise

Random circuit noise, or 'white noise' is an important factor in determining the maximum data signalling rate which can be achieved on a circuit. It can be of any frequency and when it is severe can be heard as a hissing sound. In table 4.5, the figure for random circuit noise in Schedule D is —45 dBm0p. dBm0 refers to the ratio (expressed in decibels) of the noise power to the test level at a particular point in a transmission path known as the relative zero level point. The p shows that the measurement is taken using a psophometer – a device which measures only significant noise. On a circuit to the specification in Schedule D we have:

$$10 \log_{10} \frac{\text{noise power at a relative zero point}}{\text{test power at a relative zero point}} \quad \text{—45 dBm0p (maximum)}$$

The test level is 1 milliwatt and if the transmission system is close to the target there will be no loss at the relative zero point. The maximum level of random noise will, therefore, be approximately —45 dB relative to 1 mW, ie about 0.04 microwatts or 40,000 pico watts.

More important than the actual power of the random noise is its power relative to the actual signal power – the signal/noise ratio. The maximum permissible signal power level is —10 dBm0 so that with a maximum random circuit noise of —45 dBm0p the signal to noise ratio will be in the order of 35 dB, ie 3300 to one.

Impulsive noise

Impulsive noise is the main factor which determines the error rate of a circuit and is discussed in chapter 8. It is measured using an impulsive noise measuring instrument complying with CCITT Recommendation V55.

Signal to quantizing noise

Quantizing noise, or quantizing error, only occurs on PCM links. It is caused by the process of coding and de-coding an audio signal. Although the majority of private circuits will not be routed over PCM links for many years, manufacturers of equipment must assume that any 'wires only' private circuit may include PCM sections. Signal to quantizing noise must, therefore, be taken into account in the manufacture of private equipment and the limits are quoted for the convenience of manufacturers.

Maximum frequency error

Carrier systems used in multiplexing telephone channels may introduce slight changes in the frequencies of signals transmitted. This is known as frequency error or frequency offset and the specified limit of ±2 Hz is recommended by CCITT.

Transmit to receive crosstalk

On a poor telephone connection, we may occasionally hear another faint conversation in the background. This is crosstalk which is caused by induction between different telephone channels. In table 4.5, reference is made to the transmit to receive crosstalk attenuation on four-wire presented circuits. It means that if a signal is transmitted in one direction the induction or crosstalk arising from it in the other channel should not be less than 45 dB relative to the transmitted signal, ie 40,000 to 1. Transmit to receive crosstalk of very low levels such as this is not significant in data transmission.

Signal to listener echo ratio

Signal to listener echoes can cause errors if they are of a sufficiently high order and were discussed earlier in this chapter.

Variation with time of the insertion loss at 800 Hz

The insertion loss of a circuit will vary over time so that a circuit in table 4.5 with an insertion loss of $+10$ dB at 800 Hz may vary between $+7$ and $+13$ dB. The Post Office will take this into account when the maximum tolerable insertion loss is quoted by a customer.

The Characteristics of Switched Connections

It is not possible to be precise when describing the characteristics of public switched telephone network (PSTN) connections as the telephone plant used for each call is selected on a purely random basis.

The present aim of the UK Post Office is to ensure that the limiting insertion loss between local exchanges does not exceed 20 dB at 800 Hz (approximately 30 dB between customers' premises). However, until this target is achieved, there will be occasions when connections can have an insertion loss greater than 30 dB. The combined effect of severely attenuated signals and more impulsive noise produces a poorer error performance than that achieved on private circuits.

The loss/frequency and group delay distortion characteristics likely to be encountered on the PSTN will vary considerably depending on distance and the type of plant over which calls are routed. the curve for loss/frequency response shown in figure 4.44a was produced by combining the results of a survey of PSTN connections with estimates based on the known factors which can affect this characteristic.

Although the survey was conducted several years ago and the trunk and junction network has been improved since then, the curve serves to show the

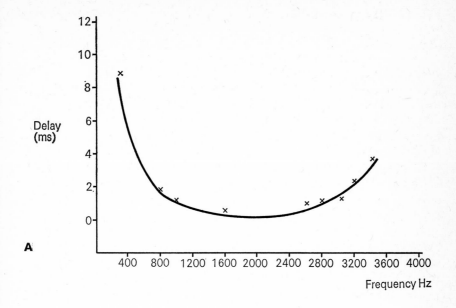

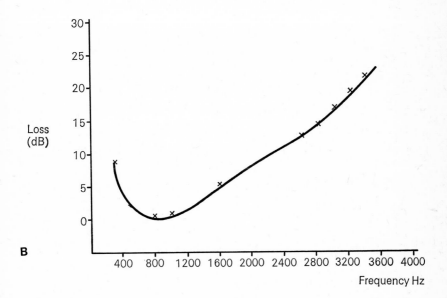

Figure 4.44 Nominal loss/frequency and group delay/frequency characteristics of an extreme connection including long junction and
trunk circuits

kind of extreme condition which can still be met. Figure 4.44b shows the group delay/frequency characteristics which may be expected on such a connection.

Although such connections are adequate for speech, they pose serious problems in data transmission. If, for example, we consider the FSK modem used on the UK Datel 600 service operating over a circuit such as this, a data signalling rate of 1200 bit/s would not be possible. At this rate the frequencies used are 1300 Hz and 2100 Hz. It will be seen that at 2100 Hz the attenuation could be as high as 40 dB (ie in connection with a loss of 30 dB at 800 Hz, plus an attenuation loss of 10 dB at 2100 Hz relative to 800 Hz, *see* figure 4.44a) and the weakness of the signal would make detection difficult. Added to this is the fact that both random noise and impulsive noise levels would be too high in relation to the signal strength. The possibility of picking up such circuits as this on the PSTN explains why the Post Office cannot guarantee 1200 bit/s data signalling rates with the Datel 600 service on the PSTN. It should always be possible, however, to obtain a connection which enables data to be exchanged at 600 bit/s. The frequencies

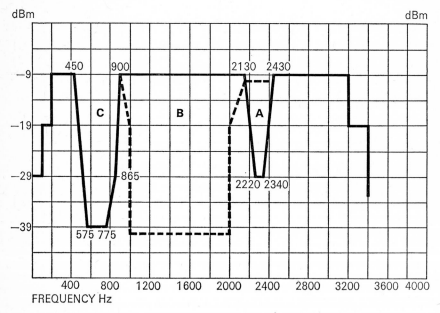

Notes: (1) Signals are permitted in Area A only if accompanied by signals in Area B
at a power level not lower than 12 dB below the power level of the signal
in Area A.
      (2) Signals are permitted in Area C provided that there is no false operation of
trunk signalling equipment (SSAC 1).

Figure 4.45

used at the lower rate are 1300 Hz and 1700 Hz and in this range loss/frequency response is less of a problem.

On the switched network, voice frequency signalling systems are used to establish, control and release connections. It follows that if signals are transmitted on an established connection, which in some way simulate those of the signalling system, then false operations such as cleardown may occur. Two inband signalling systems are in use in the UK, either or both of which may be encountered on a single connection. These signalling systems impose a constraint on the bandwidth which is available for use on the PSTN. Figure 4.45 shows the areas of sensitivity for the 1 VF and 2 VF receivers and the signal power level restrictions. Although it will be seen from Notes 1 and 2 that in some circumstances signal components in the areas of sensitivity may be allowed, the bandwidth available for medium speed data transmission is virtually limited to about 1200 Hz (between 900 Hz and 2100 Hz). Lower speed data transmission is possible by using frequencies in the lower end of the spectrum; the Datel 600 service, for example, uses the frequencies 390 Hz and 450 Hz for a low speed (75 bit/s) simultaneous supervisory channel.

5 Data Terminals

Almost any device which is capable of sending or receiving information (or both) may be regarded as a data terminal. With the progressive reduction in the costs of logic circuitry and the recognition of the need to optimise the distribution of intelligence in data communications networks, the production and use of 'intelligent' terminals is growing. Many of these are computers in their own right and defining the term 'terminal' becomes difficult. Any measuring device such as a temperature gauge or an electrocardiograph can be regarded as a potential data terminal if there are benefits to be gained in reading the information it provides remotely. When we consider also that such familiar devices as the domestic television set and telephone are likely to be used extensively in the future for data communications, precise definition of a terminal becomes impossible and indeed unnecessarily constraining. Although definition is impossible, categorisation is merely difficult as there are broad classes of terminals which have sufficient distinguishing features for the attempt to be made. There are, however, grey areas and the reader should be prepared to encounter terminals which do not fall clearly into any of the broad categories of terminals now in use which are described later in this chapter.

The Determination of Terminal Requirements

The variety of terminals on the market today makes terminal selection difficult. Nevertheless, the problem of selection is not so mountainous that a particular terminal should be chosen merely because it is there. A great deal of analysis is necessary in finding out the overall system requirements in order to specify the functional terminal requirements for a particular system. The specification of terminal requirements and the subsequent selection of suitable terminals is of major importance in the systems design. The two prime factors to be considered are, firstly, the functions which the terminal will be required to perform in the data handling operation to meet the needs of the business, and secondly, but of no lesser importance, the needs of the people who will be required to operate the terminals.

Terminal Requirements

The overall needs of the business may well influence the functions that a terminal has to perform. For example, there may be a requirement for using the terminal for sending plain language messages with 'hard' copy (printed copy) between different locations. This might then become a factor in the choice of the type of keyboard required.

Message handling

There may be a number of different types of messages to be handled. It must be decided from an analysis of these messages whether hard copy is essential or whether a video display from a cathode ray tube (CRT) is more suitable. In some applications, a voice response from a computer may be required.

If forms are to be handled, then this will determine a whole range of machine characteristics. For example, the width of the widest forms will determine the size of platen required on a dataprinter (printed copy device) or the number of characters per line on a visual display unit (VDU). The length of the form will indicate the 'form feed' requirements which are necessary in order to automatically feed out one form and substitute another on a dataprinter; 'page flip' or 'page roll' can give equivalent facilities on a VDU. On hard copy machines, 'sprocket feed' facilities are provided to lock the form in position to avoid the paper slipping or jamming. Form handling usually requires tabulator facilities so that the type head can be positioned accurately and quickly on a dataprinter; similar facilities on VDUs are provided by cursor controls.

The messages themselves may have special characteristics which require unusual characters such as those used in mathematics. It may be necessary to have different types of print which will require a machine with inter-changeable type heads.

Message storage may be necessary at the terminal. Commonly, messages are prepared at the terminal and corrected for errors before transmission at the maximum speed of the machine and line; this requires some form of storage. Similarly, a programmer may wish to retain a copy of a program which he has prepared on-line to a computer and which he can enter again without having to re-key. Many machines provide punched paper tape facilities for such purposes and an increasing number use magnetic tape cassettes.

Facilities are available for sharing local storage in magnetic tape form amongst a number of terminals.

In some real-time applications, messages consist of a highly sophisticated dialogue between the operator and the computer and this may be a determining factor in specifying the terminal input requirement.

In an extreme case, only two keys labelled 'yes' and 'no' would be required on the terminal with the computer asking questions via a simulated voice unit.

Interfacing with the computer

In any data communications system, the computer must be programmed to receive data in a prescribed format; any transmissions which transgress this format will be rejected as invalid. Similarly, the code used and the procedures necessary to control transmission will to some extent determine the type of terminal which can be used.

It is obviously important that the terminal and the computer are kept in step when transferring messages; some form of synchronisation will therefore be required. It is equally important to recognise that the slowest input device to a computer system may be a human being and some form of buffering will be necessary to equate these different speeds; in an on-line system, this buffering is often at the terminal. Timing is also important when 'polling' or selection techniques are employed; in those cases, the terminal will not only have to identify itself but generate responses automatically, all within a critical time period. It follows that the method of synchronisation (asynchronous or synchronous), the buffering capability and the timing of the control procedures must all be taken into account in selecting a terminal which is compatible with the computer system.

Interfacing with the communications network

The first factor to be considered under this heading is whether the terminal has been given permission to be connected to the communications authority's lines. Different criteria are applied depending on whether the terminal is to be connected to the public switched telephone network (PSTN) or to a private circuit. If permission has been given to connect to a private circuit, it cannot be assumed that the terminal can be connected to an exchange line. In some applications, it may be desirable to 'fall back' to the PSTN under failure conditions, the terminal being normally connected to a private circuit; in these circumstances, a terminal must have been given permission by the communications authority to be connected to the private circuit and the PSTN.

If the terminal is to be used for data collection on the PSTN, and data is collected automatically by dialling the telephone number to which the terminal is connected, an 'automatic answering' facility must be provided; this is a facility which cannot be provided by some terminals.

Speed

The speed at which data should be entered by the terminal and received from the computer will be determined by a combination of several factors, these are:

– The response time required. This applies only to two-way, on-line systems.

– The volume of input and output information and maximum times required to move the information.

– The maximum information transfer rate provided by the lines and modems to be used.

– The keying speed of an operator. This is not likely to exceed five characters per second.

– Whether synchronous timing is required by the computer or communications controller. If it is, then transmission at a fixed speed is mandatory.

– The output speed required by an operator. If the output is to be read by an operator in an enquiry/response situation, then 30 characters per second is about right. If, on the other hand, an operator requires a full frame of information to 'scan', as when checking an item on a telephone bill, to be displayed on a VDU, then he should ideally be provided with the information at a minimum of 10 times this rate, ie 300 characters per second.

– The speed of peripheral devices. If output is not to be read immediately by an operator, then it is desirable for the speed to be geared to the maximum speed of the fastest peripheral device at the terminal. For this reason, remote batch terminals with fast line printers usually operate between 300 and 1200 characters per second.

– Cost. In general, the faster the terminal operates the more costly it becomes. Although this is also true of the modems and lines to which the terminals are connected, there may be savings in overall costs at higher speeds because of improved circuit utilisation.

The user and the terminal

One of the major factors in choosing a terminal is to give very careful consideration to the people who will be using it. What kind of people are they – computer professionals, for example, skilled operators or casual untrained users? What are their physical characteristics? Are they heavy-handed people who might make short work of a sophisticated, but dainty keyboard?

Having established the sort of people who will be using the terminals, consideration should be given to the environment in which each terminal will be working. What accommodation is available for example? Will there be adequate power supplies? Do the terminals need to be portable? Are aesthetics important – as in a modern office – or is robustness more important – as in a factory?

There are many such questions, all of them based on simple common sense. However, anyone who has witnessed the obvious difficulties which some operators experience in operating the terminals and the contortions of maintenance engineers in installing them will vouch for the fact that they are occasionally overlooked.

Interfacing with other terminals

If the organisation in which the new terminal is to be installed uses other type terminals, there may be a requirement for intercommunication between these and the new terminal and again the question of compatibility arises.

Reliability

Terminal failures must be expected; the extent to which these can be tolerated will depend both on the application for which the terminal is to be used and the service which is given by the supplier or his maintenance agent in getting the terminal back in working order.

Error handling

Errors, like failures, are inevitable. A terminal's handling of errors may be judged under two headings, firstly, its ability to detect input errors and bring these to the attention of an operator and, secondly, by its ability to control line transmission errors (*see* Chapter 8).

Types of Terminals

Categorising terminals presents problems but there are broad classes of machines which have sufficient distinguishing features for an attempt to be made. There are a number of different ways which can be used for categorisation; for example, by the speed range of terminals, by the applications for which they are used, by the method of data entry, etc. All of these methods have their merits depending on the context in which terminals are discussed. None of these are suitable for a chapter of this kind which seeks to provide a general description of different types of terminal for a wide range of readers, some of whom might never have seen one.

Terminals are, therefore, discussed below under headings which it is hoped will be familiar to people already involved in data communications and which will best help newcomers to the field in getting to know the machines which are used.

Dataprinters

A number of data communications applications require basically an alphanumeric keyboard and hard (printed) copy of messages sent and received. The wide range of machines which are manufactured to provide these facilities are referred to here as dataprinters but may also be called tele-typewriters, character printers, keyboard printers or serial printers. The speed of operation of dataprinters, the way in which the basic facilities are provided and the extent to which other facilities are added varies considerably. Many dataprinters are multiple purpose devices and the machine characteristics are usually determined by the main use of the machine.

Operational speed

More than half the dataprinters in Europe are used predominantly for direct keyboard communication; for example, between operators on distant terminals, from an operator to an unattended remote station or interactively between an operator and a computer in a 'conversational' mode. In these circumstances, the main factors determining the operational speed of the machine are the needs of the operator and these needs vary with the application. The speed at which data can be entered and transmitted is not a problem with direct transmission – few operators can exceed five characters per second. The speed at which messages can be read (rather than scanned) by an operator is often a critical factor, however. A fast reading speed for a human being is 400 words per minute (40 characters per second); 250 words per minute (25 characters per second) is average and 150 words per minute (or 15 characters per second) is considered slow. Dataprinters used mainly for direct transmission generally operate, therefore, at print speeds between 10 and 30 characters per second. Machine costs rise substantially with speed (line costs may also be affected, *see* Chapter 4) and for this reason 10 character per second machines are still very popular.

Some dataprinters are used mainly for direct transmission from the keyboard, but are also used for sending or receiving fairly small quantities of data automatically in paper tape, magnetic tape or punched card form. In these circumstances, the operational speed is again dictated by the predominant direct keying use of the terminal and low speed automatic send and receive equipment (between 10-30 characters per second) is generally used. In addition to direct keyboard transmission, some applications require facilities to automatically transmit and receive fairly large quantities of information. In these cases, the needs of the operator may become secondary to other factors such as the need to make economic use of lines. To provide these facilities, a number of data printers have been designed to use faster printers, paper tape readers, paper tape punches, and, increasingly, magnetic tape cassette reader/recorders. Most terminals of this type use data transmission services between 600 and 2400 bit/s which allow for the terminal devices to operate up to a maximum of about 240 characters per second.

Where a number of on-line dataprinter terminals are employed, they may be grouped on to a multipoint network or a network using concentrators (*see* Chapter 9). In these circumstances, the transmission speed will be determined by the line loading, and buffers are used (usually in the terminals) which effectively separate the input/output of the terminal from that of the lines.

Transmit/receive capability
This is conventionally described in three ways:

– Keyboard Send and Receive (KSR)
A KSR dataprinter has an alpha-numeric keyboard for data entry and a character printer.

– Receive only (RO)
No keyboard is provided on RO machines. These machines are used in situations where either there is no requirement at the terminal to transmit messages or to provide occasional hard copy when used in conjunction with video display terminals.

– Automatic Send and Receive (ASR)
ASR machines employ local storage, usually in paper tape or magnetic tape, and have automatic send and receive equipment. Data can be stored for repeat messages or used to provide local hard copy. Received messages can be punched into paper tape as hard copy is being produced on the machine.

Generally, the paper tape reader, which is used to transmit the message, operates at the maximum speed of the machine and offers the following advantages:

– operator verification of the text before transmission;

– maximum utilisation of line time.

An alternative to paper tape is magnetic tape cassettes. These are being used increasingly for they offer similar facilities to paper tape but are easier to handle and store.

Punched cards may be used with the appropriate reader and printer but their use is less common than paper tape.

Dataprinter terminals are typified by the Teletype 33 of the Teletype Corporation. A Teletype 33 ASR is shown in plate 5.1.

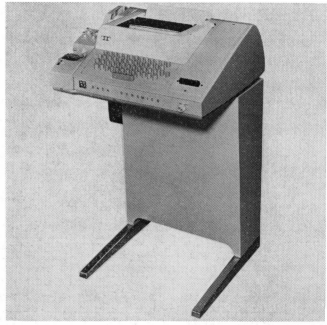

(Courtesy of Data Dynamics Ltd)

Plate 5.1   Teletype 33 (ASR)

Buffered terminals

Strictly speaking, any machine which has a tape reading facility could be termed 'buffered'. However, in a buffered terminal, the buffer is an integral part of the hardware of the machine – data is held in store, rather than on a removable tape or card. Such a terminal offers automatic send and receive facilities but additionally the buffer can hold data and transmit when called upon to do so by a polling computer at higher speed than the terminal itself.

Message handling

Dataprinters are often multipurpose devices and may be required to handle different kinds of messages. Commonly, messages are entered and received on pre-prepared forms and this may determine a whole range of machine characteristics. For example, the width of the widest form to be handled will determine the size of platen required; the length of the form will indicate the 'form feed' requirements necessary to automatically feed out one form and substitute another (this is often achieved by a sprocket feed facility which locks the form in position to avoid the paper slipping). Form handling requires tabulation facilities so that the print head can be positioned accurately and quickly. The variety and complexity of the forms to be handled will be a major factor in determining the size of the character set required.

Keyboards and codes used

Keyboards vary considerably both in layout and the character set used. Most dataprinters use a 4-row keyboard with keys for the alpha-numeric input arranged as for a conventional typewriter. Plate 5.2 shows the keyboard of a Teletype 33 which uses an abbreviated version of IA 5 code.

(Courtesy of Data Dynamics Ltd)

Plate 5.2   Keyboard layout of a Teletype 33 (ASR)

There are 50 keys plus a space bar and shifts are kept to a minimum by having letters, figures and the most commonly used punctuation signs as primary characters. On this machine, shifts from primary to secondary characters or vice versa are performed by depressing the shift key and at the same time depressing the selected character key. Like many other data-printers, the Teletype 33 does not provide lower case letters as these are not required in most applications.

Some dataprinters use five unit codes, such as, IA 2 but a more extensive character set is usually needed than this provides. More commonly, seven or eight unit codes such as IA 5, ASC II, or EBCDIC are used (*see* Chapter 1).

Character framing
All dataprinters, with the exception of some 'buffered' terminals, employ start/stop synchronisation (ie the receiver is kept in step with the transmitter during a character but not between characters). Figure 5.1 shows the bit positions allocated on a typical 10 character per second dataprinter using the seven unit IA 5 code.

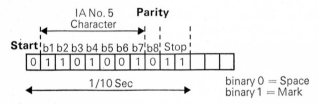

Figure 5.1   Character framing on a typical 10 characters per second data-printer

The seven information elements are arranged so that the least significant bit (b1) is transmitted first; these are preceded by a start element. Although the parity bit in the eighth position can be used for error control (*see* Chapter 8), it is not used on most dataprinters. If a parity check is employed, the parity bit is chosen in such a way that the number of '1' bits is even in the sequence of eight bits (b1-b8). In many dataprinters, the bit in b8 has no significance; the Teletype 33, for example, always produces a binary '1' in this position. The stop element in figure 5.1 is shown as being twice the duration of the information and start elements. CCITT recommends that a stop element with a duration of two unit intervals is used at the transmitter with IA 5 code over the public switched telephone and telegraph networks with electro-mechanical data terminal equipment operating at modulation rates up to and including 200 baud. In other cases, the use of a stop element with a duration of one unit interval is preferable and figure 5.2 shows the character framing of a typical 30 character per second machine using IA 5 code.

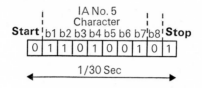

Figure 5.2 Character framing on a typical 30 character per second data-printer

During manual operation, there may be a considerable time elapsing between key depressions and the stop condition is maintained on the line during this period.

Transmission requirements

Let us now consider transmitting the IA 5 character shown in figure 5.3 on a 10 character per second dataprinter. There are 11 unit signal elements to be transmitted as shown in figure 5.3, each one of these is 1/110 second in duration. The circuit carrying these signals must, therefore, have a modulation rate which is equal to the reciprocal of 1/110, ie 110 baud.

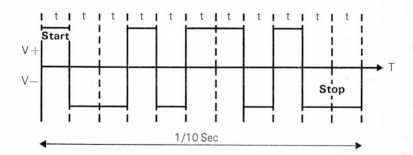

Figure 5.3 Signal elements of IA 5 character

A 30 character per second machine (*see* figure 5.2) would use only one unit signal element for the stop signal, and 10 unit signal elements would be needed to transmit each character, each one being 1/300ths of a second in duration. A circuit with a modulation rate of 300 baud would be necessary to carry these signals.

Leased telegraph circuits are available in the UK which have a modulation rate of 110 baud and therefore allow for 10 characters per second operation without the need for modems. Alternatively, the Datel 200 service can be used on the public switched telephone network; this normally provides for a modulation rate of 200 baud but has been extended so that transmission of 30 characters per second (300 baud) can often (but not always) be achieved.

Printing

Two basic types of printing are used, 'impact' and 'non-impact'.

Impact printers come in a number of different types, but they all depend on the physical impact of some kind of typehead on to paper. Non-impact printers transfer the selected character to the paper without contact, commonly, by thermal transfer or some form of ink spray.

Print speeds of single character impact printers used on dataprinters vary between 10 characters per second and about 30 characters per second. Electro-mechanical or semi-electronic machines are used within this speed range, the major restraint on speed being the physical movement of the printing device. The faster impact printers use fixed platens with extremely light moving type heads but it is unlikely that reliable and economic impact printers can be developed to operate at speeds much above 30 characters per second.

Impact printing has the advantage that undercopies can be produced economically; all machines can produce at least one good copy whilst some will produce up to 14 copies.

Non-impact printers are electronic or semi-electronic in construction. Although they are faster and – because they have fewer moving parts – quicker than impact printers they also tend to be more costly. Some non-impact printers can operate at over 120 characters per second.

Although at least one manufacturer is developing a machine which will produce one undercopy using special paper, copies are not usually available from non-impact dataprinters. Most dataprinter users do require additional copies and these must, therefore, be obtained by photocopying the original — which adds to the running costs. The poor character definition of the original produced by some dotmatrix printers may in fact not be good enough to produce satisfactory photocopies. A further disadvantage with some machines is the relatively high cost of the special paper they use.

Error control

There are three distinct levels of error control facilities provided by dataprinters and these are discussed over page. For a fuller description of error control techniques see Chapter 8.

1   *No automatic error detection or correction:* In some direct keying applications, transmission errors are of only minor importance. For example, an experienced programmer using a dataprinter and a remote computer to develop a new program will quickly detect from the responses he receives whether an error has occurred. In circumstances such as these, transmission errors are merely a nuisance and the cost of sophisticated and expensive error control equipment cannot be justified. Many dataprinters are, therefore, used without any error control facilities at all. Others use the duplex facilities offered by many standard services to 'echo' back the transmitted data. The local copy on these machines contains the data which has been transmitted and returned on the transmission link and the operator at the transmit station may then detect transmission errors visually.

2   *Automatic error detection – no automatic correction:* Where the detection of line errors is important, a variety of error detection methods such as single parity, two co-ordinate parity and cyclic redundancy checks are available on some dataprinters to indicate a transmission error by a print statement (typically 'E') and/or by an error lamp lighting at the receive terminal. If a message in, say, paper tape form is being received, the paper tape punch is usually inhibited at the receiver on receipt of an error. Correction of such errors is achieved in a number of ways but all of these require a manual operation at the transmitting terminal when only forward error detection is provided. Typically, the operator at the receive machine presses a NAK key (NAK may be a secondary character or be provided on a separate key). The return of this negative acknowledgement signal to the transmit station locks the keyboard, inhibits tape transmission and gives an alarm indication to the operator. The message, or part of the message, is then re-transmitted.

3   *Automatic error detection and correction:* Again, a variety of error detection techniques, such as two co-ordinate parity, are used to detect errors. In order to automatically correct errors, dataprinters must be capable of automatically generating and responding to the special characters (ACK, NAK) used in decision feedback error control; they must also be capable of storing information so that a block in error can be re-transmitted. A data-printer which has these capabilities will, on receipt of a block which is in error, automatically return a NAK character to the transmitter. On receipt of this character, the transmitter will, depending on the type of machine, either repeat the block from a buffer store or automatically backspace a tape to the beginning of the faulty block in order to re-transmit.

Input errors

Techniques used to control line errors can only ensure that data transmitted is received correctly. Errors due to an operator or those which exist in a pre-prepared storage medium such as punched paper tape are usually more frequent than line errors and cannot be detected by these methods. Input errors can only be found by programs or hard-wired logic which can detect invalid or incorrect input. To choose a simple example, an operator may key a letter in error instead of a figure in a box on a prepared document reserved for numeric data; this can easily be detected as an invalid input by program and can be brought to the attention of the operator in a number of ways by lamp indication, locking the keyboard, etc. In order to detect errors of this kind, the dataprinter input must, therefore, be vetted by some intelligence built into the system. The terminal itself may include a small computer or it must be connected on-line to a programmable controller or a main frame computer.

Video display units (VDUs)
Video terminals fall into two main categories, graphic displays and alphanumeric displays.

Graphic displays
Graphic displays are often used for computer-aided design and for simulation and modelling. For design work, information is entered using a device such as a 'light pen' (*see* plate 5.3). Drawings are displayed on the screen and in

(Courtesy of IBM (UK) Ltd)

Plate 5.3   Visual Display Unit being used for circuit design using a light pen

some cases can be adjusted to alter perspective. The designer works interactively with the computer by amending the design with the input device, the
amendments being instantly displayed on the screen. Most of the graphic
display terminals in use employ special-purpose, directed beam cathode ray
tubes (CRTs) with high accuracy analogue circuitry. Because transmission
speeds up to one million bit/s are required, it is not normally economic
as yet to use normal data transmission lines to connect graphic displays
to central computers and such terminals are normally located 'in-house'
close to the computer. However, some graphic terminals have their own
small computer and in these circumstances may be connected via a circuit
to a central computer. The high speed link is between the terminal and its
own computer and a relatively slow transmission link is required for
occasional communication with the main computer.

Alphanumeric displays

Alphanumeric (A/N) displays have a keyboard and a cathode ray tube which
displays letters, figures, and other symbols. They are widely used in data
communications for applications where hard copy is not usually required
at the terminal.

Figure 5.4 shows a functional schematic diagram of a single or 'stand alone'
A/N display terminal where all the elements, with the exception of the
modem, are included in one case.

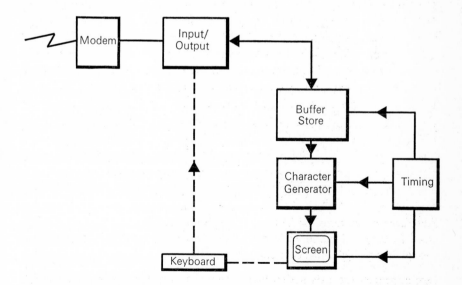

Figure 5.4   Functional elements of a stand alone alphanumeric display
                terminal

An operator using an A/N display terminal enters data, using the keyboard, into a buffer store. A wide variety of edit facilities may be offered by these terminals and the buffer usually stores the data so that the location of a character in this memory corresponds with the position selected on a screen. Characters are displayed on the screen via a character generator and as the illuminated characters decay quickly the screen must be continually 'refreshed'.

Data is not transmitted to line direct from the keyboard as is the case with the unbuffered dataprinters discussed earlier. The complete message to be sent may be assembled, checked and corrected on the screen before the operator depresses the transmit key; the contents of the buffer are only then transmitted to line via the modem.

Editing and formating

The ability to detect and simply correct input errors before transmission is a considerable benefit and A/N displays are markedly better in this respect than hard copy dataprinters. Unlike a printed character, a character displayed on a screen in error can be deleted and overwritten by another. A wide range of editing and formating facilities are, therefore, possible on display terminals which cannot be achieved on a dataprinter.

The keyboard

The keyboard design for A/N display terminals has taxed the skill of many designers and will continue to do so. Ergonomists are playing an increasing part in this interesting field where there is a particular need to fit the keyboard to the person using it – and not vice versa. The problems are more acute in the display area than in others because of the wide variety of applications in which they are used and the wider variety of people who use them.

There can be no universal keyboard design for these terminals. While the conventional typewriter layout may be satisfactory, where operators are either dedicated to their task or at least knowledgeable about (and therefore tolerant of) computers, the A/N display operator may be very different. He is likely to be a casual user, rather than a dedicated operator, who has never typed a letter in his life and is apprehensive about and aggressive towards an over-complex keyboard (or computer dialogue). Such ordinary people as these are proven terminal benders and system wreckers and it is now recognised by terminal manufacturers and systems analysts alike that they have special needs which must be met.

One approach towards a simplified keyboard layout is shown in plate 5.4. The letters are presented in alphabetical order and there are no shift keys making the keyboard much easier to use for the unskilled operator.

(Courtesy of Plessey Telecommunications Ltd)

Plate 5.4   Simplified keyboard

In other applications with A/N display terminals the users are specialist operators and the conventional typewriter layout is more suitable.

Being wholly electronic, display terminal keyboards are virtually silent in operation. Although this is an obviously desirable feature the silence can be unnerving for the terminal operators and re-assuring noises are provided by some terminals on a small loudspeaker when each key, or when the transmit key only is pressed.

Most A/N display terminals use abbreviated forms of seven unit codes such as ASCII and IA 5 although at least 64 characters are usually provided.

The screen
The effects of artificial and natural lighting falling directly on an illuminated screen are obvious and this should, of course, be avoided. Nevertheless, terminal environments will differ considerably in this respect and most screens have brightness controls and are screened in some way. The needs of the operator should, of course, be paramount and the choice of contrasting colours of the characters and background are a problem tackled differently by manufacturers. Similarly, the shape of the characters are important and on many A/N display terminals these are presented on the screen in a dotmatrix; commonly, five dots wide and seven dots high. As characters are continually

refreshed on the screen, a flickering effect must be avoided. The number of repetitions is known as the 'refresh rate' and usually exceeds 50 frames per second; at this rate, the human eye and brain do not notice these changes and flicker is avoided; some terminals offer a 'blinking' facility at a much lower rate than this to highlight a particular field.

No two operators are alike and facilities to adjust the size, colour and brightness of the characters displayed are a desirable feature of any display terminal.

Screens used on A/N displays differ considerably both in their size and the number of characters they can display. The factors affecting this capacity of a screen, in terms of the characters which can be displayed, are determined by the dimensions of the screen, the size of the characters, the distance between characters and between lines and in some cases the size of the buffer store. The number of lines on a screen vary between 12 and 40, while there may be from 30 to 80 characters per line giving a maximum capacity range for A/N displays of between 360 and 3200 characters per screen. Most terminals, however, have a maximum capacity within the range 400 to 2000 characters. On some machines, the number of characters which can be displayed is limited by the buffer capacity which is smaller than the maximum number of character positions on the screen. In practice, a screen is never completely filled with characters and buffer savings can be made by not actually storing space characters.

Editing

The editing on A/N displays is controlled by the use of special keys; the position on the screen where an edit function is to be performed being indicated by a 'cursor'. A cursor is a symbol displayed on the screen as a small bar above or below a character position; its position on the screen corresponding to a location in the buffer store. When keying alphanumeric data, the cursor automatically steps to indicate the position of the next character to be inserted. Its position on the screen can be altered quickly by the operator using cursor control keys. Having positioned the cursor, the operator may then use other control keys such as:

Delete – to delete a character.

Line erasure – to erase a complete line (leaving the remaining lines where they are or moving them up one line).

Tabulate – to indicate tabulation stops.

Space – to insert a space in a line (simultaneously moving the rest of the characters on the line left and right).

Clear – to delete a complete page.

Formating

A variety of displayed formats are possible on A/N display terminals. For example, an operator using a terminal for order entry may key in a code combination which results in an order 'form' being displayed on the screen. The code combination is recognised by the control computer which responds by transmitting fixed field information such as column headings, goods in stock, etc, into the A/N terminal buffer. The operator can then 'fill in' the form displayed using the keyboard and TAB key which moves the cursor from one fixed field to another, the fixed field information being protected while this takes place. When the order form is completed, the operator presses the transmit key and the order is entered by transmitting only the variable information; this is sometimes called 'split screen mode' or 'partial transmission' and can result in considerable savings in line transmission time.

In some applications, the screen capacity may not be large enough to display the whole form and more than one 'page' may be required. This is achieved on some machines by using a 'page flip' facility; extra buffer capacity is

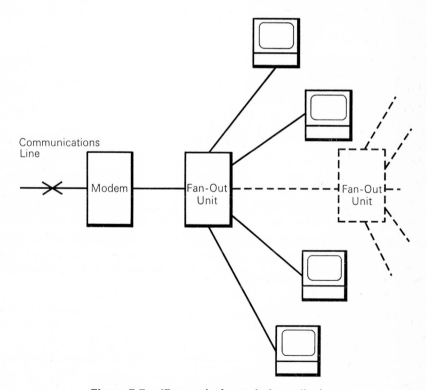

Figure 5.5   'Fan-out' of stand alone displays

required to store the information. 'Page Roll' provides similar facilities but instead of a complete page being changed the screen is 'rolled' so that the bottom line moves up to show another line and the top line moves off the screen.

A/N display configurations

A/N display terminals can be used as single 'stand alone' terminals (*see* figure 5.4) or in various combinations.

A number of stand alone terminals can be concentrated on one line using a fan out unit (*see* figure 5.5).

Where there are a number of terminals at the same location, further economies can be made by concentrating some of the functions in a control unit. The common functions performed by display controllers vary, but generally include buffer storage, character generation, and all the logic circuitry for

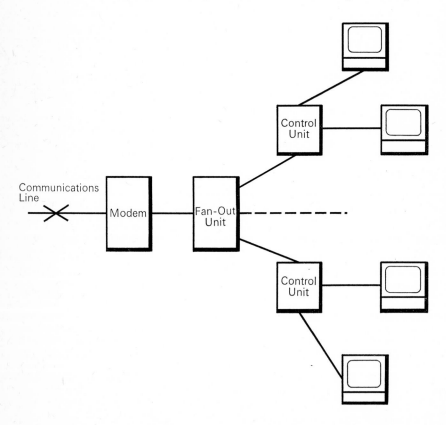

Figure 5.6   Clustered displays

editing, formating, etc. A configuration with a fan out unit and two control units is shown in figure 5.6.

Communications requirements

The communications requirements of A/N displays are often very different to those for the dataprinters described earlier. In the previous case discussed, the response time on a single unbuffered dataprinter being used interactively with a problem solving computer could be defined as 'the time which elapses between the last key being depressed by the terminal operator and the first printed output character being received on the terminal page'. In this case, the data preceding the last character keyed had already been transmitted to line; additionally, the received message from this computer would very likely be read rather than scanned. Conversely, A/N displays are often used in circumstances where incoming messages to the terminal are scanned rather than read. Also, no data is transmitted to line until the depression of the 'transmit' key on the keyboard releases the contents of the terminal buffer. A different view of communication requirements emerges from a consideration of these two factors. Response time may now be defined as 'the time between the transmit key being depressed by the terminal operator and the first output character being displayed on the terminal screen'. However, this ignores the fact that the incoming message may be scanned extremely quickly – a complete screen full of information can be scanned in some circumstances in less than two seconds. For example, on a terminal being used for customer enquiries, the operator may be searching for an item on a disputed bill held on the computer files. In this case, he would probably only scan over one column on the displayed form – say, the date, to find the item in question. In cases such as this, a more practical view of response time might be 'the time between the transmit key being depressed by the terminal operator and the last character of the response being displayed on the screen'. It can, of course, be argued that the first character to be displayed is the most critical for, until this arrives, the operator is unsure whether a response will arrive at all. Whatever the approach to response time, the time to display incoming messages on the screen must be taken into account, for messages displayed too slowly will cause a great deal of operator frustration and inevitably the system will suffer. Obviously this factor is more important in applications where long rather than short incoming messages are the norm. Response time requirements are an important factor in design calculation and are a prime factor in determining the transmission speed required. Most on-line A/N display terminals use transmission facilities in the range 1200-4800 bit/s.

Transmission time can be saved by using data compression techniques and in alphanumeric displays the number of 'space' characters sent to line is often reduced. Figure 5.7 shows simple data compression in a before and after situation where a number of blanks have been removed by a symbol signifying space, the actual number of spaces being determined by the numeric character immediately following.

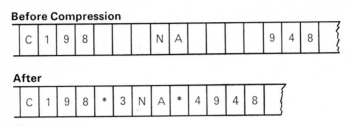

Figure 5.7   An example of data compression

Although there may be savings in line costs by using these techniques on A/N displays, this has to be set against the costs of the additional logic required on the terminal or terminal controller to provide these facilities.

Key to tape

A/N displays are being used increasingly for off-line data preparation, a number of displays being connected to a controller which captures the prepared data on magnetic tape. The editing capability of A/N displays makes them suitable for this kind of work. Communication links may or may not be employed between the controller and the central computer depending on the timescale requirements for the data to be processed; in many cases, the prepared data is despatched by using delivery services. In cases where data transmission lines are used, the large quantities of data involved usually necessitate transmission speeds of at least 2400 bit/s.

Peripheral attachments

A number of add-on facilities can be provided by peripheral equipment attached to A/N display terminals. Some of these are:

Printers   Although A/N displays are not used in circumstances where hard copy is frequently required, an occasional copy is sometimes necessary. In these circumstances, a hard copy printer can be provided with the terminal, or shared between a number of terminals, the contents of the buffer store being transmitted to the print device. Read only (RO) high speed character printers are often used for this purpose to obtain a copy as quickly as possible and allow the A/N display to handle the next transaction.

Badge readers   For security reasons, it is sometimes necessary to identify the terminal operator before allowing access to programs and files in the computer system. Although this is often done by the operator keying into the terminal an identification code, special badges containing coded information may be provided which can be automatically read by a badge reader associated with the terminal. From this information can be determined the degree of access into the system which can be allowed the badge holder.

Paper tape/Magnetic tape devices   Paper tape punches/readers or magnetic tape cassette reader/recorders can be used in place of a printer for recording input and output data.

Remote batch terminals (RBTs)

Unlike the dataprinter or the A/N display terminal, the name 'remote batch terminal' describes the function the terminal performs rather than the terminal itself. This function is to act as a satellite to a central computer to allow batch processing to be achieved remotely, and a brief description of this type of processing might be useful to some readers.

Batch processing can be defined as 'the method of computer usage whereby transactions are collected together in a batch before a computer run'. This is the historical use of computers and is still the way in which the majority of computers are used. Payroll is a typical batch processing job in which data is prepared into machine readable form, such as punched cards, punched paper tape or magnetic tape, by keying in on data preparation machines the information contained on source documents. This data, which contains variable information for the people on the payroll such as the number of hours worked, sick absences, etc, is collected together in a batch. This batch of data is sorted and loaded with the payroll program for processing on the central computer during a scheduled period. Results in the form of payslips, etc, may be printed out during the run, or, more commonly, are stored on magnetic tape for printing later. Multiprogramming allows a number of jobs to be done at the same time. The extremely fast central processing unit (CPU) supports a number of lower speed peripheral devices such as paper tape readers and punches, punched card readers and punches, magnetic tape units, disc units and line printers.

There are economies of scale to be gained in batch processing and for this reason many big organisations use large centralised computer systems. In these cases, problems can arise in moving the large quantities of data involved from different locations, processing it, and returning the results in an acceptable timescale. Other smaller companies, who cannot justify the purchase of a large computer for their own batch processing work, wish to take advantage of the computer bureaux facilities which are available on large powerful machines. These factors led to the development of a range of devices known as remote batch terminals (RBTs). They provide a means of transmitting large quantities of data to a central computer for processing and accepting the results in a suitable form. A simple RBT configuration is shown in figure 5.8.

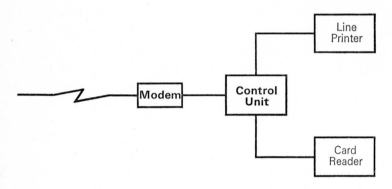

Figure 5.8   A simple RBT configuration

This terminal consists of just two peripheral devices, a line printer (with buffer) and card reader, and could be used in one of two ways:

– Data entered at the card reader could be transmitted and collected 'off-line' on a card punch or another type of peripheral at the computer centre. Although the data sent from the remote location could be preceded by punched cards containing the program to be performed, this program information is more frequently held at the computer centre. The complete job would be run at its scheduled time and results produced, typically on to magnetic tape. The results would be transmitted later, again off-line to the RBT, and printed on the line printer. For this type of operation, a terminal is sometimes provided at the computer centre to serve a number of remote machines.

– The terminal could be connected 'on-line' to the computer via an adaptor unit and an input/output channel so that the RBT line printer and card reader would appear to the computer as ordinary peripheral devices. It is common practice on these terminals to load the whole job to be processed and program information is sent preceding the data – this method of working is sometimes known as remote job entry; the user may also be able to access centrally held programs. Once data transmission has started from a RBT, there is no interaction between the user and the batch process and the time taken for the whole operation

will depend on the amount of data to be transferred and the batch processing time. There are three distinct phases involved – input, processing
and output. Only after the input has been received will the central
processor schedule the job to be done so that the best use is made of the
central processing unit memory and computer peripheral equipment.

Some RBTs include a small processor which enables local programs to be
run; communication to the central processor is only established when greater
processing power is needed.

Figure 5.9 shows a different type of RBT configuration supporting a
number of peripherals. These can be even more extensive depending on the
form of the data collected and input devices might include magnetic ledger
card readers, optical mark readers and magnetic ink character readers. Some
form of data capture facilities are usually necessary at the remote location
for data preparation. The machines used may be conventional punches and
verifiers but key to magnetic tape or disc devices are also used which may be
an integral part of the RBT configuration.

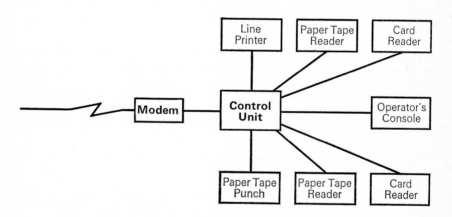

Figure 5.9   A typical RBT configuration

Communications requirements

Although the peripherals used on a RBT are similar to those used in a
computer environment, they are usually slower. Whereas a typical line printer
working to a computer may operate at 1200 lines per minute most RBT line
printers operate between 200-300 lines per minute, with transmission rates
in the range 2400 to 4800 bit/s. Data compression techniques are often
employed to reduce the amount of data transmitted. For example, to
operate at 300 lines per minute, with 136 characters per line and eight bits per

character a minimum of 5440 bit/s would apparently be required to transmit the information – this ignores time losses due to errors, etc. In practice, space characters are suppressed and this reduces the data transmitted considerably – the actual amount depending on the format of the transmitted messages. Faster line printers are used with some RBTs where the volume of the data to be transmitted is large enough to justify the increased cost of the faster printers and modems required.

The line printer is the highest speed device used on most RBTs and, therefore, determines the rate of transmission required. Although faster devices are available, typical speeds for the other peripherals are in the order of 200 cards per minute for a card punch, 100 characters per second for a paper tape punch, 300 cards per minute for a card reader and 500 characters per second for a paper tape reader.

Other terminals used for batch processing

Another group of terminals are used in batch processing systems which perform only some of the functions of the RBTs described earlier. These machines may be 'transmit only' devices, 'receive only' or transceivers which are capable of both transmitting and receiving information. All these terminals operate with pre-prepared information and very little operator activity is involved except loading the data or taking it off the machine. There are a wide variety of these terminals and the storage media used may be punched cards, punched paper tape or magnetic tape.

Figure 5.10 shows a transmit only paper tape reader at a remote station being used to transmit data off-line to a computer centre where the data is received

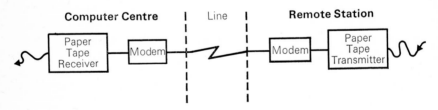

Figure 5.10   Off-line transmission using punched paper tape terminals

on a paper tape receiver. This is an example of data collection and may be used where the results are required in a different location. For example, in a stock control system, the sales data captured from a number of stores may be processed and the results despatched to a head office or warehouse. Switching could be provided at the computer centre so that the data from a number of remote stations could be handled by one machine. In this case, unattended answering facilities could be used; the terminal operator at the computer centre establishing a call to each store in turn where the paper tape would be pre-loaded on the terminals.

The terminal at the computer centre could be adapted for on-line working by attaching a data adaptor unit as shown in figure 5.11.

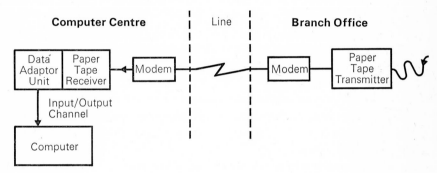

Figure 5.11   Input only on-line transmission using paper tape terminals

Receive only devices situated at remote sites can present information in readable form. In figure 5.12, a terminal at the remote station has a line printer.

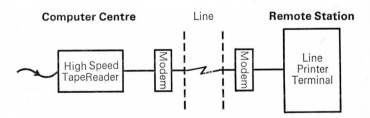

Figure 5.12   A receive only terminal with line printer

In this example, a high speed paper tape reader operating at up to 1000 characters per second is used to drive the remote line printer.

Figure 5.13 shows two transceivers which can be used for transmitting data on punched paper tape in either direction. A printed copy of the processed information could be obtained by using an off-line character printer.

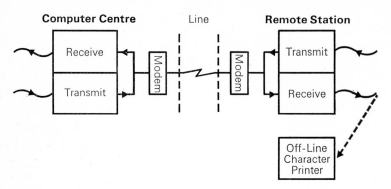

Figure 5.13   Configuration of two paper tape transceivers

As the machines described here are usually employed for batch processing work, considerable volumes of data are transmitted or received. Typically transmission rates between 600 and 2400 bit/s are required.

Special terminals
The majority of the terminals in use fall into the categories covered earlier. There are numerous other terminals often specially designed for a particular rather than a general purpose and it is not possible to cover every single type in a book of this nature. Nevertheless, they might be usefully discussed under a number of broad headings.

Point-of-sale terminals
These machines are located in stores, shops, etc, where transactions between staff and customers take place. Ideally, they should be simple to operate, reasonably quiet and inexpensive to provide and use – particularly where large numbers of terminals are needed. Usually, they are used to perform one, or a combination, of the following functions:

    (a) for data capture – to record the details of the sale in machine readable form for processing;

    (b) to issue a receipt to a customer;

    (c) to maintain a local record of transactions;

    (d) for credit verifications.

Functions a, b, and c can be handled by an off-line terminal – typically, by cash register type devices fitted with special keys which capture transaction data on paper tape or magnetic tape for onward transmission later via a concentrator unit using send only devices. Tag readers may also be used which can read pre-coded tags fastened to the goods for which transaction details are required.

Only function d (credit verification) requires on-line access to direct access storage files and this facility may be provided on a terminal which combines all the four functions described above or on a separate terminal as described below.

Terminals for credit verifications

Credit verification demands a simple means of input. This can be provided by means of a simple keyboard where customer details such as the account number can be entered or, alternatively, by using an attachment which can read a specially encoded customer credit card (this attachment may also read the pre-coded tags mentioned earlier under point-of-sale terminals). Output from the computer is obtained in one of two ways; firstly, by providing a simulated voice unit at the computer to give response via a telephone receiver at the terminal, or by using a simple printer at the terminal to accept hard copy messages – this might also be required to provide a local copy of messages entered at the terminal. To connect these terminals to communications lines requires some form of modulation device at this terminal; de-modulation is also required unless voice responses are used.

Factory floor terminals

The function of these terminals is to capture data at source accurately and transmit it (usually on-line) to a central computer. The terminals may be installed, for example, at points on a production line so that completed tasks can be quickly entered into a computerised production control system. These terminals have to be simple to operate and may be manufactured to suit a factory environment. Keyboards are unsuited to very dirty conditions and other types of foot or hand operated controls may be necessary. Input devices for reading job cards, badges, etc, may be provided for entering fixed data.

A large number of these terminals may be necessary in a factory, and where they are connected on-line the computer is usually situated close to the factory.

The Telephone Terminal

The standard dial telephone instrument cannot be used for data transmission. The dial is used to set up a call using loop-disconnect pulses which are digital in character, but once established the connection is only capable of accepting analogue signals and the dial becomes ineffective.

The push button telephone (PBT)

A PBT has a keyboard to replace the rotary dial, the key pad being an integral part of the instrument. Although PBTs are more convenient to use and are proving to be popular, calls in Strowger-based systems are not established any quicker using these instruments. The Keyphone, as it is called (*see* figure 5.14) stores the digits (which may be keyed very quickly) and transmits these to lines as loop-disconnect pulses with an inter-train pause between each digit. This is necessary to operate the electro-mechanical Strowger equipment in the telephone exchanges and the inherent slowness of this equipment presents constraints. The push buttons are ineffective when a connection is made and the instrument is therefore a convenience to customers in setting up calls and offers no data transmission benefit.

MF key pads

In some countries, there are electronic and Crossbar exchanges which are capable of responding to multi-frequency (MF) signals for call set-up. There is an international standard (CCITT Q23) for MF key pads and signalling codes. A '2 out of 8' signalling system is used with the following frequencies:

Group 1:   697, 770, 852, 941 Hz
Group 2:   1209, 1336, 1477, 1633 Hz

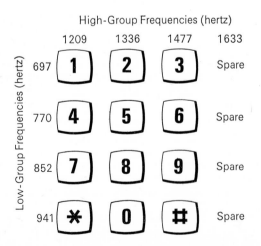

Figure 5.14   Standardised keyboard layout and signalling code for voice frequency push button signalling (CCITT Q23)

The depression of a key transmits two tones simultaneously to line (in parallel). For example, if the 5 key (*see* figure 5.14) were pressed the two frequencies 770 Hz and 1336 Hz would be transmitted to line and they can be heard in the earpiece of the receiver.

These signals can not only be used for setting up calls to those exchange systems which will respond to the signals but can also act as low speed data terminals with in built transmission facilities, after a call has been established. PBTs fitted with key pads to CCITT standard Q23 and which can provide both these functions in the one instrument are in use in the USA. This is not possible on the PSTN in the UK because of the need for loop disconnect pulses to establish the call. However, separate MF key pads of the type shown in figure 5.15 are available which have been given permission to be used over the PSTN.

Figure 5.15   Dial telephone with separate multi-frequency (MF) key pad

The telephone dial is used to set up the call and the MF key pad used for data entry and transmission. This simple installation might be used either:

– as a transmit only data terminal;
– as an interactive data terminal.

In the latter case, audio responses would be provided by the computer. Voice response units have been developed largely as a result of the data communications potential of the telephone. The voice response may consist of a prerecorded vocabulary of words or syllables which are selected by the computer and assembled into messages, or the 'voice' can be synthetically produced by modulating the white noise in the computer. In both cases, the result is a realistic, pleasing and probably 'female' voice.

Potential application areas for these terminals are credit verification, order entry, seat reservations, stock market quotations, etc. Although terminals of this kind are relatively cheap, reliable and easy to maintain, there are a number of disadvantages. Audio response units are as yet costly and the dialogue between the operator and the computer has to be carefully structured and kept as simple as possible. Conversation between the operator and the computer is of the step by step question and answer variety, the question being asked on the key pad and the answer being provided by the simulated voice. Mistakes in entry can occur either because of misoperation or because of ignorance of the procedures (particularly in businesses with a high staff turnover) and the operator must be guided carefully through the dialogue.

Error control

A rudimentary but effective form of error detection is inherent with this type of signalling for if only one, or more than two, frequencies is received, then that particular signal is ignored.

6 Line Control

Line control can be regarded as a discipline which enables data communications devices connected on the same line to communicate.

There are similarities in the type of control required for communication between machines and that which we ourselves use in day to day conversation. Although we do not usually associate discipline with conversations, it is nevertheless nearly always present and we can usefully examine the form it takes.

Consider, for example, the familiar situation where we wish to say something of importance to just one other person.

Before we begin speaking, we first try to gain his or her attention. If he is in the same room, we make sure that he is within earshot, that he is looking towards us, or giving some other indication that he is being suitably attentive. We may prefix our message to him by calling his name, thumping his table or, somewhat illogically, asking him to excuse us. Whichever of the numerous methods we adopt, our aim will be to make sure that when we begin speaking he is prepared to listen; in other words, we are making certain that he is synchronised with us at the start.

As our message is important (and our messages invariably are), we will strive to make the other person understand us. The first requirement after we have his attention is that he continues to listen, and we may go to extraordinary lengths to achieve this, varying our approach to suit different circumstances. Most of us are rather better at transmitting than receiving and are skilled in detecting when another's attention begins to wander. When this happens, we may cough loudly, move a chair, tell a funny story or, if the situation calls for more desperate measures, even throw something at him to make sure he does not drag behind – or leap ahead. More rationally, perhaps, we may break our message up into a number of sections and ask questions periodically about what has just been said.

When we have come to the end of our important message, we are likely to give some indication that we have finished. Although this might simply involve stopping talking, in many situations we will use a recognisable end of message phrase such as 'Well that's it Fred' or a final question such as 'now are you sure you've understood?'

Finally, no matter how we have finished our message, we will usually wait for some kind of response from the other person before we break off the conversation.

In this simple example, we can see the essential control elements which are involved in data communications.

The first requirement is for synchronisation to ensure that the receiver is 'in step' with the transmitter; this must be established before any effective communication takes place and maintained during the communication. If, for some reason, synchronism is lost, then steps must be taken to regain it; for without synchronism, communication is impossible.

The next requirement is to ensure that the message is received correctly. In speech communication, we naturally adopt a half-duplex method of control to maintain a check on understanding; similarly, half-duplex error control procedures are still the most commonly used in data communication.

These two requirements for synchronisation and error control, present in speech conversation, are, therefore, vital factors in the design of line control procedures. Of necessity, however, the disciplines involved must be more rigid when machine talks to machine; for there can be no allowances made for discretion and intuition. Also, the fact that in data transmission the basic unit of information is a binary digit poses different problems than in speech where the basic unit is a word. In this chapter, we will examine these basic control problems and discuss some of the ways in which they may be overcome.

Synchronisation

For one machine to communicate with another machine on the same line, there must be synchronisation on at least three distinct levels:

– bit synchronisation
– character synchronisation
– message synchronisation.

Bit synchronisation

The need for bit synchronisation can best be illustrated by a simple example.

Figure 6.1 shows a simple system using *commutators*. A five unit character is presented to the commutator at A by simultaneously placing an appropriate ON/OFF electrical condition on each of the five inputs; this is done every tenth of a second. The commutator at A rotates 10 times in one second and, therefore, data is passed to the commutator at B at a rate of 50 bit/s. If the commutator at B starts at the same time and also rotates at 10 times a second, all will be well and bits will be delivered to the correct output leads.

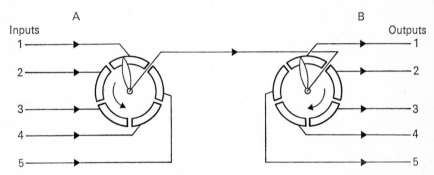

Figure 6.1   Synchronisation of the commutators at A and B

If, however, the commutator at B is slow in relation to A and rotates at say 9.8 times per second, one bit will be lost every second and incoming bits will be delivered to the wrong output leads resulting in incorrect character formation. Similarly, if the commutator at B is fast in relation to A bits will be gained through double sampling.

Character synchronisation

The need for character synchronisation can also be illustrated by referring to figure 6.1. If characters are presented on the output lead at B at the rate of 10 characters per second, then some kind of character clocking is needed to ensure that the leads are checked every tenth of a second for the presence of a character. Should this clock be out of step with A, then whole characters could be lost or gained.

Methods of obtaining bit and character synchronisation

Start/stop systems

The easiest and simplest way of obtaining bit and character synchronisation is to use a start/stop system. This method is used in teleprinters and was discussed earlier in Chapter 5. A start element ('space' or binary '0') is inserted at the beginning of each character and a stop element ('mark' or binary '1') at the end. The stop element is of a certain minimum length but, as it is maintained between characters, it has no defined maximum length. The start and stop elements are of different polarity so that, when a start signal is received, the transition in polarity clearly indicates the beginning of a character. When the receiver detects the transition, a local clock is started which controls the instants at which the line is sampled for information elements. When the stop condition is received, the receive clock is switched off and awaits the next transition. The receive clock is, therefore, only operating during a character and is reset for every new character received. Even though the receive clock may be fast or slow relative to the transmit clock, it is unlikely to drift far enough during the time of one character to cause an error.

Character synchronisation in a start/stop system is a fairly simple matter. There are a fixed number of units within a character and a count of these can be derived directly from the bit clock.

Figure 6.2 shows an example of receiver bit and character timing being derived from a line signal with start/stop elements.

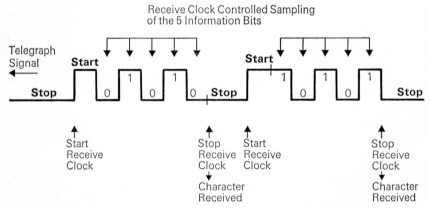

Figure 6.2   Receiver bit and character timing derived from a line signal with start/stop elements

Start/stop synchronisation is simple to achieve by hardware and is ideal when low speed terminals are used which are operated manually from a keyboard;

for, by the nature of this operation, there are frequent long pauses between characters.

Synchronous systems

The start/stop method is inefficient for higher speed transmission, because of the additional time needed to transmit start/stop signals, and other means of synchronisation are used.

In a synchronous system, the transmission is controlled by timing derived from electronic clocks at the originating station which may be in the terminal or in the modem. The data is, therefore, transmitted to line at a fixed rate, the duration of each unit signal element being the same.

At the receive end, the modem itself may be synchronous and will usually derive its timing from the line transitions. An electronic clock in the modem controls the sampling of the line conditions. This is kept in continuous step with the transmit clock by corrections made for each transition of the line signal. It follows from this that there must be sufficient changes in the line conditions to keep the receive modem synchronised and to avoid bits being lost or gained. Special techniques are sometimes used to ensure that the necessary transitions happen and to overcome the problems of code sensitivity which may occur if long strings of data with a repetitive pattern are transmitted. For example, the transmit modem may scramble the data, superimposing a random data pattern on the data to be transmitted; this is then de-scrambled at the receiver. Alternatively, a number of special synchronising characters (SYN) may be inserted in the data itself by the transmit terminal to establish and/or maintain synchronisation.

Receiver timing is needed by the receive terminal so that it can clock in the incoming digital data from the modem. Synchronous modems will usually provide the data terminal with the necessary receiver timing information on a separate interchange circuit (circuit 115 on the CCITT V24 interface). When synchronous modems do not supply separate timing information, timing must be derived from the incoming digital data stream at the modem. The electronic clock in the receiver must then be corrected from transitions in the data itself and again the problem of code sensitivity at the bit level arises; repetitive data patterns such as long strings of zeros or ones may cause the clock to drift 'off sync'. This problem is usually overcome either by the insertion of SYN characters within the data or by restricting the size of blocks transmitted.

Once bit timing has been recovered, the problem remains of obtaining character timing. Unlike the receivers used in the start/stop systems described earlier, a receiver on a synchronous system has no clear indication of the beginning and end of each character and this must be achieved in some other way.

The most common way of achieving character recovery is to use SYN characters at the beginning of each block transmitted. Figure 6.3 shows the unique bit pattern used in the SYN character of International Alphabet No. 5; the use of these characters enables a receive terminal having the necessary logic to establish (or recover) character timing. It can be seen that none of the characters shifted left in Fig. 6.3(a) are duplicated in figure 6.3(b). Also, it is not possible for bits in a following or preceding character to form the same combination as SYN. It is possible, therefore, to logically detect SYN characters if any of the shifts numbered 1 to 5 occur, identify whether it is shifted left or right and by how many bits. The necessary adjustments can then be made. This process is often referred to as 'character framing'. Only 2 SYN characters are required for this purpose and these are usually transmitted prior to all other sequences of characters. At the beginning of a transmission, 3 or 4 SYN characters may be transmitted to establish bit synchronisation.

SYN (IA 5) = 0 1 1 0 1 0 0

←	b_1	b_2	b_3	b_4	b_5	b_6	b_7		←	b_1	b_2	b_3	b_4	b_5	b_6	b_7
	0	1	1	0	1	0	0			0	1	1	0	1	0	0
1	1	1	0	1	0	0	F		1	P	0	1	1	0	1	0
2	1	0	1	0	0	F	F		2	P	P	0	1	1	0	1
3	0	1	0	0	F	F	F		3	P	P	P	0	1	1	0
4	1	0	0	F	F	F	F		4	P	P	P	P	0	1	1
5	0	0	F	F	F	F	F		5	P	P	P	P	P	0	1

(a) left shifted   (b) right shifted
F = bit from following   P = bit from preceding
      character   character

Figure 6.3   Character framing with Synchronous Idle (SYN) of International Alphabet No 5

Message synchronisation

In order to achieve message synchronisation, a receiver must be able to identify the beginning and end of each message. If hard copy plain language text is being transmitted between start/stop machines, there is no problem; the first character received is taken as the beginning of the message and the end of the message may be indicated by a signing off procedure.

With synchronous communication, the beginning and end of each message are usually indicated by special characters. If fixed field messages are transmitted or a message is divided into a number of fixed length blocks, a character count is sometimes used as an alternative to an end of message or end of block indication.

The Error Control Requirement

Decision feedback is the most widely used error control technique used in data communications for the reasons discussed in Chapter 8. This requires that a receiver will return a short message indicating whether or not a block, which it has previously received, is in error. In the majority of systems in use today, each acknowledgement will refer to the block just received and the transmitter will not proceed to transmit the next block until it has received a positive acknowledgement from the receiver. This idle-RQ method of error control has been a major constraint on the design of most of the line control procedures in use today with the result that, on most data communications systems, communication is half-duplex.

Line Control Procedures

A line control procedure is a formalised method used in transferring information between terminals separated by distance.

The complexity of line control procedures varies considerably and it is useful to begin by examining a simple hypothetical example.

Consider, for example, transmission of punched paper tape information from A to B between two terminals which operate synchronously at 2400 bit/s. We will assume that a private circuit and synchronous modems are used and that the transmission will be in fixed length blocks with a longitudinal parity check. For simplicity, we will also assume that the message is only two blocks in length. The half-duplex information flow is shown in figure 6.4.

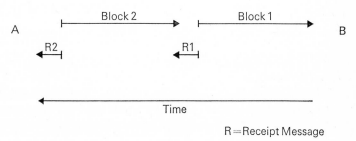

R = Receipt Message

Figure 6.4   Typical half-duplex transmission

We will begin at the point where the necessary 'handshaking' between the terminals and modems has been completed and that they are conditioned for transmission in the direction A to B. The problems now involved are simply those concerned with synchronisation and error control.

Before the information in the punched paper tape can be transmitted from the terminal at A, bit and character synchronisation must be established between the two terminals. As synchronous modems are used, we can assume that they will provide bit timing of the transmitter and receiver. Two SYN characters will, however, be necessary at the beginning of the transmission for character framing and these characters will also be needed at the beginning of each block.

Although SYN characters could be punched into the prepared punched paper tape, this would be a laborious and unreliable process. The transmit terminal must, therefore, add these characters from memory and the receive terminal must be capable of both detecting SYN and logically framing characters.

When bit and character timing have been established, the start of message synchronisation must be achieved. For this, we will use another character STX (start of text) and again we will assume that this is added by the transmit terminal.

The message is to be transmitted in two blocks and the block size will probably be determined by the size of the buffers in the terminals – typically 256 characters. It would be possible for a count to be started at the beginning of the block to give an end of block indication, but we will adopt the alternative method of using another special character ETB (end of transmission block). We will now add the BCC (block check character) which is a longitudinal redundancy check (*see* Chapter 8) so that our transmitted block now looks like this:

```
B   E                   S   S   S
C   T   —  TEXT  —   T   Y   Y     →
C   B                   X   N   N
             BLOCK 1
```

This simple message introduces an important concept. The line control must be able to recognise certain characters (ie the line control system is code sensitive at the character level as well as the bit level). This means that certain characters must not be allowed to appear in the text and this is an undesirable restriction. Ideally, the text of a message should be transparent, which simply means that any combination of any code may be used. This problem is overcome in some sophisticated line control systems which give 'transparent text transmission'.

Assuming that the first block has been received without error, the receiver now has to assemble a suitable receipt message to be returned to the transmitter. If an asynchronous return channel were available and the terminal equipment provided the necessary facilities, this could be achieved by returning one character ACK (acknowledge). The alternative is to turn the modems round and return the message synchronously which is the alternative we will choose for the example.

The receipt message will therefore be:

```
        S   S   A
   ←    Y   Y   C
        N   N   K
```

RECEIPT BLOCK 1

The next and final block transmitted from A must have a start of block indication and we will again use STX. There must also be an end of message indication ETX (end of text) and we will also use an end of transmission symbol (EOT) to advise the receiver that no further messages will follow on this particular transmission. The complete block will then read:

```
   B   E   E               S   S   S
   C   O   T  —  TEXT  —   T   Y   Y   →
   C   T   X               X   N   N
```

The receipt would be as for block 1.

This fictitious example illustrates the extent to which line controls are necessary on even the simplest synchronous system. In this particular case, the line control would almost certainly be provided by hard wired logic in the terminals. In more complex systems, the line control functions can be provided by a combination of hardware and software (communications control programs).

Roll-call polling and selection procedures

In the example above, only two terminals were connected on the same line. Line control procedures become more complex when more than one station is connected on the same line, and roll-call polling, and selection in particular, illustrate the sophistication of some of the control procedures which are required.

Figure 6.5 shows a simple star configuration on which polling and selection techniques may be used.

Polling

The purpose of polling on such a network is to provide concentration without the formation of queues of messages in the system. The way in which this is achieved is to exercise control on the network so that each terminal can only transmit a message to the central computer when it is invited to do so.

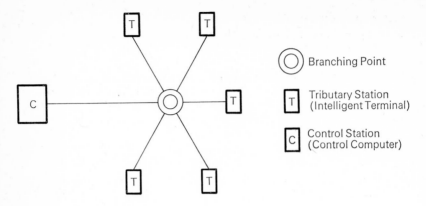

Figure 6.5   A simple star configuration

Because each terminal is buffered and the number of terminals connected in one multi-point network is restricted by the total data traffic on the system, any delays due to polling are hardly noticeable to the terminal user. Terminals on a multi-point network cannot communicate with one another.

One station only on the network controls all the procedures. This is termed the 'control station' and is usually a central computer or its 'front end processor'. The other stations (in this case the 'intelligent' terminals) are termed 'tributary stations'.

On a multi-point network, only two stations can communicate at once and these two stations take on new identities when a link has been established:

    – The 'master' station is the station which, at any given instant, has the right to select and to transfer an information message to a 'slave' station and has the responsibility of ensuring that the information is transferred. Only one 'master' station can be on a data link at any one time.

    – The 'slave' station is one which, at any given instant, is intended to receive an information message from a master station.

This master/slave relationship is an important concept. Polling is, in fact, an invitation from a control station to each one in turn of the tributary stations on its polling list to become a 'master' station. If an invitation is accepted, the tributary station concerned becomes the master and the control station becomes the slave until the information message has been transferred. Thus, any station, including the control station, can become at different times a master or a slave station.

There are normally three types of messages which are used in a polling system:

- forward supervisory sequences;
- backward supervisory sequences;
- information messages.

The examples of *typical* messages, which will be given, are drawn from the 'basic mode control procedures' of the British Standards Institution, but only sample messages can be given in a book of this kind. (For a full description, the reader is referred to the British Standard – BS 4505 part 1.)

The control characters used in the message sequences are from the IA 5 code. A fuller description of the control characters used in this code is given in Appendix 3 but the meaning of the abbreviations used in the examples is given below for convenience.

CONTROL CHARACTERS

ACK	–	Acknowledgement (affirmative)
NAK	–	Acknowledgement (negative)
EOT	–	End of transmission
ETB	–	End of transmission block
ETX	–	End of text
ENQ	–	Enquiry
SOH	–	Start of heading
STX	–	Start of text
SYN	–	Synchronous idle
BCC	–	Block control character

Forward supervisory sequence (*polling*)   A forward supervisory sequence (from a control station to a tributary station) may consist of the following sequence of characters:

$$
\begin{array}{ccccc}
E & & & S & S & S \\
N & & \text{Polling} & T & Y & Y & \rightarrow \\
Q & & \text{Address} & X & N & N \\
\end{array}
$$

The EOT character is used in this instance to condition all tributary stations to anticipate the reception of a forward supervisory sequence. After the polling address, the ENQ is used when a response is required from the addressed station. If the polling is successful, the addressed station will become the master station and will initiate its own information message sequence (*see* below).

Backward negative reply sequence (*polling*)   If the addressed station does not wish to transmit, it will send the following negative reply:

$$
\begin{array}{ccccc}
 & S & S & & E \\
\leftarrow & Y & Y & \text{(PREFIX)} & O \\
 & N & N & & T \\
\end{array}
$$

A 'prefix' sequence of characters may precede EOT in some cases to define or qualify the meaning of the sequence (eg the terminal's identification or status).

When a negative reply is received to a forward polling supervisory sequence, the control station polls the next tributary station on its list.

Information messages   SOH, STX, ETB and ETX are used as information framing characters and there must, therefore, be at least two in all information messages or blocks transmitted. In the simplest case, it may only be necessary to indicate the beginning and end of a text. Assuming that the information message to be transmitted is a positive response to a poll, we have:

$$
\leftarrow \quad
\begin{array}{ccc}
S & S & S \\
Y & Y & T \\
N & N & X
\end{array}
\; - \; \text{TEXT} \; - \;
\begin{array}{cc}
E & B \\
T & C \\
X & C
\end{array}
$$

The BCC or block check character is a longitudinal parity check which starts the check at STX and ends at the character immediately preceding BCC.

If a heading was required and the message was transmitted in a number of blocks, the first block could have the following sequence:

$$
\leftarrow \quad
\begin{array}{ccc}
S & S & S \\
Y & Y & O \\
N & N & H
\end{array}
\; - \; \text{HEADING} \;
\begin{array}{c}
S \\
T \\
X
\end{array}
\; - \; \text{TEXT} \;
\begin{array}{cc}
E & B \\
T & C \\
B & C
\end{array}
$$

Each intermediate block must begin with STX to give:

$$
\leftarrow \quad
\begin{array}{ccc}
S & S & S \\
Y & Y & T \\
N & N & X
\end{array}
\; - \; \text{TEXT} \; - \;
\begin{array}{cc}
E & B \\
T & C \\
B & C
\end{array}
$$

and the final block must indicate the end of the message:

$$
\leftarrow \quad
\begin{array}{ccc}
S & S & S \\
Y & Y & T \\
N & N & X
\end{array}
\; - \; \text{TEXT} \; - \;
\begin{array}{cc}
E & B \\
T & C \\
X & C
\end{array}
$$

Each information message or block requires a response and these are as follows —

Positive reply:

$$
\begin{array}{c}
A \\
C \\
K
\end{array}
\; \text{(PREFIX)} \;
\begin{array}{cc}
S & S \\
Y & Y \\
N & N
\end{array}
\; \rightarrow
$$

Negative reply:

```
N              S  S
A  (PREFIX)    Y  Y    →
K              N  N
```

Selection

On some multi-point networks, polling is only one of the main sequences which are used. The other, 'selection', is used when a control station wishes to send a message to a tributary station. Selecting is the process of inviting a station to receive and therefore the opposite to polling which is an invitation to a station to transmit.

A list of selecting addresses is held at the control station and to select a particular station the following type of sequence is transmitted —

Forward supervisory sequence (selection):

```
E              E  S  S
N  Selecting   O  Y  Y    →
Q  address     T  N  N
```

A negative response to such a sequence is as follows:

```
     S  S              N
←    Y  Y  (PREFIX)    A
     N  N              K
```

And a positive response:

```
     S  S              A
←    Y  Y  (PREFIX)    C
     N  N              K
```

The information messages used in selection and the responses to them have the same format as those described earlier under polling.

Transparent Mode Control Procedures

The procedures discussed so far rely on the fact that the line control is sensitive to a number of control characters. This means that none of these control characters, with the exception of SYN (synchronous idle) may be allowed to appear in the heading or text of a message. This not only reduces the characters, which are available for use in a particular code, but prevents other codes being used in which combinations of bits could coincide with those of control characters.

Procedures have been developed which will allow control characters to be used within a text. These usually involve the use of one or two DLE (Data Link Escape) characters inserted in a message which indicates that a number of following contiguous characters are to be ignored by the receiver line control. In this way, control characters, which would normally trigger some action at the receiver, can be used in the text of a message.

A newer more fundamental way of achieving complete transparency in a text is to dispense with the use of conventional control characters. This method, which was developed by IBM, is known as Advanced Data Communications Control Procedure (ADCCP) – or Synchronous Data Link Control (SDLC) and uses a special control character called a 'frame' which has the following bit sequence 01111110. All transmissions must begin and end with a frame.

Each message must have the following format —

$$F - A - C - TEXT - BC - F$$

where: F is the frame
          A is an eight bit address field
          C is an eight bit control field
and   BC is the CCITT V41 polynomial (*see* Chapter 8).

As the text is transparent, combinations of bits in the text could coincide with 'frame' and this must be avoided. This is achieved by examining the message 'at input after frame' and, if five ones in a row are encountered, inserting a zero after them. In this way, 'frame' cannot be duplicated and, at the receiver, A, C, text and BC can be identified by the 'frames' at the beginning and end. Any zero, which appears after five ones in this sequence, can be discarded by the receiver and A, C and BC can be identified, because of their position, as the first and last sixteen bits in the sequence. All the necessary control information is included in the eight bit address and control fields.

Duplex Control Procedures

Many systems using half-duplex line control procedures use full-duplex lines and modems to avoid the modem turn around problem. This is an inefficient use of a full-duplex facility, as one channel of communication is always idle. There are, however, difficulties in adopting the alternative of using full-duplex procedures.

Consider, for example, a situation in which it is desirable to transmit large quantities of data between two points A and B in both directions simultaneously. This situation is fairly common and can arise typically in remote batch applications when the results of a particular process are being transmitted to the RBT's line printer and at the same time data is waiting to be transmitted from the RBT to the computer.

The major problem in the implementation of full-duplex line control, in circumstances such as this, is in arranging decision feedback error control. Before transmitting a second message from A, it is desirable to have an acknowledgement from B that the first message has been received correctly. This presents a problem because B is transmitting a message to A; to wait for B to finish before receiving an acknowledgement is a waste of line time.

There are a number of ways this problem can be overcome. For example, an acknowledgement *may* simply be inserted into the text of the message being transmitted from B. This is not a very reliable method because bad character framing in any part of the text could result in false acknowledgements being produced.

A better method is to insert the acknowledgement into the incoming message from B but to precede the ACK or NAK with an ETB (end of transmission block) and start the text again with an STX (start of text). An acknowledgement could then be regarded as genuine only if it were preceded by an ETB.

Another approach, which has been used, is to dispense with positive acknowledgements altogether. If a negative acknowledgement is not received from B within a fixed time period, it is assumed that the previous message from A has been received correctly and it can then proceed to send the next message. A logical development from these procedures is continuous mode working. In this, acknowledgement messages are expected but transmission of the next block commences before the acknowledgement of the first block is received. Such a system requires the transmitter to 'remember' the previous block in case a NAK requires retransmission. This may be done either by providing an additional buffer, or by mechanically back-spacing the input medium (paper or magnetic tape).

Cost and the logic complexity usually limit the storage to one block, and, if short blocks are being sent on a long line with a considerable transmission delay time, operation may degenerate to block-by-block transmission (*see* Chapter 8).

Message Error Conditions

In the simple examples given so far, it has simply been stated that if an error condition is found at the receive end, a NAK signal is sent which should initiate retransmission of the faulty block. In the majority of cases, this is the situation which occurs; but a look at some of the special conditions, which arise, will focus attention on some of the logical complexities of designing satisfactory line control procedures.

Let us consider the situation which arises if station A sends a block of data to station B and receives no response. The simple assumption is that, because of a line fault, the complete block never reached B and it should be retransmitted. However, suppose B had received it correctly but the acknowledgement message was corrupted? Retransmission will now give B a duplicate block.

One way of dealing with this type of problem is to give each block a sequence number so that the receiving terminal or subsequent programmed device can bypass any duplicate block. Another alternative is to avoid retransmission in the first place. Instead, station A, when it receives no acknowledgement of the block sent, sends a special (REP) message requesting a repeat of the acknowledgement signal from station B. If this arrives correctly, the system is back in step again and A transmits the next block.

This time, however, suppose this block is never completely received at B. Now, after waiting the appropriate time, A will again send its REP message which B will respond to with ACK, because, after all, the last full block it received was correct. Station A will now start transmitting the third block, with the second one not having been received by B.

The block sequence number again can give protection against this error, or, alternatively, two different ACK messages can be used alternately. Simple logic can then easily identify that the transmitter and receiver are out of step and take the appropriate action to rectify the error.

If the line is noisy, it is quite probable that successive messages may be corrupted. Usually some provision is made for limiting the number of attempts at retransmission. If this is exceeded, a special error message can be transmitted inviting manual intervention.

If these, and other complicated error situations (*see* Chapter 8), are moved into the context of continuous mode operation on a full-duplex line it can be seen why the design and standardisation of efficient line control procedures is in fact one of the biggest problems in data communications today. Historically, computer equipment manufacturers have either developed their own procedures or have emulated those of their larger brethren. Although with time, standards are emerging, this is a slow process and there is still a proliferation of line control procedures, many of which make inefficient use of the lines they are intended to control.

7 The Communications Interface

An interface is a concept which involves the specification of the conditions necessary for interconnection between two parts of a system which have different functions. A telephone dial is a typical example of what is often called the *man/machine interface*. The human side of the interface requires, for example, that it should have clearly printed letters, that the holes be of a certain size, that it should rotate with a certain minimum pressures and so on. The machine side of the interface (the equipment at the telephone exchange) requires that digital pulses will be produced at so many pulses per second, that each pulse and the space between the pulses are of specific durations and that there will be a minimum pause between each train of dial pulses. The steering wheel of a car, a teleprinter keyboard, the tuning control and dial on a radio are other examples of that most difficult interface to define and design that lies between man and machine. To design any interface between any two parts of a system, it is necessary to have a complete understanding of how each part functions and how they interact with one another. The whole scientific field of ergonomics is devoted to the task of deciding how people might best interface with machines; whether we should push or pull a lever, press buttons or rotate a dial and so on. The man/machine interface is a vital part of all on-line data communications systems and the ergonomist deserves our best wishes and sympathy in tackling the difficult problems he faces.

The man/machine interface is only one of a number of interfaces to be found in any data communications system. The others, being involved with the interaction between equipments, lend themselves to precise definition. When an interface can be precisely defined there are considerable advantages to be gained from international standardisation so that equipment made by different manufacturers may work together. Although international standard-isation of many interfaces could be of considerable benefit to systems designers and to manufacturers as a whole, we have seen, as so often in other fields, that even national standards can be slow to develop and be even slower to be adopted. In data communications, we are fortunate that the interface between data terminals and modems (or other data communications equipment) are the subject of the International Telegraph and Telephone Consultative Committee (CCITT) recommendations which have gained world-wide acceptance by telecommunications authorities and manufacturers. These recommendations precisely define the type, quantity and function of the interconnecting (or 'interchange') circuits as they are called and the type and form of signals to be interchanged between these circuits.

Before examining these interchange circuits in detail, it is useful to consider a simple example where data is being exchanged between two points so that the inter-relationship between the modems and the data terminal equipments can be seen more clearly. We will assume that punched paper tape informa-tion is to be transmitted off-line from A to B, over the public switched telephone network. Decision feedback will be used to acknowledge each block transmitted and the system will operate in half-duplex mode at the same data signalling rate in each direction. For convenience, it will also be assumed that one modem at each end can provide the necessary facilities (*see* figure 7.1).

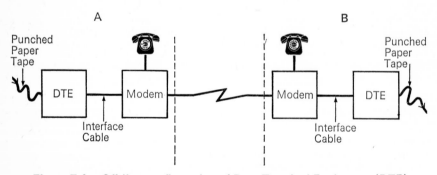

Figure 7.1   Off-line configuration of Data Terminal Equipment (DTE)

Before data can be exchanged, it is necessary for a connection to be established through the telephone network. We will assume that a call has been set up, that the operators have spoken at each end and that they are ready for the transmission of data to proceed. The interaction between the equipments involved can now be conveniently described as a conversation which takes place in a series of steps.

Step 1

The modems at each end must be advised that the data terminal equipment (DTE) is ready to operate. The modems must also be switched to the line. These two requirements could be achieved in a number of ways, but the two most common methods are shown below as steps 1a and 1b.

(a) A single signal can be sent from each data terminal equipment to its associated modem.

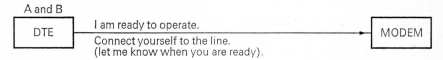

(b) The DTE can merely advise its modem that it is ready to operate. The switching of the modem to the line will not take place until it receives a signal from another source (eg a switch on an associated telephone).

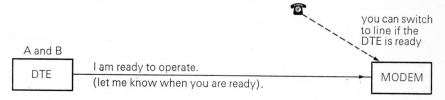

Step 2

The modems at each end advise their associated DTEs that they have switched to line and are ready to accept further instructions.

Step 3

No indication has yet been given of the direction of the transmission which is to take place. The modem at A must be conditioned to transmit and the modem at B conditioned to receive. The first action must be from the DTE at A.

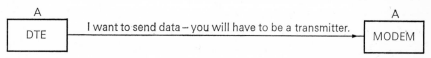

Step 4

The modem at A must send a signal to advise the modem at B that it wishes to transmit.

Step 5

When the modem at B is satisfied that it is receiving a satisfactory line signal from A it will advise its DTE to organise itself as a receiver.

Step 6

After a pre-set time to allow the distant end time to be conditioned for receiving, the modem at A can give an affirmative response to the request to send data from its DTE.

We will assume that a block of data is successfully passed from A to B. The DTE at B will assemble a receipt message and steps 3-6 will be followed again in the reverse direction beginning with a 'request to send'.

It will be seen that, even in this simplified example, a strict discipline is necessary to successfully bridge the demarcation between modems and the terminals which work with them. It will also be clear that standardisation of the interface is essential if there is to be compatibility between a wide range of different equipments.

CCITT Recommendation V24

The CCITT approach to this problem has been to include in one recommendation (V24) all the interface conditions which are likely to be involved in any configuration of data terminal equipments and modems; each interface circuit being defined in terms of its use, direction of responsibility and electrical conditions. It can be regarded as a shopping list of interchange circuits. Each circuit is given a 3 digit number; the 100 series of numbers refer to interchange circuits for general application while the 200 series covers those used for automatic calling. The numbers do not refer to the pin and socket positions on the 25 way adaptor which connects the modem to the DTE; this is the subject of an ISO recommendation.[1]

Line of Demarcation
Figure 7.2 illustrates the general layout of communications equipment and the line of demarcation. The connector (or connectors) is the interchange point between the data terminal equipment and the data communications equipment (DCE).

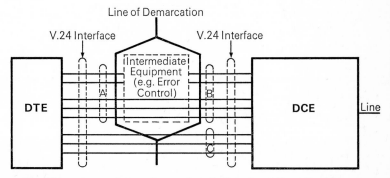

NB   Without intermediate equipment the selections A and B are identical.
     Selection C may be a selection specifically for automatic calling

Figure 7.2   General layout of data communications equipment

The data communications equipment may include signal convertors, timing generators, pulse generators and control circuitry together with equipment to provide other functions such as error control, automatic calling and automatic answering.

The 100 series interchange circuits
Table 7.1 shows the 100 series interchange circuits by category.

V24 was described earlier as a shopping list of interchange circuits, and how many of the 37 listed in table 7.1 are actually required will depend on the modems used and the facilities to be provided. CCITT give separate recommendations for modems of different speeds and each recommendation

---

Document ISO/TC97/SC6 No. 315.

stipulates which of the 100 series interchange circuits are needed. For example, tables 7.2 and 7.3 show the interchange circuits which are essential for the 600/1200 bit/s modems covered by CCITT recommendation V23 when these are used on the general switched telephone network and on non-switched leased telephone circuits.

It will be seen that between 8 and 18 of the interchange circuits are necessary depending on the facilities required.

Interchange circuit number	Interchange circuit name	Ground	Data		Control		Timing	
			From DCE	To DCE	From DCE	To DCE	From DCE	To DCE
1	2	3	4	5	6	7	8	9
101	Protective ground or earth	X						
102	Signal ground or common return	X						
103	Transmitted data			X				
104	Received data		X					
105	Request to send					X		
106	Ready for sending				X			
107	Data set ready				X			
108/1	Connect data set to line					X		
108/2	Data terminal ready					X		
109	Data channel received line signal detector				X			
110	Signal quality detector				X			
111	Data signalling rate selector (DTE)					X		
112	Data signalling rate selector (DCE)				X			
113	Transmitter signal element timing (DTE)							X
114	Transmitter signal element timing (DCE)						X	
115	Receiver signal element timing (DCE)						X	
116	Select standby					X		
117	Standby indicator				X			
118	Transmitted backward channel data			X				
119	Received backward channel data		X					
120	Transmit backward channel line signal					X		
121	Backward channel ready				X			
122	Backward channel received line signal detector				X			
123	Backward channel signal quality detector				X			
124	Select frequency groups					X		
125	Calling indicator				X			
126	Select transmit frequency					X		
127	Select receive frequency					X		
128	Receiver signal element timing (DTE)							X
129	Request to receive					X		
130	Transmit backward tone					X		
131	Received character timing						X	
132	Return to non-data mode					X		
133	Ready for receiving					X		
134	Received data present				X			
191	Transmitted voice answer					X		
192	Received voice answer				X			

Table 7.1   100 series interchange circuits by category

No.	Designation	Forward (data) channel one-way system				Forward (data) channel either way system	
		Without backward channel		With backward channel		Without backward channel	With backward channel
		Transmit end	Receive end	Transmit end	Receive end		
101[a]	Protective ground or earth	X	X	X	X	X	X
102	Signal ground or common return	X	X	X	X	X	X
103	Transmitted data	X	–	X	–	X	X
104	Received data	–	X	–	X	X	X
105	Request to send	–	–	–	–	X	X
106	Ready for sending	X	–	X	–	X	X
107	Data set ready	X	X	X	X	X	X
108/1 or	Connect data set to line	X	X	X	X	X	X
108/2 (Note 1)	Data terminal ready	X	X	X	X	X	X
109	Data channel received line signal detector	–	X	–	X	X	X
111	Data signalling rate selector (DTE)	X	X	X	X	X	X.
114 (Note 3)	Transmitter signal element timing (DCE)	X	–	X	–	X	X
115 (Note 3)	Receiver signal element timing (DCE)	–	X	–	X	X	X
118	Transmitted backward channel data	–	–	–	X	–	X
119	Received backward channel data	–	–	X	–	–	X
120	Transmit backward channel line signal	–	–	–	–	–	X
121	Backward channel ready	–	–	–	X	–	X
122	Backward channel received line signal detector	–	–	X	–	–	X
125	Calling indicator	X	X	X	X	X	X

[a] May be excluded if so required by local safety regulations.

NOTE 1   This circuit shall be capable of operation as circuit 108/1 (connect data set to line) or circuit 108/2 (data terminal ready) depending on its use. For automatic calling it shall be used as 108/2 only.

NOTE 2   Interchange circuits indicated by X must be properly terminated according to Recommendation V24 in the data terminal equipment and data circuit-terminating equipment.

NOTE 3   These circuits are required when the optional clock is implemented in the modem.

Table 7.2   Interchange circuits essential for V23 modems when using the Public Switched Telephone Network (PSTN)

Interchange circuit		Forward (data) channel one-way system				Forward (data) channel either way or both ways simultaneously system	
No.	Designation	Without backward channel		With backward channel		Without backward channel	With backward channel
		Transmit end	Receive end	Transmit end	Receive end		
101[a]	Protective ground or earth	X	X	X	X	X	X
102	Signal ground or common return	X	X	X	X	X	X
103	Transmitted data	X	−	X	−	X	X
104	Received data	−	X	−	X	X	X
105	Request to send	X	−	X	−	X	X
106	Ready for sending	X	−	X	−	X	X
107	Data set ready	X	X	X	X	X	X
108/1 or	Connect data set to line	X	X	X	X	X	X
109	Data channel received line signal detector	−	X	−	X	X	X
111	Data signalling rate selector (DTE)	X	X	X	X	X	X
114 (Note 3)	Transmitter signal element timing (DCE)	X	−	X	−	X	X
115 (Note 3)	Receiver signal element timing (DCE)	−	X	−	X	X	X
118	Transmitted backward channel data	−	−	−	X	−	X
119	Received backward channel data	−	−	X	−	−	X
120	Transmit backward channel line signal	−	−	−	X	−	X
121	Backward channel ready	−	−	−	X	−	X
122	Backward channel received line signal detector	−	−	X	−	−	X

[a] May be excluded if so required by local safety regulations.

NOTE 1   This circuit shall be capable of operation as circuit 108/1 (connect data set to line) or circuit 108/2 (data terminal ready) depending on its use. For automatic calling it shall be used as 108/2 only.

NOTE 2   Interchange circuits indicated by X must be properly terminated according to Recommendation V24 in the data terminal equipment and data circuit-terminating equipment.

NOTE 3   These circuits are required when the optional clock is implemented in the modem.

Table 7.3   Interchange circuits essential for V23 modems when used on non-switched leased telephone circuits

Notes on the 100 series interchange circuits

Some explanatory notes on the thirty-seven 100 series interchange circuits defined in the recommendation are given below. Although it is hoped that these will be helpful to the reader in understanding the functions of the various circuits, they should not be taken as being a substitute for the recommendation itself.

Because the data communications equipment (DCE) referred to in the recommendation is usually a modem, the term modem has been used in the explanatory notes on this series. The abbreviation DTE is used for data terminal equipment. The ON and OFF conditions referred to are logical conditions; ON is given the binary value 0 and is expressed by a positive voltage; OFF is given the binary value 1 and is expressed by a negative voltage.

- **Circuit 101 – Protective ground or earth**

    It is desirable to extend the protective earth condition from the DTE to the modem and this circuit is allocated for this purpose.

- **Circuit 102 – Signal ground or common return**

    This circuit is the common earth return for the signals on all the interchange circuits (except 101). At the modem, this circuit may be connected to circuit 101 by a wire strap.

- **Circuit 103 – Transmitted data (DTE → modem)**

    Data signals transmitted from the DTE to the modem are passed over this circuit.

When no data is being transmitted, circuit 103 is held in the OFF condition (binary '1'). The DTE cannot transmit data on this circuit unless an ON condition (binary '0') is present on all the following circuits, where these are implemented.

    Circuit 105 – Request to send
    Circuit 106 – Ready for sending
    Circuit 107 – Data set ready
    Circuit 108.1/108.2 – Connect data set to line/data terminal ready.

- **Circuit 104 – Received data (modem → DTE)**

    Analogue signals received from the line are converted into digital signals and transmitted from the modem to the DTE on this circuit.

    NB   To prevent spurious signals being sent to the DTE due, for example, to excessive noise on the line this circuit may be held in the OFF condition until an ON condition on circuit 109 indicates that a signal within appropriate limits is being received from the line (*see* circuit 109 below). This procedure is termed 'clamping'.

● **Circuit 105 – Request to send (DTE → modem)**

When the DTE wishes to send information, it applies an ON condition on this circuit causing the modem to assume the transmit mode. The OFF condition signifies that the DTE does not wish to transmit.

● **Circuit 106 – Ready for sending (modem → DTE)**

Replies from the modem to the DTE, in response to a request to send, are passed on this circuit. An ON condition indicates that the modem is ready to accept data from the DTE on circuit 103 (transmitted data).

> NB The delay between an ON condition being applied by the DTE to circuit 105 and the answering ON condition being sent from the modem to the DTE is termed the 'ready-for-sending delay'. This delay is built into the transmit modem to give time for a distant modem to condition itself to receive signals from the line.

There are a number of factors which can influence the ready-for-sending delay, which is required, and the number of times that this delay occurs:

– If automatic calling and answering are used, a time allowance is required to allow the calling condition to be detected at the receive modem; the detection of the calling signal (typically ringing current) allows the call to be automatically answered. For example, on the 600/1200 bit/s modem to CCITT recommendation V23, the initial ready-for-sending delay is between 750 and 1400 ms; after the call has been established, this time is reduced to between 20 and 40 ms.

– If uninterrupted transmission is maintained in one direction (simplex) or in both directions simultaneously (duplex), there are no ready-for-sending delays after the first one. Users are, however, encouraged to switch off circuit 105 (request to send) whenever there are breaks in transmission to reduce the power loading of carrier circuits; in these circumstances, whenever transmission re-starts, there is a further ready-for-sending delay.

– If the modems and/or the lines cannot give duplex facilities and a half-duplex method of transmission is adopted, it is necessary to 'turn round' the modems at each end whenever there is a change in the direction of the transmission. Two ready-for-sending delays are therefore incurred for each change of direction. This important factor, which considerably reduces throughput efficiency, is discussed more fully in Chapter 8.

– Some modems require longer ready-for-sending delays than others. Generally speaking, the slower, asynchronous or unclocked modems merely require a carrier to be on the line for a brief period (typically 20-40 ms) to ensure that the receive modem is receiving it at the right power level.

The ready-for-sending delay is, therefore, the same whether the request to send is the first one in a transmission or one which occurs subsequently. The higher speed modems (over 2400 bit/s) are usually synchronous and may employ adaptive equalisers. An 'initial training pattern' is sometimes sent which enables the receive modem to synchronise with the transmit modem and to allow time for the adaptive equalisers in the receive modem to adjust to the line conditions. Subsequent training patterns between blocks may be considerably shorter as the timing and equalisation elements in modern modems will remain stable and will require little adjustment once they have been set.

- **Circuit 107 – Data set ready (modem → DTE)**
  The signals on this circuit indicate to the DTE that the modem is ready to receive its next instruction. The transmission of line signals for equalisation, etc, will not take place unless this circuit is switched on.

- **Circuit 108 (DTE → modem)**
  There are two options for the use of this circuit to meet different user requirements.

  108/1 – *Connect data set to line*   An ON condition on this circuit will immediately connect the modem to line; this results in circuit 107 (data set ready) being switched to ON. An OFF condition on 108/1 disconnects the modem from the line when data on circuit 103 has been transmitted.

  108/2 – *Data terminal ready*   An ON condition on this circuit from the DTE informs the modem that the data terminal is ready to operate. It is not in itself an instruction to connect the modem to line and before this can be done a subsidiary signal is necessary. This signal may be given by an operator pressing a 'data' button on the telephone associated with the modem. Alternatively, the signal may be derived from the automatic answering equipment in the modem which detects automatic ringing current on the line. When the ON condition on circuit 108/2 and the subsidiary signal are both present, the modem will switch to line and an ON condition is applied on circuit 107 (data set ready) from the modem to the DTE.

- **Circuit 109 – Data channel received line signal detector (modem → DTE)**
  An ON condition on this circuit indicates to the DTE that the received signal is within the appropriate limits. These limits are specified in the

CCITT recommendations for the type of modem being used. For example, V23 (600/1200 bit/s) modems will apply on ON condition on circuit 109 when a signal greater than 43dBm is received. This circuit may be 'clamped' to circuit 104 to avoid false signals being passed to the DTE.

● **Circuit 110 – Data signal quality detector**
Data signal quality detection is a method of error control whereby the line signal is checked for certain characteristics which are likely to cause errors (*see* Chapter 8). An ON condition on this circuit indicates that there is no indication from the line signal that an error has occurred. An OFF condition indicates that there is a reasonable probability that the distortion detected on the line signal will cause an error.

Data signal quality detectors are not used in the current range of serial modems covered by CCITT recommendations. Circuit 110 is, however, included as an option in recommendation V30 which is concerned with parallel modems.

● **Circuit 111 – Data signalling rate selector (DTE → modem)**
When modems offer a choice of two fixed data signalling rates or a choice between two ranges of data signalling rate, the selection is usually made at the DTE. An ON condition on circuit 111 from the DTE directs the modem to adopt the higher rate, or range of rates and an OFF condition indicates that the lower mode is selected.

Either (but not both) circuit 111 or circuit 112 can be used for data signalling rate selection.

● **Circuit 112 – Data signalling rate selector (modem → DTE)**
This is an alternative to circuit 111, choice of data signalling rate being made from the modem.

● **Circuit 113 – Transmitter signal element timing (DTE → modem)**
When synchronous modems are used, the signal elements from the transmitting modem must be sent to line at a fixed rate. The timing information which is necessary may be provided from the DTE in which case circuit 113 will be used. The signals on this timing circuit are square waves with ON and OFF conditions of equal periods. Transitions from ON to OFF indicate the centre of each data bit being transmitted to the modem on circuit 103 (transmitted data). Timing information on circuit 113 is provided at all times when circuit 107 (data set ready) is in the ON condition.

Either (but not both) circuit 113 or circuit 114 can be used to provide transmitter signal element timing.

- **Circuit 114 – Transmitter signal element timing (modem → DTE)**

  This circuit is an alternative to circuit 113 and is used when the timing information is provided from the modem. Transitions of data bits on circuit 103 (transmitted data) to the modem occur at the time of the transitions from OFF to ON conditions of the square wave signals from the modem on circuit 114. Timing information on circuit 114 is provided at all times when circuit 107 (data set ready) is in the ON condition.

- **Circuit 115 – Receiver signal element timing (modem → DTE)**

  When synchronous modems are used, timing information for the received data (circuit 104) may be provided from the modem on circuit 115. Transitions from ON to OFF on circuit 115 indicate the centre of the data bits being sent to the DTE on circuit 104. This timing information is provided at all times when circuit 109 (data channel received line signal detector) is in the ON condition.

  Either (but not both) circuit 115 or circuit 128 may be used for receiver signal element timing.

- **Circuit 116 – Select standby (DTE → modem)**

  When standby communication facilities are provided, such as a standby exchange line, this circuit may be used for selection between the normal and standby facilities.

- **Circuit 117 – Standby indication (modem → DTE)**

  The signals on this circuit indicate to the DTE whether the normal or standby facilities which have been selected are conditioned to operate.

- **Circuits 118 to 124 inclusive**

  Used only when backward channels are provided by the modems. A backward or 'supervisory' channel operates at a lower data signalling rate (typically 75 bit/s) than the data channel and is intended to be used for the return of short supervisory or error control messages. The interchange circuits used are equivalent to other circuits described above except that they are associated with the backward channel rather than the data channel; they are listed below with their equivalents:

- **Circuit 118 – Transmitted backward channel data (DTE → modem)**

  Equivalent to circuit 103 (transmitted data).

- **Circuit 119 – Received backward channel data (modem → DTE)**

  Equivalent to circuit 104 (received data). This circuit may be clamped to circuit 122 just as circuit 104 may be clamped to circuit 109.

- **Circuit 120 – Transmit backward channel line signal (DTE → modem)**
  Equivalent to circuit 105 (request to send).

- **Circuit 121 – Backward channel ready (modem → DTE)**
  Equivalent to circuit 106 (ready for sending)

- **Circuit 122 – Backward channel received line detector (modem → DTE)**
  Equivalent to circuit 109 (data channel received line signal detector).

- **Circuit 123 – Backward channel signal quality detector (modem → DTE)**
  Equivalent to circuit 110 (data signal quality detector).

- **Circuit 124 – Data channel receiver cut off (DTE → modem)**
  This circuit can only be used when the clamping option (*see* circuit 104 above) is not used.

An ON condition causes the modem to put an OFF condition on circuit 104 (received data). Conversely, an OFF condition allows data to be received on circuit 104.

- **Circuit 125 – Calling indicator (modem → DTE)**
  An ON condition on this circuit notifies the DTE that a calling signal is being received from the line.

- **Circuit 126 – Select transmit frequency (DTE → modem)**

- **Circuit 127 – Select receive frequency (DTE → modem)**

- **Circuit 128 – Receiver signal element timing (DTE → modem)**
  This circuit is used as an alternative to circuit 115, the difference being that the receiver signal element timing is provided by the DTE rather than the modem.

- **Circuit 129 – Backward channel receiver cut-off (DTE → modem)**
  This circuit is equivalent to circuit 124 (data channel receive cut-off). An ON condition on this circuit results in circuit 119 (received backward channel data) being switched to OFF. Circuit 129 cannot be used when the 'clamping' option is used.

- **Circuit 130 – Transmit backward tone (DTE → modem)**

An ON condition on this circuit conditions the modem to transmit a single tone on the backward channel. A potential use of this circuit is in a system using push button MF telephones. The in-station modem could be conditioned to transmit a single tone as an audible acknowledgement to a person listening on the telephone that data had been received correctly.

- **Circuit 131 – Received character timing (modem → DTE)**

Any signals on this circuit provide the DTE with character timing information. This information cannot normally be provided. Most modems transmit and receive data serially bit by bit and do not know when characters begin and end. The circuit is only used in conjunction with parallel modems which accept data from the line and pass it to the DTE a character at a time.

- **Circuit 132 – Return to non-data mode (DTE → modem)**

An ON condition on this circuit instructs the modem to return to a non-data mode (eg a telephone) without losing the line connection to a remote station.

- **Circuit 133 – Ready for receiving (DTE → intermediate equipment)**

This circuit is optional when there is intermediate equipment between the DTE and the modem (eg error control equipment to CCITT recommendation V41). An ON condition on circuit 133 is an indication to the intermediate equipment that the DTE is ready to receive a block of data on circuit 104 (received data).

- **Circuit 134 – Received data present (intermediate equipment → DTE)**

This circuit is only used when error control equipment is provided between the modem and the DTE. The intermediate equipment notifies the DTE on circuit 134 which of the bits in a block transferred on circuit 104 are information (ON condition on circuit 134) or supervisory (OFF condition on circuit 134).

The 200 series interchange circuits

The 200 series of interchange circuits are all related to the operation of automatic calling over the public switched telephone network. A similar interchange of circuits is provided for automatic calling over the Telex network; these are covered in CCITT recommendation (V2).

Automatic calling over the PSTN involves a disciplined interchange of responsibility between the DTE (which is computer-related equipment of some kind) and the automatic calling equipment provided by the telecommunications authority. The 200 series interchange circuits are shown in table 7.4.

Interchange circuit number	Interchange circuit name	From DCE	To DCE
201	Signal ground or common return	X	X
202	Call request		X
203	Data line occupied	X	
204	Distant station connected	X	
205	Abandon call	X	
206	Digit signal (2^0)		X
207	Digit signal (2^1)		X
208	Digit signal (2^2)		X
209	Digit signal (2^3)		X
210	Present next digit	X	
211	Digit present		X
212	Protective ground or earth	X	X
213	Power indication	X	

Table 7.4   200 series interchange circuits by category (CCITT V24)

Notes on the 200 series interchange circuits

Some notes are given below on those 200 series interchange circuits which require some explanation; again, these should not be taken as being a substitute for the CCITT recommendation.

With automatic calling, there is an interaction between the modems and the automatic calling equipment and this is not standardised by CCITT. Because of this, a non-standard term, PTT equipment (PE), will be used in these notes for simplicity. PE may refer to automatic calling equipment or a modem. DTE is again used to denote data terminal equipment.

● **Circuit 202 – Call request (DTE → PE)**

An ON condition on this circuit instructs the PE to condition the automatic calling equipment to originate a call and to switch to line. The circuit must be switched OFF between calls or call attempts and cannot be turned ON again until circuit 203 (data line occupied) is turned OFF.

- **Circuit 203 – Data line occupied (modem → PE)**

An ON condition on this circuit indicates that the communications channel is in use. An OFF condition indicates that the DTE may originate a call provided that circuit 213 (power indication) is ON.

- **Circuit 204 – Distant stations connected (PE → DTE)**

When a connection to a remote data station is established, a 2100 Hz signal is received from the distant modem. When this is detected, an ON condition is applied to circuit 204; this condition must be maintained until circuit 202 (call request) is switched off.

- **Circuit 205 – Abandon call (PE → DTE)**

This circuit is used to indicate to the DTE whether a pre-set time has elapsed between successive events in the calling procedure. If these pre-set times are exceeded, an ON condition on the circuit instructs the DTE to abandon the call. The OFF condition on circuit 205 indicates that the call can proceed; this condition must be maintained after the distant station has been connected, ie after circuit 204 is switched ON.

The initial time interval starts when circuit 202 (call request) comes ON. Subsequent time intervals start each time circuit 210 (present next digit) is turned OFF. As an example, the timings involved in the UK when *Data Control Equipment 1A* is used are as follows:

- The time allowance between call request (circuit 102) and dial tone being received from the telephone exchange is pre-set to between 2 and 10 seconds.
- The period between dialled digits is between 350 ms and 1300 ms.
- After the last digit has been sent by the *Data Control Equipment 1A*, an answering tone of 2100 Hz must be received from a remote data station within a time which is selectable within the range 10-40 seconds.

- **Circuits 206 to 209 – (DTE → PE)**

The DTE presents the numbers to be dialled and control characters to the automatic calling equipment by placing binary conditions on 4 digit signal circuits. The conditions are held on these circuits while circuit 211 (digit present) is ON. Table 7.5 shows the standard code sequence adopted.

The control character EON (end of number) causes the data communications equipment to take the appropriate action to await an answer from the called data station. The control character SEP (separation) indicates the need for a pause between successive digits and causes the automatic calling equipment to insert the necessary time interval. For example, if the automatic calling equipment is dialling out from an extension on a private automatic branch

Information	Binary states			
	209	208	207	206
Digit 1	0	0	0	1
Digit 2	0	0	1	0
Digit 3	0	0	1	1
Digit 4	0	1	0	0
Digit 5	0	1	0	1
Digit 6	0	1	1	0
Digit 7	0	1	1	1
Digit 8	1	0	0	0
Digit 9	1	0	0	1
Digit 0	0	0	0	0
Control Character EON	1	1	0	0
Control Character SEP	1	1	0	1

Table 7.5

exchange (PABX), an initial digit may have to be dialled to obtain access to an exchange line. In these circumstances, the DTE sends a SEP character to the automatic calling equipment which instructs it to apply the time interval for awaiting dialling tone. If this was not done, the shorter time interval resulting from the inter-digital pause would not be long enough to allow the exchange equipment to prepare itself for dialling.

- **Circuit 210 – Present next digit (PE → DTE)**
     Signals on this circuit indicate whether the automatic calling equipment is ready to accept the next code combination on digit signal circuits 206, 207, 208 and 209 from the DTE.

The ON condition indicates that the automatic calling equipment is ready to accept the next code combination and the OFF condition indicates that it is not. When circuit 210 is turned OFF, it cannot be turned ON again until circuit 211 is turned OFF.

- **Circuit 211 – Digit present (DTE → PE)**
     An ON condition on this circuit is an instruction to the automatic calling equipment to read the code combination presented on the digital signal circuits.

Before an ON condition can be put on this circuit from the DTE, there must be an indication that the automatic calling equipment is ready to accept the next code combination (an ON condition on circuit 210). Also, the required code combination must have been presented on the four digital signal circuits by the DTE.

- **Circuit 212**

  Protective ground or earth.

- **Circuit 213 – Power indication**

  An ON condition on this circuit indicates that power is available within the automatic calling equipment.

The CCITT recommendation V25 is concerned with the setting up of a data connection over international circuits when automatic calling and/or answering equipment is used. The standard describes the sequence of events involved in establishing a connection between an automatic calling data terminal and an automatic answering data terminal for the cases of V21 (200 bit/s) and V23 (600/1200 bit/s) modems.

8 Data Errors

'Anybody can make a mistake' is a truism in which most of us have taken refuge at some time. The fact that people make mistakes is accepted as inevitable and is regarded with varying degrees of tolerance depending on the consequences of the errors and the frequency with which they occur. If the result of a human error is likely to be serious, it is intuitive to go more slowly, 'taking pains' to avoid mistakes and then to check and double check if necessary. Even so, 'residual errors' may remain after the checking process. Typists typify the fallibility of human beings. Their errors are often glaringly obvious to everyone but themselves and often the results are more comic than calamitous.

Errors will occur in any data communications system, certain elements within the system producing more errors than others. Although data communications links are prone to errors, they are by no means the worst offenders; sadly, that title must fall to the people within a system. Terminal operators in an on-line system are often the weakest link in an otherwise reliable installation and very high keying errors indeed are to be expected – particularly, it seems, in the critical early days of operations. In batch processing systems, the very best operators dedicated to a particular task such as card punching produce a high proportion of errors. In a field study[1] involving more than 1000 operations of IBM card punches and bank proof machines

---

[1] 'Productivity and Errors in Two Keying Tasks: A Field Study', Klemmer, B. T. and Lockwood, G. R. *Journal of Applied Psychology,* 1962 Vol. 46, No. 6, 401-408.

in 20 different installations in the USA it was found that experienced punched card operators averaged between 1600 to 4300 key strokes per undetected error, experienced bank proof machine operators averaging 3500 cheques per undetected error. The study revealed the interesting facts that the least accurate operators make ten times as many errors as the most accurate, and that fast operators tend to make fewer errors. Intuition, it seems, is not always to be trusted! These figures emphasise the inevitability of human error and indicate an upper limit of error performance in the order of 2×10^4 characters. This, of course, is way beyond the reach of most on-line terminal operators who may be performing a variety of tasks in very different conditions to the punch room. In many on-line systems, a good performance is regarded as being nearer 1 in 100, while horror stories of the system bender with a 1 in 10 error rate may be heard in hushed whispers on those occasions when on-line computer professionals congregate.

Reliable but costly means are, of course, available to detect errors both in data preparation for batch processing and for on-line terminals. Various methods of detecting punching errors are employed, the most common of these involving the use of special verifying machines. The input documents together with the punched cards or punched paper tape are handed after punching to a second operator; the information on the input documents is then keyed by the second operator, the verifier comparing the new input to that produced by the first punching. A so-called 'clean' output is, therefore, produced by the verifier – although this itself may contain errors if, for example, the second operator has made the same mistake as the first. Although verification will reduce the number of errors, they are never completely eradicated, typically the residual error rate will be in the order of 1 in 10^4 to 1 in 10^6.

Just as anyone else the computer professional himself may be fallible. Many residual program bugs are lurking now in computer systems seemingly ready to pounce at the most critical moment and then retire to await their next opportunity. The communications and computer professionals have many things in common and this is perhaps symbolised by their approach to such inexplicable errors. The term 'right when tested' of the communications engineer is perhaps less elevating than the 'act of God' of the computer professional, but it means the same thing. The real problems begin when a 'right when tested' meets an 'act of God'; in such circumstances the close affinity between brother professionals may not always be apparent! Computers themselves can make mistakes and the transient errors such as a dropped bit caused perhaps by dust particles on a magnetic tape or disc are familiar to computer programmers and operators.

The recognition of the inevitability of errors in any part of a data communications system is the first step towards a remedy. The next steps are to evaluate the likely costs of errors and to examine the probability of their occurrence. A very high degree of error control can be applied to any part of a system although it should be emphasised that the cost of guarding against errors must not be allowed to exceed the cost of allowing them to occur. Errors can be expected on data communications links and the nature of these and the available means of error control are discussed in this chapter. Much attention has been given to this interesting subject in recent years and initial fear of transmission errors has been replaced to some extent by an enthusiasm to control them. There is, however, a need for consistency of approach to the problem. Residual error rates can now be reduced to infinitesimal proportions but it is unrealistic to design for a residual error rate of, say, 1×10^{-14} in this area without protection of the same degree in other equally important parts of a system.

It is also useful to remember that an error which remains undetected on a transmission link may be detected elsewhere. Simple validity checks can be included in 'data vet' programs to ensure, for example, that fixed data field sizes are not exceeded or that numeric information is not received when alpha is expected. Reasonable checks can be included in application programs, so that in a payroll program, for example, the caretaker is not paid more than the chief executive. Protection against transmission errors must, therefore, be seen in perspective as only part of a solution to a total systems problem.

The Transmission Error Problem

The only statement that can be made with certainty about transmission errors is that they will occur. How often they will do so and what the distribution of errors will be on a particular circuit is a forecast which the bravest communications engineer would not attempt.

Private circuits can be provided with defined characteristics which indicate the distortions and disturbances on the line which are unlikely to be exceeded. To what extent errors result from these imperfect line conditions will depend to a great extent on the modems and transmission techniques used. All telecommunications authorities are naturally reluctant to quote guaranteed error rates on their networks because of these factors and because inevitably some circuits will give a poorer performance than others. Table 8.1 shows, however, the maximum bit error rates recommended by CCITT for different types of connection. These show only the maximum average number of error bits to correct bits and, while being useful to telecommunications engineers for maintenance purposes, they are not very helpful either to designers of error control systems or to systems analysts.

Modulation rate (bauds)	Connection	Maximum bit error rate
1200	switched (when possible)	10^{-3}
1200	leased	$5\text{-}10^{-}$
600	switched	10^{-3}
600	leased	$5\text{-}10^{-5}$
200	switched	10^{-4}
200	leased	$5\text{-}10^{-5}$

Table 8.1   Maintenance limits for errors on the PSTN and leased terms (CCITT Green Book, Vol. VIII 1973, recommendation V53)

Transmission errors in fact pose different problems for three different groups of people. The telecommunications engineers – and here modem manufacturers are included – must study the transmission problems which are likely to cause errors so that circuits can be engineered and modems designed to minimise their effects. In addition, the telecommunications engineers, through their PTTs, have the added responsibility of providing as much information as possible regarding the frequency and distribution of those conditions on their networks which are likely to cause errors and to recommend means of controlling them. A great deal of detailed work has already been done and published in this direction by PTTs through their international body CCITT[2] and the work continues.

The designer of an error control system is primarily concerned with the control of errors with a view to providing the maximum protection against them with the minimum amount of redundant information. His prime interest is the distribution or pattern of errors as well as the frequency with which they are likely to occur and he will conduct his own laboratory and field experiments as well as using CCITT statistics in order to obtain the information he requires.

The systems analyst working on data communications systems apparently has the easiest transmission error control problem. Indeed he can – and some do – ignore the problem altogether in the belief that he can readily obtain the level of protection which he needs against this type of error. This is understandable, for, with modern data communications systems, retransmission of blocks in error takes place automatically and the presence of transmission errors is rarely evident. He could be forgiven for wondering what the fuss is

---

[2] CCITT Blue Book, Vol. VIII 1968,
  CCITT White Book, Vol. VIII 1969, and
  CCITT Green Book, Vol. VIII 1973.

all about and devote himself to other more pressing or exciting tasks. He may well be right in this for, if the communications hardware has already been purchased and manufacturers' communications control software is being used, there may be very little he could do about transmission errors anyway. However, a knowledge of data transmission error control may help a systems designer in a number of ways.

By considering carefully the effects of errors in a proposed system, the analyst can determine the proper degree of protection required and try to select an error control method which will give him the necessary residual error rate with the minimum redundancy. From then on, the systems analyst can regard errors as delays, delays which can increase costs or lengthen response times or both. These delays can be reduced considerably by careful attention to the block sizes and the error control procedures used. Later in this chapter, different types of error detection and correction codes will be discussed and the throughput of information in the presence of errors will also be considered. Before examining these subjects, it is useful to clarify what is meant by the various terms used to describe errors and to have some idea what causes them. First of all, the term 'error' itself. This could not be easier, for the nature of computer data is such that the symbols 0 and 1 are mutually exclusive. If, therefore, a binary '1' is received when a binary '0' has been transmitted, an error has occurred. This is described as a single bit error if the bits on either side are received correctly. Errors also occur in groups and a two bit error group for example is two consecutive erroneous bits with correct bits either side. Table 8.2 shows the recorded distribution of error groups found on a series of tests on a looped private circuit in the UK using FSK modems at 1200 bit/s.

Number of 1 bit errors	584
Number of 2 bit errors	204
Number of 3 bit errors	73
Number of 4 bit errors	43
Number of 5 bit errors	16
Number of 6 bit errors	9
Number of 7 bit errors	5
Number of 8 bit errors	3
Total number of error groups	937

Table 8.2 Distribution of error groups from tests on a private circuit in the UK at 1200 bit/s (CCITT White Book, Vol. VIII. Supp. 15)

The results of these tests, which were conducted using a 4082 bit pseudo-random pattern, cannot be regarded as typifying those to be found on other private circuits, but they serve to illustrate the fact that a variety of error groupings can be expected. In this case, only 62 per cent of the error groups were found to be single bit errors, the average number of bits in an error group being 1.68.

Line disturbances also cause bursts of errors to occur. An error burst is defined by CCITT as a group of bits in which two successive erroneous bits are always separated by less than a given number (X) of correct bits, the definition going on to state that the last erroneous bit in a burst and the first erroneous bit in the following burst are accordingly separated by X or more correct bits. Such precise definition is necessary in international communications but can pose problems of understanding similar to those conundrums beloved of the Zenn Bhuddist. The reader may be relieved to learn that CCITT have not so far attempted to define an 'erroneous bit'. Burst errors, in fact, are not as incomprehensible as they sound and are extremely important. If errors are to be detected, it is necessary to find out more about the way in which they are distributed. To say that an average error rate is say, 1 in 10^4 tells us very little, for errors will certainly not be conveniently slotted into data stream 1 every 10,000 bits. Error groupings, as in table 8.2, are helpful but give no indication of the distances which separate the errors – a key factor in the design of effective error detection and correction codes. The analysis of data in terms of error bursts is very useful and fairly simple. Consider the small block of data shown in figure 8.1.

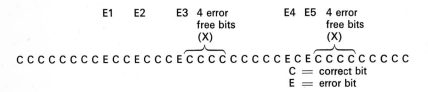

Figure 8.1   Analysis of a block for burst errors

An error burst must begin and end with an error but may or may not contain other error bits; the term therefore describes a 'span' rather than a number of errors. We could, therefore, consider first of all the span E1 to E2 as being a four bit burst. However, if we were to require the transmission of four error free bits (ie X) to indicate the end of an error burst, we would have considered the burst to be terminated by E3. The block in fact contains an eight bit burst E1-E3. This is followed by a three bit burst E4-E5.

Figure 8.2 gives a typical graph of error burst size distribution.

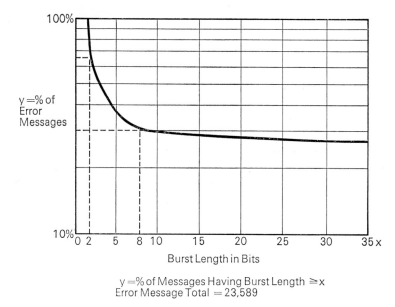

y =% of Messages Having Burst Length ≥x
Error Message Total = 23,589

Figure 8.2 Error burst size distribution (CCITT Blue Book, 37/22)

Transmission Errors

Transmission errors are caused by a number of factors but impulsive noise is probably the major problem. The main source of impulsive noise is switched connections through automatic telephone exchanges.

The electro-mechanical switches in the exchanges cause vibrations which create movement on contact surfaces resulting in noise peaks or spikes with typical peak to peak values of 100 milli-volts. There is also some evidence[3] to suggest that the quality of the final selectors in the called exchange exert a considerable influence on the level of impulsive noise. Noise power is normally expressed in dBm0 which refers to the ratio of the noise power at a point in the transmission path to the test level measured at that point (expressed in decibels). The maximum number of noise peaks which occur during any period of 15 minutes on *private* circuits are published in the relevant PTT circuit specifications. For example, on a UK Post Office schedule D circuit, a threshold level of —21 dBm0 is set which must not be exceeded more than 18 times in any period of 15 minutes (*see* figure 8.3).

---

[3] CCITT White Book, Vol. VIII, Supp. 14.

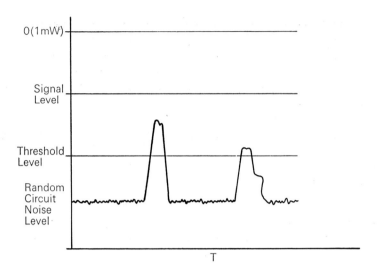

Figure 8.3   Noise peaks

Signal power and transmission errors

As the most important factor affecting transmission error performance is the ratio of impulse noise power to the signal power, it would obviously be advantageous to increase the signal power of the modems used on telephone circuits. Unfortunately, there are limits which must be observed and these have been agreed internationally (CCITT recommendation V2). The reasons for this are, firstly, to avoid overhearing or cross-talk which can be caused in the local cable network by excessive signal power and, secondly, because the multi-channel carrier systems used on the networks have design tolerances which limit the power values of individual channels.

The CCITT has recommended a maximum send level of —10 dBm0 from subscribers' equipment into simplex private circuits and —13 dBm0 for duplex circuits. The BPO stipulates a send level not exceeding —13 dBm0 on all private circuits. An inland private circuit to schedule D specification and an international circuit to M102 specification conform to CCITT recommendations regarding impulsive noise levels. Noise levels exceeding a threshold level of —21 dBm0 are measured and a count is made of the number of times the noise exceeds the threshold level. On private circuits, the signal to noise power level at the noise threshold point is therefore 8 Db (signal level —13 dBm0, noise level —21 dBm0). The count should not exceed 18 during any 15 minute period.

In the UK, modems attached to the PSTN are provided by the Post Office and are adjusted on installation so that the sending level is —10 dBm at the Group Switching Centre. This complies with the international agreement (CCITT recommendation V2) that systems transmitting continuous tones should have the power level of the customer's equipment adjusted so that on international calls the level of the signal at the international circuit input shall not exceed —10 dBm0 for simplex systems or —13 dBm0 for duplex systems. Calls connected on the PSTN are not only more subject to impulsive noise and interruptions than private circuits but the ratio of the level of these disturbances to the signal power is likely to be very much higher because of the greater attenuation of the signals (*see* Chapter 4). It follows from this that the error rate of calls over the PSTN will be considerably worse than on a private leased circuit.

Telephone traffic and transmission errors

The incidence of errors on telephone circuits tends to follow the same pattern as that of the exchange traffic. The typical telephone traffic graph is shown in figure 8.4.

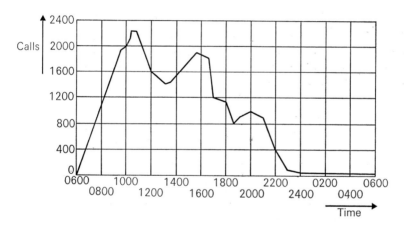

Figure 8.4   Telephone call distribution

This close correlation between busy hour traffic and data errors is an international phenomenon and can be seen clearly by comparing figure 8.4 with figure 8.5 which shows the distribution of erroneous blocks transmitted on the PSTN in Chile.

The error peaks are due to the additional impulsive noise introduced by automatic selectors in automatic telephone exchanges during busy periods.

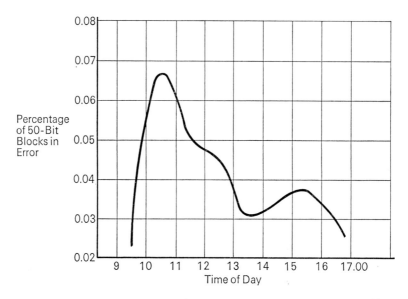

Figure 8.5   Time distribution of erroneous blocks on the PSTN in Chile

The same effect can be seen on private circuit connections. The tests referred to earlier on a private circuit in the UK (CCITT White Book, Vol. VIII, Supp. 14) show a different distribution but the influence of peak traffic can be seen clearly in table 8.3.

9.00 – 10.00 hrs	1 bit in	75,343
10.00 – 11.00 hrs	1 bit in	14,378
11.00 – 12.00 hrs	1 bit in	46,014
12.00 – 13.00 hrs	1 bit in	1,277,811
13.00 – 14.00 hrs	1 bit in	12,876,768
14.00 – 15.00 hrs	1 bit in	79,529
15.00 – 16.00 hrs	indeterminate, better than 1 bit in	6,425,000
16.00 – 17.00 hrs	1 bit in	10,261
17.00 – 17.30 hrs	indeterminate, better than 1 bit in	2,140,000

Table 8.3   Bit error rates against time of day. Tests on a private circuit in the UK (CCITT White Book, Vol. VIII, Supp. 14)

The results shown here, and other tests throughout the world, suggest that the error performance of data links in traffic off-peak periods will yield better results than in the busy periods. This is particularly true of calls on the PSTN where there is the added incentive to use off peak periods because of reduced call charges.

There may be a wide variation of bit error rates over different days of the week and again there are indications that this is probably due to variations in telephone traffic density. Table 8.4 shows the results found on the UK tests (CCITT White Book, Vol. VIII, Supp. 14).

Monday	1 bit in	1,647,283
Tuesday	1 bit in	1,272,290
Wednesday	1 bit in	55,770
Thursday	1 bit in	3,006,290
Friday	1 bit in	647,140

Table 8.4   Variations in bit error rates Monday to Friday. Tests on a private circuit in the UK (CCITT White Book, Vol. VIII, Supp. 14)

Although over 300 million bits were transmitted during these tests, they were conducted over a period of only three weeks and it would be unwise, therefore, to draw any other conclusions from these figures alone except that considerable variations in error rates from day to day may be experienced. The figure for Wednesdays is interesting and, although considerable efforts were made to find the reasons for the relatively poor performance on that day, no convincing explanation could be found. The perversity of errors being so great on Wednesdays during these tests is further evidence that average bit error rates are not to be trusted.

Short breaks in transmission

A problem which occurs in all telephone networks is that of short interruptions in transmission during which the line signals may be lost completely. Table 8.5

Duration of interruption (milliseconds)	Total number of interruptions	Number of interruptions whose cause could not be identified
<10	4	4
10-20	16	7
20-50	21	3
50-100	7	0
100-300	20	1
300 to 1 minute	25	1
>1 minute	7	2
TOTALS	100	18

Table 8.5   Distribution of durations of interruptions recorded on a 200 mile channel during two weeks

shows the results of an investigation during a two-week period in January 1966 on a channel with a total length of 200 miles.[4]

The channel measured was set up on a through-supergroup over three, old type, coaxial systems. The majority of causes for the interruptions were identified and it is expected that with the more modern design features of newer systems and the improved maintenance procedures which have been and are continuing to be introduced that the incidence of short interruptions will be reduced. However, it is most unlikely that these breaks will ever be eradicated and data will not be transmitted during the periods they are present. With modern error control procedures, the majority of these shorter breaks will result in the blocks of data in which they occur being retransmitted and data will not be lost but delayed. Longer interruptions may cause further delays if synchronisation is lost and some systems will register a failure if a number (typically 3) of retransmissions is unsuccessful. Unless each block of data is clearly identified, there is a danger that a line interruption may result in a message being lost – particularly, when continuous automatic retransmission methods are used (*see* Chapter 6).

Echoes

In speech conversations over long distance circuits, a person's voice may be returned or echoed back to him. These echoes are due to reflections which can occur whenever there is a change of impedance in the line such as a 2 to 4-wire conversion through hybrid transformers.

This talker echo effect is a nuisance when measured in tens of milliseconds, and above 500 ms will inhibit speech altogether; some long distance circuits are fitted with echo-suppressors to prevent echoes being returned but these can be disabled when the circuit is used for data transmission as it may be essential to have the return channel open (eg for 75 bit/s control procedures).

Echoes have a different effect on data transmission. The problem is that data transmitted may be followed by a delayed replica of itself (*listener echo*) which may interfere with the operation of the data receiver. Delays of fractions of a millisecond may be significant and, if the echoes are of sufficient amplitude, errors may be produced.

On schedule D circuits, for example, the maximum level will be 20 dB. On the public switched telephone network, some connections may have a signal to listener echo ratio of worse than 15 dB.

---

[4] 'Characteristics of Telephone Circuits in Relation to Data Transmission', Williams, M B, *POEEJ*, Vol. 5, Part 3, Oct. 1966.

There are other factors such as the level of random noise, frequency distortion, and phase distortion which may contribute towards data errors. However, good modem design can minimise the effect of these factors on data errors to negligible proportions.

Error Control Systems

The two basic functions of an error control system are, firstly, to detect the errors which occur and, secondly, to correct them. The way in which these functions are provided varies considerably but a prime consideration is the availability of a return path on the transmission system. In situations where no return channel is provided, sufficient redundant information must be added to the message so that the receiver can not only detect but also correct errors which occur. This type of system is known as 'error correction' or 'forward error correction' and is discussed on page 206. There are few situations, however, where a return path of some kind is unavailable on data communications links and most of the error control methods used utilise this path for feeding back information or decisions related to the message to the transmitter; messages in error are then retransmitted. These systems can be distinguished according to the type of communication used on the return channel as either 'information feedback' or 'decision feedback'.

Information feedback

In these systems, information about a message is referred to the transmitter where the decision to accept or reject a message is made.

Most of us have used a form of information feedback error control during telephone conversations. A person receiving a list of figures on the telephone naturally repeats the information back, the decisions regarding the correct reception of the message being made by the originator.

The same principles are applied in information feedback systems used in data communications, except that communication is in duplex rather than half-duplex mode. A method sometimes referred to as 'echo checking' or loop checking is often employed on data printers when used for direct keying. The conventional method of obtaining a 'local copy' of messages transmitted on a data printer is shown in figure 8.6, the transmitter 'looping' the data being transmitted to its own receiver.

On a data printer using information feedback techniques the information sent is received at the receive station and simultaneously fed back to the transmit station to produce the local copy as shown in figure 8.7.

This is a simple and inexpensive form of error control and is often used when the terminal operator is working interactively with a time sharing bureau.

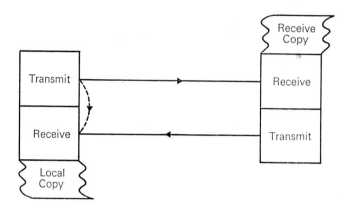

Figure 8.6   Production of 'local copy' – not using information feedback

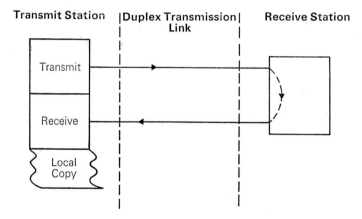

Figure 8.7   Production of 'local copy' – using information feedback

For example, a programmer might be developing a program with the aid of a remote computer and he can be reasonably confident that if the characters he keys are reproduced on his page copy that they have been received correctly at the computer. Error correction is arranged manually by backspacing and deleting character errors which have been detected.

The time delay between a key depression and the character being printed will be apparently negligible on a terminal having the exclusive use of a circuit; the delay being made up of the propagation time for the signals to go round the circuit. If the terminal is connected on a character interleaved time division multiplexed (TDM) link, however, there may be a noticeable delay; information feedback on multiplexed links is sometimes known as 'echoplexing'.

There are a number of disadvantages with using information feedback. Because errors can occur in the backward path as well as the forward path, errors are detected which never happened! This in effect doubles the incidence of transmission errors. On the other hand there is the possibility that a disturbance might occur at the same time in the transmit and receive channels which will cause an error in the forward direction to be compensated by an error in the return direction. A further potential disadvantage is the need to use duplex transmission facilities. Information feedback, therefore, utilizes a facility which would not otherwise be used on terminals which operate in a conversational or half-duplex mode.

Decision feedback

All the error control methods using decision feedback employ some means of providing additional or 'redundant' information with the transmitted data to enable the receiver to check its accuracy. A decision, as to whether the information has been received correctly or not, can then be fed back to the transmitter in the form of an acknowledgement (ACK) or a negative acknowledgement (NAK); the need to repeat all the information in the return direction is, therefore, avoided. Most of the data communications systems in use today employ half-duplex control procedures (*see* Chapter 6). Data is transmitted a block at a time and at the end of each block an ACK or a NAK character is returned from the receiver to the transmitter to indicate whether the data has been received correctly or not. If the transmitter receives an ACK character in return, it proceeds automatically to send the next block; if a NAK is received, it transmits the previous block again. Typically, three attempts are made to re-transmit a block in error before the terminal at the transmit station gives up and produces a visual or audible indication of failure.

In the earlier example of a group of numbers being passed between two people over the telephone, a simple decision feedback system using a 'total' method could be used. The numbers could be totalled and the total transmitted at the end of the block of numbers as follows:

$$\begin{array}{cc} data & total \\ 1521+2789+3148+2214 \quad = & 9672 \end{array}$$

The person receiving the data could perform the same addition and check his total against the total received, returning only a simple request to repeat the information or to proceed to the next block. Obviously, this would allow for faster communication, but the human calculation involved would slow things down. There would also be a problem of compensating errors, for example the following received block, which contains two compensating errors, would be accepted as being correct:

$$1521+2788+3149+2214 \quad = \quad 9672$$
$$(-1) \quad (+1)$$

Total methods are rarely used in isolation to control errors in data communications systems. The calculations involved require logic which adds to the costs, and the relatively high redundancy makes them inefficient in comparison with other methods. However, in applications where the total may be of use and is, therefore, not redundant (as in banking), total systems are used effectively in conjunction with more sophisticated error control techniques.

Parity systems

The two most common forms of error detection methods used are character (or vertical) parity and block (or longitudinal) parity.

Character parity involves the addition of an extra bit to each character. Figure 8.8 shows a character using odd parity where an extra bit is added so that the total number of 1 bits in the character is odd.

parity							
↓							
b8	b7	b6	b5	b4	b3	b2	b1
1	0	1	1	0	1	0	1

Figure 8.8

CCITT recommend[5] that the least significant bit (b1) of this information is transmitted first and that the additional character parity bit should be transmitted last (b8). At the receiver, a check is made of the number of 1 bits in the character received and, if the total is odd, it is assumed that the character has been received correctly; if an even number of 1 bits are received, a negative acknowledgement signal is returned.

Character parity can detect all single bit errors and is often used within a computer system where the transient types of error, which occur due to dust particles on magnetic tapes and discs, are of this type. Character parity

---

[5] Recommendation V4, CCITT Green Book, Vol. VIII.

cannot detect an even number of bit errors within a character and it is therefore, extremely inefficient in circumstances where multiple errors are likely to occur.

A complete character known as a block check character (BCC) may be added at the end of each block of information to give longitudinal parity checking (*see* figure 8.9).

Character Parity	b8	0	0	1	0	0	0	0	0	1	0	1	0
	b7	0	0	0	0	0	0	0	0	0	0	0	0
	b6	0	1	1	1	1	1	1	1	1	1	0	1
	b5	0	1	1	1	1	0	1	1	1	1	0	0
Information Bits	b4	0	0	0	0	0	0	0	0	1	.1	0	0
	b3	0	0	1	0	0	0	0	1	0	0	0	0
	b2	1	0	0	1	0	0	1	1	0	0	1	0
	b1	0	1	1	0	1	0	0	1	1	0	1	0
	Characters	STX	1	5	2	1	SPACE	2	7	9	8	ETX	BCC

Longitudinal Parity

NOTES
1 Odd parity is used for the character check.
2 Even parity is used for the longitudinal check.
3 The STX (start of text) character is not included in the longitudinal check.
4 Bit position 8 (b8) of the BCC is used for character parity and the sense is therefore odd.

Figure 8.9   An example of two co-ordinate parity using IA 5

The rules used for the generation of the BCC in the example shown in figure 8.9 are those of British Standard 4505: part 3. Each of the first seven bits of the BCC is the modulo 2 binary sum of every element in the same bit 1 to bit 7 column of the successive characters of the block. With modulo 2 arithmetic, any figure carried forward is discarded and only the remainder is left, eg

$$2^1 \quad 2^0$$
$$1$$
$$1$$
$$1+$$
$$\overline{}$$
$$1$$

This means, in effect, that the total number of 1 bits in each column should add up to an even number using the longitudinal parity method. The summation to obtain the block check character is started by the first appearance of either SOH (start of heading) or STX (start of text) and the starting character is not, therefore, included in the summation. In messages which begin with SOH, an STX character which follows will, however, be included in the longitudinal check. Either ETX (end of text) or ETB (end of transmitted block) signal that the next following character is the block character and are included in the summation.

Two co-ordinate parity is more suitable for data transmission purposes than simple character parity. All messages with odd numbers of error bits can be detected, also all two bit errors and some other even numbers of errors. Although the number of compensating errors are reduced, rectangular error patterns will remain undetected as shown in figure 8.10.

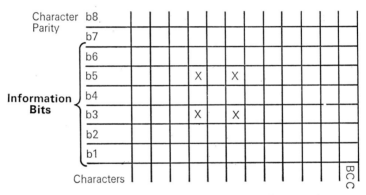

Figure 8.10   Undetected errors with two co-ordinate parity system

Constant ratio codes

In a constant ratio code, the character set is structured so that the ratio of '1' bits to '0' bits in each character is always the same, any disturbance in this ratio can then be detected. For example, a number of characters having a ratio of 3:4 of '1' bits to '0' bits can be derived from a seven unit code; the actual number of such combinations that can be obtained being given by the formula:

$$\frac{N!}{M!\,(N-M)!}$$
where N = the total number of bits in each character
and M = the number of '1' bits in each character

substituting, we have $\dfrac{7\times6\times5\times4\times3\times2\times1}{3\times2\times1\times(4\times3\times2\times1)} = 35$ characters

This type of code, where each of the 35 characters has three '1' bits and four '0' bits, is widely used in radio telegraphy.

The code shown in figure 8.11 is an example of a redundant code where more signal elements are transmitted than are actually needed to convey the

Letter and figure case	7-unit international code No. 3
A —	0011010
B ?	0011001
C :	1001100
D ¹	0011100
E 3	0111000
F ¹	0010011
G ¹	1100001
H ¹	1010010
I 8	1110000
J ¹	0100011
K (	0001011
L)	1100010
M .	1010001
N ,	1010100
O 9	1000110
P 0	1001010
Q 1	0001101
R 4	1100100
S '	0101010
T 5	1000101
U 7	0110010
V =	1001001
W 2	0100101
X /	0010110
Y 6	0010101
Z +	0110001
carriage return	1000011
line feed	1011000
letters	0001110
figures	0100110
space	1101000
(not used)	0000111
signal repetition	0110100
signal α	0101001
signal β	0101100

(permanent 0 polarity)   (permanent 1 polarity)

NB digit 0 = Space   digit 1 = Mark

Figure 8.11   Example of 3:4 constant ratio code, IA 3

information. A seven unit code without shifts can provide 128 characters: as only 35 are used in a 3:4 code, 93 of the 128 combinations are redundant. All odd bit errors up to a maximum of seven can be detected but inversions of 2, 4, or 6 bits may remain undetected. Because of the high redundancy and the limited character set available, 3:4 codes have not been used for commercial data communications. A '4 out of 8' constant ratio code has been widely used in the past which provides 70 out of a possible 256 characters; however, the redundancy is high relative to the protection it provides and this method is not now used in modern data communications equipment.

Cyclic codes

The most promising codes for error detection are known as cyclic codes. Cyclic coding involves a calculation at the transmitter station in which the block of data to be sent is treated as a pure binary number and is divided by a predetermined number. This produces a remainder which forms the check digits and is transmitted to line immediately after the block of data. The equipment at the receiving station divides the received data (including the check digits) by the same predetermined number as the transmitter and if the block has been received correctly there should be no remainder.

This process (which requires the use of 'shift registers') can best be described by using a simple example.

The data to be transmitted is:

$$1001001010$$

This will be passed into a shift register which contains an 'adder' and two 'shift stores'. The adder is used for modulo 2 addition and the two inputs have the outputs shown in figure 8.12.

The shifting stores can store one binary digit; when a '0' or a '1' is received on the input lead this replaces the original bit stored which is shifted to the next stage as shown in figure 8.13.

Figure 8.14 shows how the combination of the adder and the shift stores responds to the input of the example data block. The shift register is in fact performing a division in modulo 2 arithmetic, and the contents remaining in the shift stores at the last step (step 12) represent the remainder. The number divided is the block of data which is treated as a pure binary number as shown in figure 8.15.

The divisor is called a generating polynomial and for this simple example has been chosen as $x^2 + 1$ (which is 101).

The actual division in modulo 2 arithmetic is shown in figure 8.16 which may be compared with the sequence of figure 8.14.

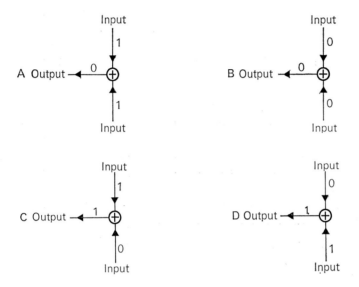

Figure 8:12   Outputs of modulo 2 addition

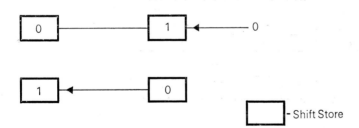

Figure 8.13   Basic function of simple shift store

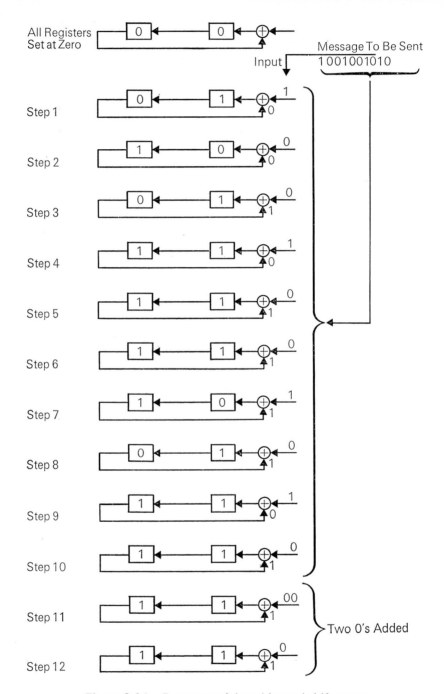

Figure 8.14   Response of the adder and shift stores

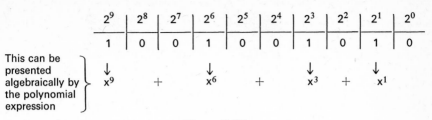

This can be presented algebraically by the polynomial expression

$$x^9 + x^6 + x^3 + x^1$$

Figure 8.15

```
                        1011110111
generating  →     101 / 1001001010:00          ←    2 zeros added to
polynomial              101          :               the original data
(x² + 1)                ───
                        110                      ←    step 4
                        101
                        ───
                        110                      ←    step 5
                        101
                        ───
                        111                      ←    step 6
                        101
                        ───
                        100                      ←    step 7
                        101
                        ───
                         110                     ←    step 9
                         101
                         ───
                         110                     ←    step 10
                         101
                         ───
                          110                    ←    step 11
                          101
                          ───
                           11                    ←    step 12
                                                      (remainder)
```

Figure 8.16

The complete block transmitted consists of the original data and the remainder stored in the shift register and is transmitted to line as follows:

original data   *remainder*

1 0 0 1 0 0 1 0 1 0   1 1

At the receiver, a similar shift register performs the same calculation on the incoming data and, if no errors have occurred on the line, the received data **should** be exactly divisible by the generating polynomial as shown in figure 8.17.

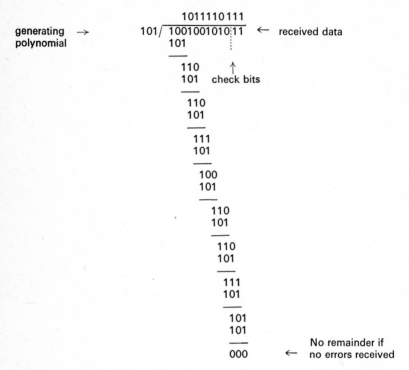

Figure 8.17   Division at the receive terminal of the received data by the generating polynomial

If the cyclic shift register at the receiver produces a remainder other than zero, this indicates that an error has been detected in the received data and the received terminal calls for a retransmission.

The polynomial used in the example (x^2+1) is too short for practical application. Polynomials used in data communications are chosen to combine powerful burst error detection with low redundancy and cyclic coding is, therefore, more efficient than the methods described earlier.

Figure 8.18 shows the arrangements for encoding the 16 bit polynomial $x^{16}+x^{12}+x^5+1$ (CCITT recommendation V41). This polynomial will be used in the UK experimental 'packet switched' service (EPSS).

It has been found from computer simulation[6] that when using a block size of 260 bits (including service bits and check bits) an improvement factor in the order of 50,000 is achieved. On a circuit with a mean error rate of 1 in 10^4, the residual error rate would, therefore, be in the order of 2 in 10^9, the 16 redundant bits comprising only 6.1 per cent of each block. All odd numbers of errors within a block would be detected, also any one error burst not exceeding 16 bits in length and a large percentage of other error patterns.

To encode, the 16 register stores are set to zero, gates A and B are enabled (opened) and gate C is shut. The data, which is headed by four service bits, is clocked into the input, passing through gate B and at the same time is leaked off into the shift register. When all the bits have passed through the shift register, a remainder comprising 16 checking bits is left in the shift stores. This represents the modulo 2 division of the block of data (service bits + information bits) and is passed to the output via gate C which is enabled.

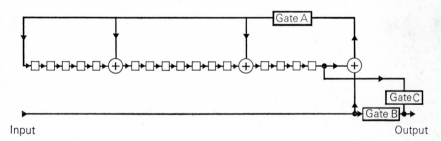

Figure 8.18   An encoding arrangement using the 16 bit polynomial
$x^{16} + x^{12} + x^5 + 1$ (CCITT Recommendation V41)

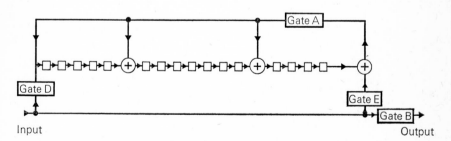

Figure 8.19   A decoding arrangement using the 16 bit polynomial
$x^{16} + x^{12} + x^5 + 1$ (CCITT Recommendation V41)

---

[6] The simulation assumed a distribution of errors as in the CCITT Blue Book, Vol. VIII, Supp. 22.

In the decoder shown in figure 8.19 the shift stores are set to zero, gates A, B and E are enabled and gate D is inhibited.

The service bits and information bits are clocked into the input after which gate B is inhibited. The 16 check bits are then clocked into the input and, if the data has been received correctly, the contents of all the 16 register stores should be zero; ie, the received data should be exactly divisible by the generating polynomial $x^{16}+x^{12}+x^5+1$.

If it is found in examination of the register content that there is a non-zero remainder, this indicates that the block is in error. Gate D is enabled when checking for block synchronisation patterns (*see* Chapter 4), gates A, B and E are then inhibited.

In order to correct a block which is in error, there must be automatic repetition of a block upon request (ARQ) from the data receiver. In order to avoid the output of erroneous blocks at the receiver, it is usual for the output from the shift register to be passed to local storage in the terminal. Blocks in error can then be erased ensuring that only 'clean' data is produced at the system output.

As with any ARQ system, storage is necessary at the transmitter so that blocks previously sent can be repeated. Storage for at least two data blocks must be provided at the transmitter.

Block Identity

As was pointed out in Chapter 6, to avoid blocks being lost, gained or transposed, some means of identifying each block is desirable. Some systems employ 'odd' and 'even' indicators by the addition of a '1' bit or a '0' bit added to the block. Others use a block sequence number indication to give more powerful protection.

Table 8.6 shows the mandatory service bit combinations used in conjunction with CCITT recommendation V41.

Combination	Function
0011	Block A sequence indicator
1001	Block B sequence indicator
1100	Block C sequence indicator
0101	Synchronising sequence prefix

Table 8.6

The first three combinations give a cyclic block identification (A B C A B . . .).

Block size

The size of the block used is often determined by the operational requirements of a system or the hardware used rather than the need to optimise the throughput of transmission links. In most cases, the blocks transmitted are of variable length although the upper limit is usually conditioned by the type of message or by terminal characteristics such as buffer capacity. On alpha-numeric display terminals, for example, the maximum block size is likely to be determined by the size of the buffer although the block sizes actually trans-mitted will vary considerably depending on the size of the input and output messages.

From an error control point of view, blocks should ideally be of fixed length; the actual length being determined by the probabilities of errors occurring and the nature of the error bursts likely to be encountered. There is, therefore, a conflict between the need for efficient transmission of information and other important design considerations. In on-line systems, it is difficult to reconcile these differing requirements and compromise is necessary. In off-line applications, there is greater scope for savings and these may be substantial if large quantities of data are transmitted. When the public switched telephone network is used for on-line transmission, very different error conditions may be met on different calls. In these circumstances, a terminal which provides facilities to choose from a range of different block sizes offers better opportunities for efficient transmission than one which does not.

There are advantages in using large blocks. Firstly, where synchronous transmission is employed with half-duplex control procedures, a significant period may elapse between blocks transmitted (*see* Chapter 6). This period is constant whether blocks are long or short and the larger the block the less time is wasted. Secondly, with a large block the proportion of redundant data to information may be smaller for a given degree of protection than with a smaller block.

There are, however, disadvantages in using large blocks. First of all, these have to be retransmitted when necessary and therefore some form of storage is required at the transmitter.

This might not be costly with paper tape or magnetic tape terminals where the tape readers can be reversed to the beginning of a block. However, on buffered terminals the increased buffer capacity required by using long blocks might outweigh other savings. The second factor is that the probability of errors increases proportionately with the block length; allied to this is the fact that the re-transmission of each block takes longer.

Some examples of the effects of these different considerations are given later in this chapter.

Data Signal Quality Detection

Data signal quality detection or analogue error detection is a means whereby a received data signal can be checked to find out whether it has departed from its original form. Unlike the other error detection methods described earlier which work on the principle of examining logically the binary information received, data signal quality detection involves the examination of the quality of the received signals. The quality criteria applied may typically be the amplitude of the signals, the signal to noise ratio, frequency distortion, phase distortion, separately or in combination. They do not, therefore, measure errors but the probability that errors will be caused by signals outside defined tolerance limits.

Data signal quality detectors are unlikely to be used as the sole means of detecting errors although a useful error reduction can be obtained by a fairly low cost amplitude tolerance detector which uses amplitude thresholds to evaluate the amplitudes of demodulated signals.[7]

There is a hidden redundancy with detectors of this kind which is produced by their tendency to indicate disturbances which would not in fact produce errors. However, there may be considerable advantages to be gained by using data signal quality detectors in combination with other apparently more powerful error control methods such as cyclic redundancy checks. While cyclic codes may be designed to be extremely efficient for error burst sizes up to the total number of check bits used, they become less efficient with larger bursts. Although an obvious answer is to increase the number of check bits used, the proportion of redundancy to information may rise to unacceptable levels to achieve the necessary protection. Data signal quality detectors become more effective the greater the burst size and a combination of techniques is likely to provide greater efficiency on circuits where long error bursts are to be expected.

Forward Error Control (FEC)

Unlike ARQ systems, forward error control (FEC) systems attempt to correct errors at the receiver without the retransmission procedures described earlier. Sufficient redundancy must therefore be contained in forward messages so that not only the presence of an error is detected but also its position within the message. After the position of an error is known, correction is achieved simply by inverting the erroneous bit from 1 to 0 or vice versa.

ARQ systems are greatly superior to FEC systems when used on telephone channels. We have seen that residual error rates can be reduced to infinitesimal

---

[7] CCITT White Book, Vol. VIII, Supp. 23 (AEG Telefunken).

levels when efficient error detection codes are allied to simple control procedures. If a code is required simply to detect errors, systems using redundant parity bits will be able to detect a very high proportion of the many different error patterns which can be expected on telephone circuits. The fraction of undetected error patterns will be only $1/2^r$ irrespective of the length of the error detection code used where r is the number of checking bits in the code. A code using eight checking bits is, therefore, capable of detecting all but 1/256th of all the error patterns which can possibly occur. The effectiveness of the codes can be further increased by careful design to give maximum protection against those error patterns which are most likely to occur. Comparatively few error patterns are correctable when using parity checking. This fraction will be no better than $1/2^k$ where k is the number of information bits in a block – regardless of the algorithm used. It follows from this that unless the error characteristics of a channel are such that only a very small number of error patterns are present the residual error rate will be high when using FEC. Forward error correction is usually used, therefore, when a return channel is not available and more efficient ARQ methods are not possible. Typically, they are designed to correct single or two bit errors but will detect other error patterns and give an error indication at the receiver when these occur – usually by printing special character symbols.

The general effect of FEC is to reduce the error rate of a channel but the high proportion of checking bits to information bits also significantly reduces the transfer rate. The transfer rate of an FEC system can be given as:

$$\frac{Rk}{n}$$

where R $\quad$ = the data signalling rate;

$\quad$ k $\quad$ = the number of information bits transmitted;

$\quad$ n $\quad$ = the total number of bits transmitted.

A general comparison between the throughput efficiency on a telephone circuit of an ARQ system and a FEC system cannot be made, as the output from a FEC system will contain a much higher proportion of uncorrected errors than the output from an ARQ system.

On switched connections where fairly high error rates can be expected, there is an argument for using a combination of FEC and ARQ techniques, the FEC reducing the number of blocks requiring re-transmission and, therefore, possibly increasing transfer efficiency. There is a trade-off between the extra redundancy introduced by FEC and the reduction in the number of re-transmissions. More practical experience is required of such hybrid systems before forming firm conclusions but it seems unlikely that they will offer any real advantages over continuous ARQ systems.

Forward error correction codes

Many complex coding schemes have been developed for forward error correction. The most common of these is the Hamming single bit error correcting code which is perhaps the simplest method used for error correction and, therefore, provides a useful introduction to the subject.

A Hamming code can be constructed for any group of data to give error correction of any one bit in the group which is detected as being in error; it can, therefore, be applied to a character or a block of information. The checking bits which are used occupy pre-determined positions within the data field, the positions being all those with the value of 2^n. For example, in a protected data field of 15 bits, the checking bits occupy the bit positions 1, 2, 4 and 8 as shown in figure 8.20.

In figure 8.21, an 11 bit data message (10101011001) is shown which is to be protected by four check bits.

Bit position	15	14	13	12	11	10	9	2^3 8	7	6	5	2^2 4	3	2^1 2	2^0 1
	I	I	I	I	I	I	I	X	I	I	I	X	I	X	X

I = Information bit
X = Hamming or check bits

Figure 8.20   Position of Hamming bits in a protected 15 bit data field

Bit position	15	14	13	12	11	10	9	8	7	6	5	4	3	2	1
	1	0	1	0	1	0	1	X	1	0	0	X	1	X	X

Figure 8.21

Bit positions 15, 13, 11, 9, 7 and 3 contain binary '1's and the binary values of these bit positions are added using modulo 2 arithmetic to produce the Hamming bits (*see* figure 8.22).

Bit position	Binary value	
15	1 1 1 1	NB: Modulo 2 addition
13	1 1 0 1	(addition without carry)
11	1 0 1 1	produces even parity
9	1 0 0 1	
7	0 1 1 1	
3	0 0 1 1	
	0 1 0 0	← Hamming bits

Figure 8.22   Hamming bits produced from a modulo 2 addition

The full 15 bit field is now shown in figure 8.23, the lowest order Hamming bits being inserted into the lowest order bit positions.

Bit position	15	14	13	12	11	10	9	X 8	7	6	5	X 4	3	X 2	X 1
Data field	1	0	1	0	1	0	1	0	1	0	0	1	1	0	0

X = Hamming bits

Figure 8.23

At the receiver, the binary value of each bit position containing a 1 bit is added using modulo 2 arithmetic. If there have been no errors, the result should be zero as shown in figure 8.24.

Bit position	Binary value
15	1 1 1 1
13	1 1 0 1
11	1 0 1 1
9	1 0 0 1
7	0 1 1 1
4	0 1 0 0
3	0 0 1 1
	0 0 0 0 ← modulo 2 result

Figure 8.24

If a single bit error occurs in transmission, the position of the error will be indicated by the modulo 2 sum. For example, assuming an error in the 11th bit position in figure 8.23, the data would be received as shown in figure 8.25.

Bit position	15	14	13	12	11	10	9	X 8	7	6	5	X 4	3	X 2	X 1
Data field	1	0	1	0	0	0	1	0	1	0	0	1	1	0	0

↑
error

X = Hamming bits

Figure 8.25

At the receiver, the binary values of positions 15, 13, 9, 7, 4 and 3 would then be added as shown in figure 8.26.

Bit position	Binary value
15	1 1 1 1
13	1 1 0 1
9	1 0 0 1
7	0 1 1 1
4	0 1 0 0
3	0 0 1 1
11	1 0 1 1 ← modulo 2 sum indicates bit position 11 in error

Figure 8.26

The modulo 2 sum in figure 8.26 indicates that the 11th bit position is in error and the bit is then inverted from 0 to 1. If two bit errors occur, the position of the errors cannot be determined from the modulo 2 result, although, as this will not be zero, the presence of a double error will be indicated. The code can correct single bit errors and detect double errors but some multiple errors will escape detection.

A wide variety of cyclic codes have been designed for error correction by Hamming, Fire, Chaudhuri, Bose and others which can provide better protection with lower redundancy than the simple example shown here. Nevertheless, it is unlikely that any of these will prove attractive on the vast majority of communications links where a return channel can be provided at little extra cost.

Failures

It is useful to distinguish between errors which are inaccuracies of some kind and failures which are breakdowns; for the problems they present are quite different. In doing so, it should be remembered that errors can cause failures. If, for example, an operator throws the wrong switch in error he may cause a failure; similarly, an invalid statement entered in error by a terminal operator may cause a system breakdown. Failures can produce errors also and line failures in particular may come to notice because of an unusually high number of retransmissions.

Failures like errors are always with us. The cost of guarding against failures should, as with error control, never exceed the cost of allowing them to happen. The cost of a failure may be very high indeed in many computer systems and this is particularly true of on-line systems where it is often difficult and expensive to recover from failures in key components in the system. If the analysis for a proposed data communications system shows that failures cannot be tolerated and yet the necessary protection against them is too costly, the system should be stifled at birth!

Some on-line systems have been designed to be 'fail-safe' or failure proof, key sections in the system being doubled or even trebled in order to provide the necessary back-up. In many others a sensible compromise solution is possible between failures and the cost of protection against them. This may be referred to as 'fail soft' or more poetically 'graceful degradation', the object being to provide a degraded service of some kind under failure conditions. For example, in the event of a hardware failure on a main frame computer a small front end processor can at least maintain communication with the terminals; terminal users can be kept informed of the state of the system and service can later be restored in a more orderly fashion than would otherwise have been possible.

Throughput Efficiency

The efficiency of an error control system must not only be measured against its ability to detect errors but also on the extent to which it reduces the amount of useful information which can be transferred in a given time. We have seen that with all error detection methods the added redundancy will reduce the information transfer rate by a fixed percentage which can readily be calculated. Even more important than this is the reduction in information transfer due to the feedback of decisions using 'return query' (RQ) methods.

In decision feedback systems there are a number of different ways of arranging for retransmission of erroneous blocks. The oldest method and the one which is still most commonly used is to transmit a block and wait for a positive or negative acknowledgement before either transmitting the next block or retransmitting the same block again. This leaves long gaps (T) when no data is being transferred as shown in figure 8.27 and is commonly known as an idle-RQ system.

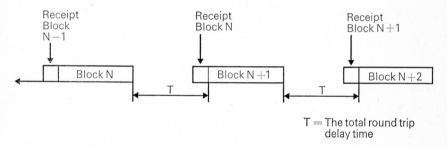

Figure 8.27 Simple half-duplex error control (idle-RQ)

The throughput efficiency of such a system in an error free situation is given by the equation:

Equation (1)

$$E = \frac{\dfrac{B}{R}}{\dfrac{B}{R} + T}$$

where
- E = the throughput efficiency
- B = the block length in bits
- T = the total round trip delay
- R = the input data rate (bit/s)

The losses due to parity bits or to control and synchronisation bits within blocks are ignored in this equation as these factors are independent of those given and their relatively minor effect is best calculated separately. Also excluded is the effect of erroneous return messages as the probability of these being in error is much smaller than in the relatively longer message blocks.

It will be seen from (1) that the duration of T is the critical factor in determining throughput efficiency. The total round trip delay T is the time delay between the end of transmission of one block (block n) to the beginning of transmission of the next (block n+1). 'T' may include:

1 *The loop propagation time of the line:* this is the time taken for a signal to travel the length of the circuit and back again. Generally, propagation time increases with distance; within the UK, loop propagation times rarely exceed 15 ms but on intercontinental circuits via satellites may be in excess of 540 ms.

2 *Modem propagation delay:* additional delays are introduced when a signal passes through filters, equalisers and other components in a modem. This delay is in the order of a few milliseconds for each modem and in the examples which follow is added to the loop propagation time of the line to give the 'total propagation delay'.

3 *Transmitter and receiver delays:* when the last bit of the last character in a block is received, the data terminal equipment at the receive end will check the accuracy of the received block and assemble a receipt message. When the receipt message is returned, the data terminal equipment at the transmit end must interpret the meaning of the message receipt and initiate the appropriate action. The delays introduced by these two operations are usually small and are ignored in the examples which follow in this chapter.

4 *The time taken to transmit the return message:* this message may be simply a binary '0' condition for a positive acknowledgement or a binary '1' condition for a negative acknowledgement (CCITT recommendation V41) in which case no time allowance need be added to the loop propagation time. However, message receipts are usually in the form of special characters (ACK and NAK) which may be accompanied by SYN and other control characters (*see* Chapter 6). In some cases, these messages comprise 32 bits and the time taken to transmit them will depend on the bit rate of this return channel. For example, 32 bits on a 75 bit/s supervisory channel would take 427 ms.

5 *Modem turn-around times:* On 2-wire circuits, there are two ways of providing a return channel. One is to have a frequency division multiplexed, narrow band, low speed simultaneous channel. The other is to reverse the direction of transmission after each block; this requires the modems at each end to 'turn-around' and introduces delay. This delay will vary considerably between modems. The most significant factor is the time which elapses between the data terminal equipment signalling 'request to send' (on circuit 105 on the CCITT V24 interface) and the

modem returning 'ready for sending' (on circuit 106 on the CCITT V24 interface). This is termed the 'ready-for-sending delay' (or 'response time of circuit 106' in the appropriate CCITT recommendation).

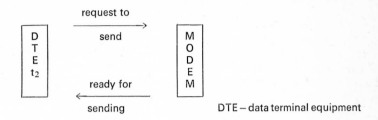

Figure 8.28 Ready-for-sending delay

Modems with data signalling rates above 2400 bit/s may be provided with adaptive equalisers – these become necessary where the modem has to automatically adapt to the range of different circuit conditions to be met on the PSTN. Early modems of this type had extremely long turn-around times of two seconds or more because the equalisers in these modems had to re-adapt to the line conditions each time the direction of transmission changed. Modern modems use adaptive equalisers which have a fairly long initial period of adjustment during which time a long 'training pattern' of signals is transmitted: this may be up to two seconds depending on the conditions found on the particular PSTN connection. The equalisers store their settings so that subsequent training patterns can be very much shorter in duration - in some modems less than 100 ms. Each time the modems turn-around this short training pattern must be sent before data can be transmitted; the duration of the short training pattern is included in the modem turn-around times.

The total round trip delay (T) has been defined as being the time delay between the end of transmission of one block (block n) to the beginning of transmission of the next (block n+1). It is useful to consider the progressive build up of T in an example of an idle RQ system on a circuit with half-duplex facilities.

(a) The last bit in the last character of a block will pass through two modems and over the transmission link. In figure 8.29 $t_1+t_2+t_3$ is the time delay between the last bit being transmitted from A and received at B, ie the propagation delay between the modem interface at A and the modem interface at B.

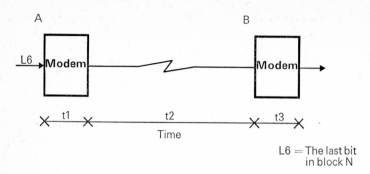

L6 = The last bit
in block N

Figure 8.29   Propagation delay between the modem interfaces at A and at B

(b)   After the last bit is received, the terminal at B will check the block and assemble the return message. This delay we will term t_4.

(c)   The terminal at B will then signal request to send to the modem at B and the modem will turn-around – delay t_5.

(d)   In figure 8.30, $t_6+t_7+t_8$ is the time delay between the first bit of the receipt message (FB) being transmitted from B and received at A, ie the propagation time between the digital interface at B and the digital interface at A.

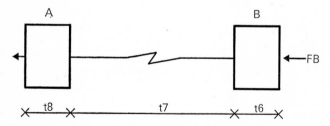

Figure 8.30   Propagation time between the digital interfaces at B and at A

(e)   The time for the receipt message to be returned will depend on the length in bits of the return message and the data signalling rate at which it is transmitted – delay t_9.

(f)   After the last bit of the message receipt arrives, the terminal at A will interpret the meaning of the message and determine the appropriate action, ie, decide whether to retransmit block n or transmit block n+1 - delay t_{10}.

(g)   The terminal at A will then signal a request-to-send to the modem at A and the modem will turn round ready to transmit the first bit of the next block – delay t_{11}, the modem at B will have turned round before t_{11} is completed.

It will be seen from this that the total round trip delay is the individual delays t_1 to t_{11} added together. The total propagation time can also be seen to be the sum of the loop propagation time of the line (t_2+t_7) and the propagation times of the two modems $(t_1+t_8$ and $t_3+t_6)$.

Consider now an idle-RQ system where a simultaneous 75 bit/s return channel is available and thus modem turn-around times can be ignored. In the first case error-free transmission is assumed so that the effect of errors on throughput efficiency may be seen in better perspective later.

Example 1 **Throughput efficiency (E) of an Idle-RQ system with a simultaneous return channel**

Equation (1)

$$E = \frac{\dfrac{B}{R}}{\dfrac{B}{R} + T}$$

E = Efficiency
Block length (B) = 1000 bits
Input data rate (R) = 1200 bit/s
Length of receipt message = 16 bits
Data signalling rate of simultaneous
  return channel = 75 bit/s
Total propagation delay = 25 ms

T = 25 ms for total propagation delay + the time taken for the 16 bits message receipt at 75 bit/s

$$T = 25 + \left(\frac{16}{75} \times 1000\right) ms$$

T = 238 ms

$$E = \frac{\left(\dfrac{1000}{1200}\right) \times 1000}{\left(\dfrac{1000}{1200}\right) \times 1000 + 238}$$

$$E = \frac{833}{833 + 238}$$

E = 77.77 per cent (933 bit/s)

In considering throughput in the presence of errors, the additional consideration is the number of blocks in error relative to the total number of blocks sent. We can now extend equation 1 to allow consideration of throughput in the presence of errors so that:

Equation (2)

$$E = \frac{\dfrac{B}{R}(1-P(e))}{\dfrac{B}{R} + T}, \quad \text{where } P(e) = \text{the block error probability}$$

Example 2 **Throughput efficiency of an Idle-RQ System with a simultaneous 75 bit/s return channel showing the effect of errors**

Using the basic data for example 1, we now assume that 1 block in 100 has to be retransmitted because of detected errors.

$$P(e) = 0.01$$

$$E = \frac{833\ (1-0.01)}{833 + 238}$$

$$E = \frac{824.6}{1071}$$

$$E = 76.99 \text{ per cent (923 bit/s)}$$

A single thousand bit block in error in every 100 is not unduly optimistic at 1200 bit/s on a private circuit. Table 8.1 (*see* page 180) shows the maximum bit error rates which are recommended by CCITT; where these are exceeded the transmission channel is considered defective.

These figures are for maintenance rather than planning purposes. Nevertheless, they do indicate that even if errors occur in a purely random fashion no more than 1 bit in 20,000 at 1200 bit/s on a leased circuit, a maximum of 5 in 100 thousand bit blocks, would be in error. Because of the clustering effect of error bursts, the proportion of erroneous blocks would probably be a good deal less than this in practice. It will be seen that from the simple example above that errors have a relatively minor effect on throughput efficiency with blocks of this size when compared to the total round trip delay T. Although it is obvious from equation (1) that increasing the block size will improve the throughput efficiency in the absence of errors, the presence of errors imposes a restraint as the block error rate will increase with block size. There is therefore an optimum block size for any given bit error rate and total round trip delay T to give maximum throughput efficiency.

However, it will be remembered that there are other factors which influence block size and the throughput efficiency of some idle-RQ systems, particularly where variable block lengths are used, may be very low indeed.

In examples 1 and 2, a simultaneous 75 bit/s narrow band return channel was used for message acknowledgements. Consider now (example 3) data being transmitted over the PSTN at 2400 bit/s; no simultaneous return channel is available and the modems, therefore, have to be 'turned-round'. Two reversals per block will be required, one to establish the return channel and one to re-establish the forward channel.

Example 3 **The effect of modem turn-around times on the throughput efficiency of an Idle-RQ System**

Assume, for convenience, an error free connection.

$$E = \frac{\dfrac{B}{R}}{\dfrac{B}{R} + T}$$

Block length (B) = 1000 bits
Input data rate (R) = 2400 bit/s
Length of receipt message = 16 bits
Total propagation delay = 25 ms
Data signalling rate of return
    channel = 2400 bit/s
Modem turn-round time = 75 ms

T = 25 ms for total propagation delay + time taken for 16 bits at 2400 bit/s + (modem turn-round time) × 2

$$T = 25 + \left(\frac{16}{2400} \times 1000\right) + 150\,\text{ms}$$

$$= 25 + 6.6 + 150\,\text{ms}$$

$$T = 182\,\text{ms}$$

$$E = \frac{\left(\dfrac{1000}{2400}\right) \times 1000}{\left(\dfrac{1000}{2400}\right) \times 1000 + 182}$$

$$E = \frac{417}{599}$$

$$E = 69.6 \text{ per cent } (1670\,\text{bit/s})$$

Example 4 **The effect of increasing data signalling on throughput efficiency of an Idle-RQ System**

There are a number of problems involved in using higher speed modems on two-wire connections such as are available over the PSTN. First of all, as the data signalling rate increases, the time to transmit each block (B/R) is reduced and T becomes proportionally bigger. Let us assume that the same conditions apply as in example 3 except that R is increased from 2400 to 4800 bit/s.[8]

$$E = \frac{\left(\dfrac{1000}{4800}\right) \times 1000}{\left(\dfrac{1000}{4800}\right) \times 1000 + 178}$$

NB: T is reduced slightly because of the reduction in time required to transmit the 16 bits return message

$$= \frac{208}{386}$$

$E = 54$ per cent (2590 bit/s)

It can clearly be seen from this example that it becomes increasingly important to use longer blocks as the data signalling rate increases. However, the problem arises that as the length of the block becomes greater the block error probability rises also. Another problem is that the adaptive equalisers used on some high speed modems may increase the modem turn-round times and throughput efficiency may suffer.

It has been found from customer experience in the UK using the Datel 2400 dial up service, transmitting at 2400 bit/s, that maximum throughput efficiency is apparently achieved with block sizes in the order of 1000 bits, although the evidence is by no means conclusive.

A much greater throughput efficiency with idle-RQ can be obtained by operating in a full duplex mode on a four-wire private circuit. In these circumstances, modems do not have to be turned-round and the effect of this on throughput efficiency can be clearly seen if we subtract the modem turn-round times from T in example 3.

Example 5 **Effect of full-duplex facilities on throughput efficiency**

$$E = \frac{417}{599-150} \text{ (from example 3)}$$

$$E = \frac{417}{449}$$

$E = 93$ per cent (2229 bit/s)

---

[8] In practice the higher speed modems would introduce different delays and T would therefore be altered.

It should be mentioned here that these calculations are only used to demonstrate the inter-relationship of the more important factors which determine throughput efficiency. Costs have been ignored for clarity's sake but it will be seen that if the throughput efficiency is known, the cost per bit or cost per thousand bits can be calculated for different circumstances.

Idle-RQ is simple and reliable and its inherent throughput inefficiency is often tolerated for these reasons. The major factor which influences the total round trip delay in the UK is modem turn-round time and this is widely avoided by using duplex facilities on four-wire private circuits. However, we have seen that, with higher speed transmission, the half-duplex facilities and the relatively poor error performance of the PSTN, compared to private circuits, restricts throughput efficiency to very low levels when idle-RQ is used. There is a problem too on long distance circuits. While loop propagation times are normally short on circuits within one country, on intercontinental circuits they may be extremely long and idle-RQ becomes unsuitable. For example, let us assume a half-duplex intercontinental connection via a satellite with a total loop propagation delay of 540 ms with the other data as in example 3; the throughput efficiency would then be an optimistic 37 per cent on a circuit with no errors at all.

Continuous RQ

An RQ system which gives greater throughput efficiency is known as 'go back' or 'continuous' RQ. In this system, data blocks are transmitted without interruption until a negative acknowledgement is received on the simultaneous return channel which must be provided. When a NAK message is received, the transmitter 'goes back' to the beginning of the erroneous block and repeats it and any other blocks it may have sent before the error indication.

Figure 8.31 illustrates the basic principles of a continuous-RQ system; it will be seen that the blocks may be transferred to line without interruption and the total round trip delay time T is, therefore, avoided. Although two-block

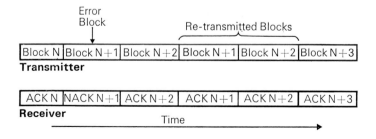

Figure 8.31   Continuous RQ using 2 block repetition

repetition is illustrated, longer sequences may be used. This method is sometimes known as the 'storage change' system because it necessitates the
provision of additional storage at the transmitter and receiver. Because of
this need, and the logical complexities of the sequencing, two block repetition
is the usual limit.

It is obviously more efficient to re-transmit only the erroneous block. However, this creates problems in maintaining the block sequence and increases
the requirement for logic and buffer storage. Even with the need to re-
transmit error free blocks which follow blocks in error, the throughput
efficiency of continuous-RQ systems is extremely high when compared to
idle-RQ systems. CCITT recommendation V41 uses a double RQ or go-back-2
system. Tests over long distance terrestrial links and satellite links have
shown an average transfer efficiency of over 98 per cent in the presence of bit
error rates averaging 5.3×10^{-5}. [9]

Continuous-RQ systems impose a constraint on the total round trip delay
time (T). For example, in a go-back-2 system the acknowledgement for
block 1 must be received during the period in which block 2 is being transmitted otherwise the transfer efficiency will be impaired. The constraint on
T can be shown as:

$$(n-1)\ (B/R) \geqslant T \geqslant (n-2)\ (B/R)$$

where B = block length
R = transfer rate
and n = the available blocks of storage

so that in a system with two blocks of storage with a block length of 980 bits
and a data signalling rate of 2400 bit/s, we have:

$$1 \times 0.4083 \geqslant T \geqslant 0 \times 0.4083$$

∴ the total round trip delay T must be between 0 and 408 ms.

Table 8.7 shows the maximum permissible line loop propagation times when
using CCITT recommendation V41. Allowances for 40 ms for total modem
delay have been made and 50 ms for detection of the RQ signal, these should
be added to the figures in table 8.7 to give the total round trip delay.

NB: In the CCITT V41 system the backward channel is monitored for a
period of 45-50 ms immediately prior to the transmission of the last of the
16 check bits in order to detect any RQ signal arising from the check on the
previous block. This period is termed 'RQ recognition time'.

⁹ CCITT COMSp A-No 34-E, November 1973.

Block size (bits)	Data signalling rate					
	200	600	1200	2400	3600	4800
260	1210	343	127	18	—	—
500	2410	743	327	118	49	14
980	4810	1543	727	318	182	114
3860	19210	6343	3127	1518	982	714

Table 8.7 Maximum loop propagation times (ms) for CCITT Recommendation V41

Availability

A key measurement of the usefulness of any system is the time when it is available for use relative to the time that it is required to be used. This measurement is termed availability and in a single unit can be given by:

$$a = \frac{\text{MTBF}}{\text{MTBF} + \text{MTTR}}$$

where a   = availability
       MTBF = mean time between failures
and   MTTR = mean time to repair

Many systems comprise a number of component units in serial so that the system availability depends upon the availability of individual units:

$$a = a_1 \times a_2 \times a_3 \ldots \ldots a_n$$

for example, a serial system has MTBF and MTTR figures for the four key components as shown below; we will assume that the availability required is not less than .95,

Unit a_1 MTBF = 600 hours ∴ a_1 = 0.9868
        MTTR =   8 hours

Unit a_2 MTBF = 200 hours
         MTTR =   3 hours ∴ a_2 = 0.9852

Unit a_3 MTBF = 200 hours ∴ a_3 = 0.9523
         MTTR =   10 hours

Unit a_4 MTBF = 200 hours ∴ a_4 = 0.9803
         MTTR =   4 hours

giving an availability of the system (a) of 0.9075. In other words, the system would probably be available for less than 91 per cent of the time required.

The effect of doubling up on components in the system can be seen if we consider doubling up on the worst unit (a_3) as shown in figure 8.32:

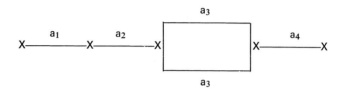

Figure 8.32

the availability of parallel components can be given as:

$$1 - (1-a_n)(1-a_n) = a$$

or in the example:

$$1 - (1-a_3)(1-a_3) = 0.9978$$

this will improve the overall system availability from 0.9075 to 0.9509 giving an availability in the order of 95 per cent. The confidence limits which can be placed on this sort of conclusion obviously depend on the accuracy of the MTBF and MTTR figures and there are problems in getting the information required. In practice, it is often impossible to obtain MTBF and MTTR figures from manufacturers or PTTs regarding hardware or communications links. Modems are exceptional in that they are extremely reliable and figures are usually readily available from which MTBF and MTTR can be derived. British Post Office modems, for example, have an average failure rate better than one in five years, the majority of these being cleared in one day.

Private circuit availability cannot be derived from published PTT figures. These circuits are themselves serial systems comprising a number of sections routed over different kinds of line plant; the failure rates may, therefore, differ widely between one circuit and another. Nevertheless, some idea of the reliability of point-to-point private circuits can be given by examining the UK national picture of faults reported per circuit and the average time out of service.

Average faults reported on amplified circuits
(over 40 kilometres)   —   2.2 faults per annum

Average out of service time per fault reported   —   15 hours

NB: Out of service time is the time between the fault being reported and the time the fault is cleared. It includes time at night and at weekends when a customer may not require a circuit.

The figures for unamplified circuits (less than 40 kilometres) are considerably better than this, averaging 0.26 fault reports per circuit per annum with similar out of service times.

It would be unwise to use the national average figures quoted above to directly calculate the MTBF and MTTR for a proposed single point-to-point circuit. Apart from the obvious danger that an individual circuit may be better or worse than the national average, the average number of faults reported per annum does not include those faults (probably few) which do occur and are cleared without being reported. Similarly, the 15 hours national average for out of service times include hours when many customers do not want to use the circuits. In spite of these problems, the quoted figures can be useful in obtaining rough estimates of MTBF and MTTR as can be seen in the following example:

A point-to-point private circuit is required from Manchester to Birmingham. The circuit will be required for use eight hours per day, five days per week, 50 weeks in the year, a total of 2000 hours. A reasonable estimate of the circuit availability is required.

On the assumption that there are no existing circuits between the points concerned that will yield some useful fault history, we must attempt an estimate derived from the national figures. Taking a fairly pessimistic view we could say that the average number of faults per annum on the proposed circuit would be twice the national average giving an MTBF of:

$$\frac{2000}{4.4} = 454.5 \text{ hours}$$

With a nationwide maintenance service which is being continually improved, it is reasonable to use the national average 15 hours out of service time to derive MTTR. As the working day is only eight hours in this case, we will make the slightly optimistic assumption that the MTTR will be eight hours (operational time) therefore the estimated availability:

$$(a) = \frac{454.5}{462.5} \simeq 0.98$$

We might reasonably assume from this that the proposed circuit from Manchester to Birmingham would be available for use approximately 98 per cent of the time it would be required to be used.

This example points to the fact that telephone circuits provide an availability which bears comparison with most other components in a data communications system. Nevertheless, let us assume that the estimated availability of 98 per cent for the line in the example is not good enough. We could, of course, rent a second line which was automatically switched in in the event of failure, this would give an estimated availability of 0.9998 but could be a costly solution. In circumstances such as this, a standby exchange line can often provide effective and cheap insurance against failure. The availability (a) of exchange lines cannot be calculated with anything approaching precision from national statistics – for example, in the UK an average of only 0.80 faults are reported per telephone station per annum and yet many others occur without being reported – in particular dialling failures. If we are to use the exchange line as standby to a private circuit then we are first of all concerned with a simple question. If I pick up a telephone in Manchester what is the probability that I will be able to obtain a satisfactory speech connection to Birmingham and how long will it take me to get through? A reasonably informed answer to this sort of question can usually be obtained by talking to the firm's telephone operators. This time we will take a very pessimistic view. We will assume that from our enquiries we can form the following general statement which is acceptable to people who frequently telephone between the points concerned:

"On 90 per cent of occasions when attempts are made to establish a call a satisfactory speech connection can be established within 10 minutes."

Such a statement, loose as it is, is quite useful to us in finding out whether to use exchange lines for standby purposes. We can now say that on the occasions when the point-to-point private circuit failed, nine times out of ten we would be able to establish a connection within ten minutes using the exchange line. Therefore in effect 90 per cent of the failures on the private circuit will have an MTTR of less than ten minutes and on only 10 per cent will the MTTR be eight hours. Such simple rule of thumb calculations show that a pessimistic view would give an availability for the point-to-point private circuit and the exchange line in the order of 0.996 for minimal cost.

On multi-point circuits, a higher availability is required on the main links which serve every terminal compared with the spurs which serve single

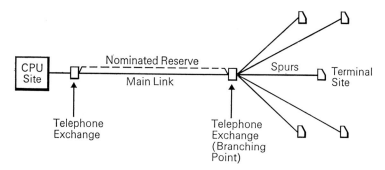

Figure 8.33   A multi-point circuit with a 'nominated' reserve for the main link

terminals. 'Nominated reserves' are frequently provided at no extra charge for these main links. A nominated reserve is a circuit which normally carries speech on the public switched network, and which is alternatively routed to the main link, but may be switched in when a main link becomes faulty (*see* figure 8.33). The switching takes place in the Post Office premises which are always manned; engineers must wait until conversations are finished on the nominated reserve circuits before switching.

In the UK, Post Office maintenance statistics and customers' experience indicate that multi-point circuits are very reliable. The average number of faults reported on multi-points is less than three a year and of these less than 10 per cent can be attributed to failures on the main links. As the national average time to switch in a nominated reserve is less than one hour (the MTTR on main links therefore being effectively less than one hour) the availability on multi-point circuits is extremely high.

9 Concentrators and Multiplexors

Concentrators and multiplexors employ two different techniques in effecting line economies. It is useful to distinguish between them, but to achieve a clear distinction becomes increasingly difficult as techniques merge and produce hybrid devices which cannot precisely be categorised. However, there are distinguishing features of multiplexors and concentrators which can be examined and which help towards a better understanding of the total subject.

There are different types of concentrators but the most important factor which distinguishes them from multiplexors is that they employ contention. Contention means that larger numbers of inputs are contending or competing for a smaller number of outputs on a demand basis, and line economies have been gained in this way since the earliest days of telecommunications. The circuit switching systems used on public telephone networks employ contention, with costly telephone plant and equipment being shared by a large number of customers. The familiar telephone switchboard is another obvious example of a line concentrator where a larger number of extensions contend for a smaller number of public exchange lines – a typical ratio being four extensions to one exchange line (*see* figure 9.1).

This simple example illustrates two important features of concentration systems, ie that high utilisation of the outputs is possible and that contention usually involves queuing. In the switchboard example, the efficiency of the operator in recording call requests and distributing calls is the key factor in

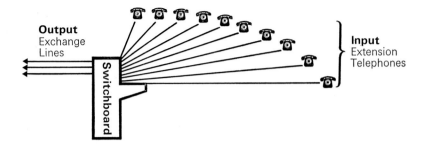

Figure 9.1   Concentration by a manual telephone switchboard (incoming calls ignored for convenience)

handling queues in busy periods, during which times a steady almost un-interrupted flow of telephone traffic should pass on the exchange lines.

Concentration takes advantage of the situation where individual inputs into a system are not all active at the same time. This is common in data communications and typically terminals are in active use only 10-20 per cent of the time available. In the familiar situation where a number of data terminals in one town (A) need to access a computer in a distant town (B), concentration in town A provides one method of sharing the data link between the two towns. Figure 9.2 illustrates the point that the sum of the total terminal

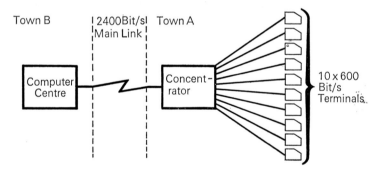

Figure 9.2   Remote concentration of data terminals

speeds need bear no relation to the speed of the main link. The number of terminals which can be handled by one concentrator will depend instead on the total amount of traffic generated by the terminals, the nature of the traffic flow and the service to be given to the terminals in terms of the tolerable delay. Concentrators in data communications systems will usually include storage and thus the terminal will in practice communicate with the concentrator; the concentrator in turn will communicate with the computer rather than the terminal having a direct link with the computer.

Multiplexing, on the other hand, is a method of sharing of a communications link which does not employ contention. The line to be shared is divided into a number of separate and simultaneous channels so that each input is allocated its own channel of communication. Multiplexing on data links avoids queuing but in consequence often gives an inferior circuit utilisation when compared with concentration. We can note that on a multiplexing system the sum of the signalling rates on the inputs (usually measured in characters per second) cannot exceed the signalling capability of the multiplexed link. A multiplexor system, therefore, enables terminal inputs to communicate directly with a distant computer port unlike the concentrator.

Having established the differences between concentrators and multiplexors, we can now consider the subjects separately.

Concentrators

Although all concentrators employ some kind of contention, there are numerous devices performing a variety of functions which might arguably be described as concentrators and this causes some confusion. The real problem lies in deciding what exactly is being concentrated, and it is a considerable help in clarifying the situation if we begin by splitting concentrators into two separate categories – line concentrators and message concentrators. Definition now becomes easier and we can say first of all that a line concentrator is "any device which enables a number of input channels to dynamically share a smaller number of output channels". Any circuit or line switching equipment can, therefore, be accurately described as a line concentrator. The fact that 'statistical time division' multiplexors also provide contention rather spoils the tidiness of this definition and they are rather conveniently classified as hybrids! A message concentrator can be defined as "any device which concentrates low density message traffic originating from a number of sources into a higher density message flow". The unit of information transmitted in this type of concentrator is a message, and messages of variable length are queued for transmission over high speed lines. Queuing necessitates some form of storage and this type of device is often referred to as a 'store and forward' concentrator.

Messages, which are concentrated in this way, are separate entities and may be switched through a network by suitable addressing techniques. The switching method employed for routing messages through a network is termed message switching and is described in Chapter 10.

Another method of concentration ensures that the capacity of a high speed line will not be exceeded, by exercising control over the low speed input line activity. This technique is known as 'hold and forward' concentration and involves a polling process.

Polling

Polling enables a common transmission path to be shared by a number of lines by a discipline which ensures that information is flowing from only one source at a time. Figure 9.3 shows a typical multipoint network on which polling techniques are employed.

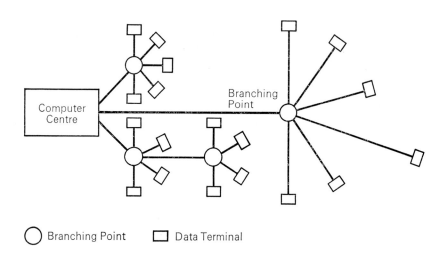

Figure 9.3   Multipoint system

The branching points shown in this figure are in Post Office maintenance control centres and do not contain any private equipment. Communication is possible only between the computer centre and each terminal, not between terminals.

In this example, polling is performed by the control computer which invites each terminal in turn to transmit a message. The terminal replies by sending an information message to the computer or a simple control message indicating that it has nothing to send. When polling techniques are employed, the addressing points will be buffered to enable transmission at the maximum rate of the main link; this also has the advantage that the intermittent dialogue between the computer and the terminal is not noticeable to the terminal user.

This method is termed roll call polling because the computer refers to lists which give the sequence in which the polling is carried out; as the frequency at which terminals are polled may be varied by changing the polling lists, a good deal of flexibility can be achieved.

Substantial savings in line costs are possible by using roll call polling on multipoint networks and this method has been widely used by commercial banks in the UK. The number of terminals which can be connected on one multipoint circuit usually depends on the amount of peak data traffic originating from each terminal, but there may be an overriding technical limitation imposed by the design of the concentrator. Further savings are achieved on multipoint circuits because only one modem is required at the computer centre for each multipoint circuit connected; on a multipoint link with eight terminals only nine modems would be required compared to the 16 needed if direct private circuits were to be provided to each terminal.

Another variant of the roll call polling network uses 'intelligent' concentrators. The concentrators, which are in fact small processors, are connected to the computer centre by good quality speech private circuits, usually transmitting synchronously at 2400 bit/s. The terminals are fairly low speed devices operating at 10 or 15 characters per second connected to the concentrators by telegraph circuits or lower quality speech circuits; in the latter case, modem by telegraph circuits or lower quality speech circuits; in the latter case, modems are necessary both at the terminal and the concentrator. These local circuits are termed 'low speed tails' and are not connected in any way to the same transmission path as the main lines. From a transmission point of view, all the circuits would be separate and there are, therefore no technical limitations on the number of low speed tails that can be served by one high speed line; the main loading factor is, therefore, the amount of data traffic generated by each terminal.

Roll call polling on a network such as this can take two different forms. Terminals can be polled from the computer centre, as described earlier, or it may be done at two levels, the computer centre polling the concentrators and the concentrators handling the local polling to the terminals. This latter method has the advantage that the number of control messages which involve the computer centre is reduced, but the flexibility of a system suffers because of the increased difficulty in altering polling lists.

The use of small computers within a network provides a number of additional advantages:

- The buffering, which is necessary for polling, can be centralised in the concentrators rather than at the individual terminals and buffer storage costs can, therefore, be reduced substantially. Small sections of buffer store at the concentrators may be permanently allocated to terminals, but the larger message buffers used for communicating with the computer centre are usually shared.

– A number of local programs can be held at the concentrator and run at the terminals. This is extremely useful in those applications – particularly banking – where terminals need to be used for a number of small routine computations. The services of the large central computer cannot economically be used for these calculations and the other alternative of providing 'intelligent' or programmable terminals is an expensive solution. Providing these programs in the concentrator enables relatively simple and cheap terminals to be used – an extremely important consideration when large numbers of terminals are necessary.

– Error checking can be provided between the concentrator and the terminals. Some concentrators may also provide format checking giving more control over operator input errors.

– Bit stripping (removal of redundant data) can be performed at the concentrator enabling more efficient use to be made of the main lines.

This type of device brings a new meaning to the term concentrator. Not only can it perform polling, which is a concentration technique, but it also can provide a local concentration of computing functions. This concept of 'distributed intelligence' is discussed further in the next chapter.

Multiplexors

The main purpose of multiplexors used in data communications systems is to reduce line costs by using a single telephone circuit to carry a number of simultaneous low speed transmissions instead of many lines each carrying a single low speed transmission. The multiplexing techniques used all fall into two broad categories, frequency division multiplexing (FDM) and time division multiplexing (TDM).

Frequency Division Multiplexing (FDM)

FDM divides the available bandwidth of a communications channel into a number of independent channels, each having an assigned portion of the total frequency spectrum. Figure 9.4 shows the frequency bands of the first four channels in a typical FDM system (UK Post Office Dataplex). The 'bearer' circuit, as the multiplexed circuit is called, has a nominal bandwidth of 3000 Hz giving 12 channels each of 240 Hz bandwidth. Four-wire circuits are used giving 12 'send' and 12 'receive' channels, enabling full duplex facilities to be given.

Each channel is modulated using frequency shift keying, the upper frequency being used for binary '0' and the lower for binary '1' as shown in figure 9.5.

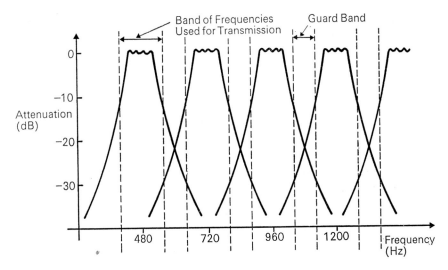

Figure 9.4   Frequency bands of a FDM system

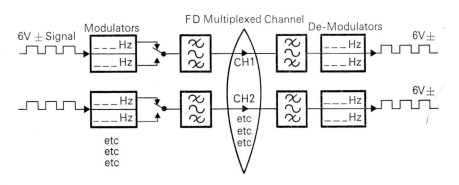

Figure 9.5   Modulation and demodulation of separate channels for a typical FDM system

One of the limitations of an FDM system will be seen from figure 9.4, guard bands or safety zones are needed to prevent overlapping of the electrical signals, resulting in under-utilisation of the available bandwidth.

The data signalling rate of each channel on the example system is 110 bit/s to cater for the numerous 10 character/second dataprinters in use. If all the channels were in use at once, a total of only 1320 bit/s would be transmitted which is far less than the data signalling rate capability of the bearer circuit (up to 9600 bit/s using suitable high speed modems). More expensive filtering equipment can improve the aggregate bit rate on FDM systems but this would not be likely to exceed much above 2000 bit/s in the example case.

A further disadvantage, inherent with FDM systems, is that the error performance of some channels may be poorer than others due to the loss/frequency and group delay characteristics of the bearer circuit (*see* Chapter 4). For example, signals in a channel in the higher part of the frequency spectrum will be more severely attenuated than the signals in a lower channel; this problem can be largely overcome by equalisation but at added cost.

The main advantage of FDM for a user is to be found in those applications where the low aggregate bit rate is not a constraint. Where only a limited number of low speed channels are required, the simplicity of FDM systems can give a lower cost per channel compared with the TDM systems which are discussed below. One of the reasons for this is that no modems are required between frequency division multiplexors – the multiplexors themselves performing the necessary digital/analogue conversion for transmission over the bearer circuit.

Time Division Multiplexing (TDM)

A time division multiplexor works on the principle of taking data from a number of sources and allocating each of these sources a period of time or 'time slots'. The individual time slots are assembled into 'frames' to form a single high speed digital data stream. PCM systems, which were discussed in Chapter 4, use time division multiplexing to interleave a number of speech conversations which are first converted from analogue into digital form. The output from data terminals is already digital and this simplifies the time division multiplexing process. The interleaving takes two different forms, 'bit interleaving' and 'character or byte interleaving'.

Bit interleaved TDM

Figure 9.6 shows a simplified representation of the bit interleaving process. It will be seen from the diagrams that, if synchronisation between the multiplexing and de-multiplexing functions is lost, there is a danger that bits may be delivered to the wrong outputs (when de-multiplexed). Synchronisation is maintained by assembling the individual bits sampled from each terminal into a frame so that nominally one frame consists of one bit from each of the terminal inputs to the system.

A unique bit sequence termed a framing pattern is included within each frame (or can be distributed throughout a number of frames) and must be

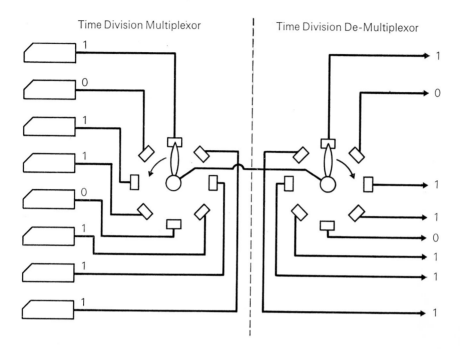

Figure 9.6 Principles of bit interleaved time division multiplexing using simple commutators

detected a pre-determined number of times by the de-multiplexing stage before synchronisation is assumed. Similarly, the loss of frame synchronisation is not assumed until the framing pattern has failed to be detected a pre-determined number of times. If synchronisation is lost due to any factor such as a line disturbance, re-synchronisation is achieved by searching for the unique framing pattern and synchronisation is not assumed until this has been detected several times.

In practice, the digital output from any time division multiplexor must be converted into analogue form for transmission over telephone circuits and

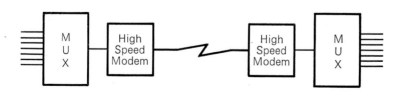

Figure 9.7 Modems required in TDM

back from analogue to digital at the distant end. The modems used may be an integral part of the multiplexor but are more often separate as shown in figure 9.7. Synchronous modems are used so that bit synchronisation can be maintained throughout the system.

Character or byte interleaved TDM

A character interleaved multiplexor interleaves characters received from low speed channels on to the high speed bearer circuit. Each interleaved character occupies eight bits in the frame, but this may vary depending on the code level being transmitted and the need for a status bit. The simplified elements of a character interleaved time division multiplexor are shown in figure 9.8. Data is received serially from each low speed channel and assembled in a serialiser. When a complete character has been received, it is shifted in parallel form into a buffer register and then transmitted in serial form to the high speed line at the high speed line rate during the time slot period allocated to that low speed channel.

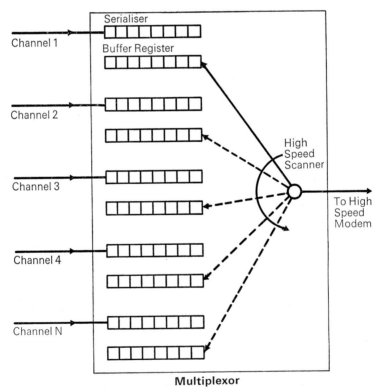

Figure 9.8 Simplified character interleaved time division multiplexor

The scanner operates at a speed related to each low speed character period. For a 10 character per second terminal, scanning for transmission to the high speed line would take place every tenth of a second. If a buffer is empty, the related byte in the transmitted frame will be padded. Each frame consists of typically nine bits per low speed channel (this will vary in accordance with the terminal code being used) plus a synchronisation sequence and frame control information, the nature and length of which varies between manufacturers. The frame structure used in a typical character-interleaved system is shown in figure 9.9.

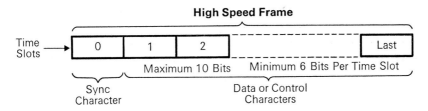

Figure 9.9   Frame structure in a character interleaved system

The effect of lost synchronisation with bit-interleaved TDM was mentioned earlier and similar schemes have been developed in order to maintain frame synchronisation on character-interleaved TDM systems. Again this involves the use of a unique framing pattern within each frame which must be detected a pre-determined number of times before frame synchronisation is assumed. Because characters rather than bits are interleaved in each frame, the frames are longer than in bit interleaved systems. This usually means that the proportion of synchronising bits to information bits is lower with character-interleaving but the greater efficiency which results is offset to some extent by the longer time taken to re-synchronise.

Because whole characters have to be assembled in a character-interleaved system, more storage has to be provided than in a bit-interleaved system and this tends to increase the costs. However, as it is unlikely that all the terminals will be in use at the same time, storage can be reduced by dynamically allocating buffers to those terminals which are actually being used. Some modern character-interleaved multiplexing designs not only reduce costs in this way but also achieve significant reductions in the size of the TDM equipment.

Character-interleaving offers a number of advantages over bit-interleaving. In particular, when used for multiplexing asynchronous terminals, they offer more efficient transmission. Start and stop elements can be simply stripped off and replaced at the de-multiplexing stage, as the units sampled are characters and not bits. This effectively compresses the data on the high speed line and improves the aggregate low speed bit rate of the TDM link. On ten character per second machines using ASCII or IA 5 code, three bits of the eleven bits per character are used for start/stop, and bit stripping, therefore, provides a potential saving of over 27 per cent of line time. IA 2 with its 7.5 bit structure with 2.5 bits used for start/stop provides even greater potential savings of over 33 per cent. Thirty characters per second machines use one start and only one stop element in a 10 bit character structure but bit stripping still offers an attractive 20 per cent improvement factor. In practice, the need for synchronisation and control bytes within frames reduces the aggregate low speed bit rate of character-interleaved multiplexors to some extent, but this is still usually between 10 per cent and 20 per cent higher than the rate of the bearer circuit; ie a 2400 bit/s circuit will typically bear some twenty-five 110 bit/s terminals – an aggregate low speed bit rate of 2750 bit/s. The actual improvement will depend on the character structure used by the terminals and whether terminals of mixed speed are being multiplexed. However, as the proportion of synchronisation bits to information bits is usually higher in bit-interleaved systems, character-interleaving gives a significant improvement in efficiency. Typically, a bit-interleaved multiplexor will support twenty-one 110 bit/s terminals on a 2400 bit/s bearer circuit (an aggregate low speed bit rate of only 2310 bit/s). Bit stripping is possible on bit-interleaved systems but the added logic necessary reduces their cost advantage. A major advantage of character-interleaving over bit-interleaving is that noise bursts affect fewer terminal users. A ten bit burst would affect a maximum of two terminals whereas up to 10 terminals would be affected in a bit-interleaved system. The relatively better error performance of character-interleaved systems has to be weighed against the added length of time they take to re-synchronise.

Most TDM systems can accept input from terminals using different speeds and codes but because the multiplexor system operates on a synchronous basis it is necessary to know in advance the speeds and codes to be handled and to program for them. TDM systems can also handle data from synchronous data terminals where the terminal transmission is in the block mode rather than character by character. For this type of transmission, bit-interleaving is usually employed as this provides a degree of bit sequence independence not possible with character-interleaved systems and in any case is cheaper and simpler. It should be remembered that data characters within a block do not usually include start and stop bits and thus the facility of bit stripping which is a significant advantage of character interleaving would not be applicable.

Figure 9.10 gives typical examples of the kind of terminal speed mixtures which can be handled on a character-interleaved multiplexor.

Low speed inputs		Data signalling rate of the bearer circuit	Aggregate low speed bit rate
Example 1	8 x 110 bit/s 12 x 134.5 bit/s 8 x 300 bit/s	4800	4894
Example 2	11 x 110 bit/s 1 x 1200 bit/s	2400	2410
Example 3	11 x 110 bit/s 12 x 134.5 bit/s 2 x 300 bit/s 2 x 600 bit/s	4800	4624

Figure 9.10   Typical examples of mixed input rates possible on a character-interleaved multiplexor

Where a TDM system is required to handle a mixture of input speeds and codes, it is usual for groups of channels and their related computer ports to be dedicated for particular speed and code operation. Some types of multiplexor, however, can provide a facility which enables some or all channels of the system to handle terminals operating at any speed or code within a pre-determined range – this facility is variously known as 'adaptive speed control' or 'automatic bit rate' and code level selection – ABR.

To provide the facility, all messages from the terminals connected to the multiplexor must be prefixed by an agreed character which, when compared with internally programmed set characters at the multiplexor, enables the multiplexor to determine the speed and code level being employed and to adapt the channel conditions to handle that type of terminal. This facility has a particular advantage for computer bureaux operators who use the PSTN to provide contention for inputs to the multiplexor. For example, if a bureau's customers in Birmingham were to be connected to a London computer centre over a TDM multiplexed link Birmingham-London, access to the TDM multiplexor would be gained by dialling a local call in the Birmingham area. If the terminals used by the bureau's customers in Birmingham were all one speed and used the same code, they could all be given the same number to dial for access to any one of the TDM ports (*see* figure 9.11). The concentration function of the PSTN can be seen in this example and,

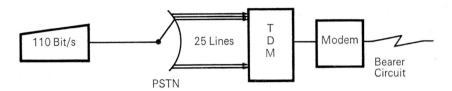

Figure 9.11 Access into a 'local' TDM using the PSTN as a concentrator

typically, a contention ratio of four terminals to one input port is used, giving high utilization of the TDM channels. The effect of having terminals of two different speeds 110 bit/s and 300 bit/s can be seen from figure 9.12.

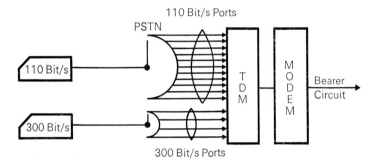

Figure 9.12 Access into a 'local' TDM from different speed terminals, using the PSTN for concentration

Different ports must normally be used for the two types of terminal and separate telephone numbers provide two distinct access routes. Because 110 bit/s ports may be free while 300 bit/s ports are overloaded the efficiency of the whole system is reduced.

Although adaptive speed control overcomes this problem, we cannot obtain 'something for nothing'. The penalty, apart from slight increased cost of the multiplexor equipment, is that the channel capacity of the multiplexor system will be restricted and must be determined on the basis that all channels may need to operate at the highest required speed, ie 300 bit/s in the example in figure 9.12; time slots are not allocated dynamically.

When using adaptive speed control, it is necessary for the computer ports also to be able to adapt to the required terminal speed and this can be arranged by sampling a prefix character in a similar manner to that described for the multiplexor – this adds to the complexity and cost of the computer system.

Software de-multiplexing

A typical configuration for a TDM system is shown in figure 9.13.

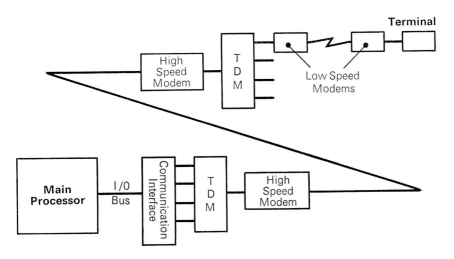

Figure 9.13   A typical TDM configuration

At the computer centre incoming data is received in a serial digital stream from the high speed modem. It is then de-multiplexed, presenting the communications interface with a number of lower speed digital data streams (usually but not always in serial form). The data is then re-multiplexed at the communications interface before being passed to the computer. The reverse process occurs when information is output from the computer. As further costs are incurred because of the need for individual terminations for each low speed channel, the whole process seems an extraordinary way to set about saving costs. However, it has its merits; standard computer/communications interfacing equipment can be used which means that terminals carried over a multiplex link can be treated just as any other terminal – the line multiplexing being virtually transparent to the computer system and the terminal user.[1] Testing arrangements are also simplified by separating the low speed channels at the computer centre.

The obvious alternative to the arrangements discussed above is to dispense with the multiplexor at the computer centre altogether. The high speed serial digital data stream can be taken from the modem straight into the communi-

[1] Some additional delays may, however, be introduced on the various interchange circuits during the setting up and clearance of calls. Delays may also occur when echo-plexing.

cations interface where it is simply converted from serial to parallel form and passed over the high speed input/output to the main processor. The main processor then has to de-multiplex the data by means of a special de-multiplexing software program. In the reverse direction, the computer software has to construct multiplexed frames of data for transmission via the communications interface and modems to the remote time division multiplexor. The process is termed 'software multiplexing' and there are savings to be gained through dispensing with one time division multiplexor and the low speed channel terminations. However, the problem arises yet again that the reduction of costs in one area results in increased costs in another. The additional software required may be fairly simple, particularly when terminals of the same speed are being multiplexed. An incoming frame, for example, has only to be read into memory and a check made for each time slot to find out whether or not a character is present. Programming can become much more complex and costly, however, when different speeds are being multiplexed. One of the most important arguments against software multiplexing is the additional work required of the central processing unit. As processing only takes place after each frame, it follows that the number of interrupts on the central processing unit will depend on the size of the frame and character-interleaving has obvious advantages in this respect over bit-interleaving.

Statistical TDM

The major weakness of all the multiplexing techniques discussed so far is that channel capacity is wasted by allocating a band of frequencies or time slots within frames to all terminals irrespective of whether they are active or not. Clearly, if time slots can be allocated only when terminals are active, a much higher line utilisation will be achieved. To dynamically assign time slots in this way implies contention amongst the terminals for the time slots available. Any multiplexor which employs contention for channels might arguably be described, therefore, as a concentrator. Such is the case with a statistical time division multiplexor which is something of a hybrid performing a multiplexing function but relying on the statistical probability of the number of terminals which will be active at any time to increase the number of terminals which can be served. Analytical studies[2] show that between two and four times as many users can be accommodated on a line using Statistical TDM as with more conventional TDM techniques. This technique obviously has its attractions but there are also attendant problems. More storage is necessary to hold incoming messages and in busy periods there is the probability that lengthy queues will occur giving unacceptable delays to system

[2] 'Design Considerations of Statistical Multiplexors', Chu W W. Proc. 1st and 2nd ACM Symp.-Prob L Optimisation Data Comm Syst, Oct 1969 and Oct 1971.

users. As each slot is allocated dynamically rather than being associated with a particular terminal, elaborate addressing methods must also be employed to ensure accurate message assembly and delivery; the added redundancy involved lessens the transmission efficiency. The extent to which Statistical TDM will be used in the future will depend on how well these problems are overcome and at what cost. It must be remembered that the justification for a multiplexor is the line costs which can be saved. Very long and therefore expensive lines may well justify the added complications and relatively high cost of Statistical TDM systems but they are unlikely to be used extensively, for example, in the UK where lines are relatively short compared to those in the USA.

FDM versus TDM

Many of the arguments for and against these two fundamentally different forms of multiplexing have been discussed, but they can usefully be summarised as follows:

– The simplicity of FDM brings cost advantages when only a few low speed channels are required. At present FDM is cost attractive when fewer than about 10 or 12 channels are needed, the actual break even figure depending on which particular manufacturers' equipments are being compared. TDM is progressively cheaper per channel than FDM as the number required rises beyond 12.

– FDM techniques offer very little scope for cost reductions through technological development. Conversely, the reduction of logic and storage costs through the use of large scale integration (LSI) could significantly reduce the costs of TDM in the future. Whether these cost reductions will be realised depends on whether the demand for time division multiplexors warrants manufacturing the large quantities needed to justify the use of LSI techniques. As TDM requires the use of high speed modems, the total system costs will obviously be reduced if modem costs are reduced, or the throughput on bearer circuits can be increased without significantly increasing modem costs.

– Because of the need for guard bands on FDM systems, the aggregate low speed bit rate achievable is less than on TDM systems on which no guard channels are required and some data compression can be applied. This not only affects the costs per channel but also limits the ability of FDM systems to expand. For example, a TDM system over a typical leased circuit could expand to accommodate up to twenty-five 110 bit/s terminals. The most modern FDM system would be unlikely to handle more than eighteen 110 bit/s terminals.

– Some FDM channels may give a worse performance than others due to the line characteristics of the bearer circuit. TDM systems give a constant performance on all channels of the same speed.

– TDM systems are more flexible than FDM systems. Time division multiplexors can intermix terminals of different speed and with different synchronisation methods; system and channel configuration changes can also be effected more easily.

– The monitoring and diagnostic facilities on TDM are very much better than on the relatively less sophisticated FDM systems. High and low speed parity check facilities can also be given on TDM but not an FDM.

– One minor disadvantage of TDM systems – particularly when character interleaving is employed – is when the low speed terminals operating through the multiplexor system use echo-checking techniques for error control. With this technique, termed echo-plexing, a character entered on the terminal is transmitted to the computer and looped back to provide a local check for the user. The effective use of this technique requires the minimum possible delay between entering the character and the subsequent print out at the terminal. However, when a multiplexor system is included in the transmission path, transmission delays do occur which are more noticeable on some types of TDM systems than on FDM systems and may prove disturbing to the terminal user.

The economics of multiplexing

A data communications system designer must decide what method will be used to connect the data terminals to the central computer. There are a number of 'closed' systems where the terminals are only used by people within one organisation, where internal security or other operational factors such as the response time or call set up time requirements will dictate the use of dedicated circuits or multi-point networks. In many other cases, the major factor will be the cost of connection and a direct comparison can usefully be made between the relative communications costs involved in using the PSTN, private circuits, multiplexed channels or any combination of these three.

The following example illustrates a simple but typical case:

Example

A problem solving computer bureau company wants to provide a service for up to 40 customers in an area centred on a town 96 km from the computer centre; 10 character per second asynchronous terminals will be used.

Three alternatives might be considered:

(a) *Connection by direct private circuits*

The 10 character/sec machines could operate over telegraph circuits. These circuits provide digital transmission at 110 bit/s and no modems would be required. The cost of each circuit would be approximately £555 per annum [3]– a total of £22,200 per annum.

(b) *Connection via the public switched telephone network*

A method of calculation for this is given in the formula below:

$$C = \frac{NXY}{100} \left[\left(\frac{n_1 \times 3600}{R_1} \right) + \left(\frac{n_2 \times 3600}{R_2} \right) \right] \times U$$

where C = total annual call charges
N = number of terminals
X = number of days per week that the terminal is used
Y = number of weeks per year that the terminal is used
n_1 = number of hours per day at rate 1 (standard rate)
n_2 = number of hours per day at rate 2 (peak rate)
R_1 = number of seconds bought for unit fee during standard rate
R_2 = number of seconds bought for unit fee during peak rate
U = unit fee in pence

For the purposes of this example we will assume that terminals will be connected to the computer centre for an average of two hours per day (one hour at the peak rate and one hour at the standard rate) five days per week, 50 weeks per year (it should be noted, however, that as customers would be billed for telephone calls there might well be a tendency on the part of terminal users to restrict the amount of usage resulting in loss of revenue to the bureau).

Substituting we have:

$$C = \frac{40 \times 5 \times 50}{100} \left[\left(\frac{1 \times 3600}{12} \right) + \left(\frac{1 \times 3600}{15} \right) \right] \times 1.5p^3 =$$

£81,000 per annum

It is of interest to note that as the charges on the PSTN do not rise with distance over 56 km the charge would be the same for a distance of 300 km.

(c) *Connect via the public switched network and a multiplexed bearer circuit*

The method of obtaining a connection using this method is shown in figure 9.14.

---

[3] Costs used in these examples are as at 1st January 1975

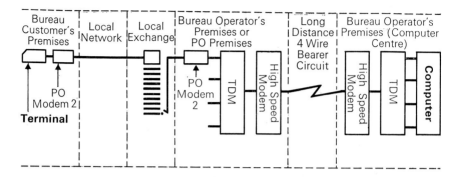

Figure 9.14   Connection via the PSTN and a multiplexed bearer circuit

The bureau customer dials a local call to gain access to the time division multiplexor.

The total costs of this system are easily calculated in two stages:

(i) the total annual call charges are calculated using the previous formula:

$$C = \frac{40 \times 5 \times 50}{100} \left(\frac{2 \times 3600}{180}\right) \times 1.5p$$

NB: There is no difference in the local call tariff during the business day.

C = £6,000 per annum.

(ii) For this example, we will assume that 15 computer ports will be provided to serve the 40 customers which gives a somewhat generous contention ratio. It is assumed that the TDM service is costed as a package and the annual costs for a system with 15 channels would be as follows:

Multiplexors and modems for 15 channels	£4,500
Bearer circuit (96 km)	£1,000
Total	**£5,500**

The total annual costs would therefore be:

£6,000 + £5,500 = £11,500 per annum.

A direct cost comparison can be made between (b) and (c) above, for annual rentals for exchange lines and modems are common to both cases showing a saving of some £69,500 per annum for the multiplexed system. Comparing (c) with (a) we have to add an annual rental for:

– 40 modems at customer's premises

   – 40 exchange lines

   – 16 modems and racking at the bureau operator's remote premises
(15 + 1 spare)

Nevertheless in this particular case the annual charges for communications
facilities would be some £4,000 less per year for the multiplex system described
than for direct private circuit connection.

This example is by no means exhaustive and there are a number of other
alternative solutions which can be tried. The alternatives given here are
intended merely to show the substantial savings which multiplexing can offer
and the type of calculations which are involved. Direct cost comparisons,
although useful, can be misleading particularly where some of the cost
elements may be difficult to determine. It is unlikely, for example, that a
multiplexor could be added to any system without the need for some re-
programming, hardware modification or changes in operational procedures.
Although, as in the example, cost is often a major factor in the choice of
system there are other important considerations. When multiplexing is being
considered the reliability and ease of fault finding and maintenance warrant
special attention; for the attraction of multiplexing must be carefully
balanced against the dangers of having too many eggs in one basket. The loss
of a bearer circuit due to a circuit, multiplexor or modem failure is inevitable
sometime and unless some alternative means of communication is given to
users it is also potentially disastrous.

10 Distributed Intelligence, Message and Packet Switching

The previous chapter has already pointed to some of the advantages of giving concentrators and multiplexors some decision logic of their own – making them 'intelligent'. It also showed some of the complexities of keeping track of the message elements, at bit and character level, and making sure that they arrived at their correct destination at the correct time. The logical extension of these 'low-level' activities is the creation of networks with 'distributed intelligence' and complete flexibility for transferring data between nodes of the network – message switching. It is the purpose of this chapter to examine these broader concepts and to show some of the developments which have resulted.

Historically, the main purpose in providing a data communications system was to connect a number of geographically separate locations to a powerful central computing resource. Yet, in recent years, we have seen an increasing use of small computers in different parts of data communications systems. These 'intelligent' or programmable modules are now to be found in terminals, terminal controllers, concentrators, and 'front-ends' located at the main computer centre between the 'main-frame' computer and the communications lines.

We are not witnessing nor are we likely to in the near future, a movement towards de-centralising all those computing facilities provided by a large central processor. Only when very long and costly communication links are needed can this be justified. It remains economic to centralise large and complex application programs on one powerful machine shared amongst a number of on-line terminals. The high cost of mass storage devices and the complexity of establishing and maintaining large databases continues to act against the de-centralisation of computer files. Expensive peripherals, such as high speed printers and microfilm output devices, are usually only justified at a central location. If we add to this the fact that costly specialist programming staff cannot realistically be spread thinly around a system, it is plain that the demise of the medium and large central computer is not yet foreseeable. We must, therefore, look elsewhere for reasons why small computers are being used in a system in addition to a central main-frame machine.

If a powerful central computer is to continue to handle the large jobs for which it is ideally suited, it is useful to examine those other logical operations which it may be called upon to perform in handling a number of remote terminals. In this way, we can consider whether these functions are best performed by the central processor or whether they should be handled elsewhere.

As most of the existing telecommunication-based computer systems have evolved from batch processing installations, we will begin by examining the following problems involved when just one remote 10 character/sec, start/stop terminal is given direct access to an application program in a large central computer:

    – Communication with the terminal must be in bit serial form (one bit at a time) whereas normal communication within the computer system will be in parallel or byte serial form (one byte or eight bits at a time).

    – The terminal is painfully slow compared with other peripheral devices, as shown in table 10.1.

Peripheral	Typical transfer rate (char./sec.)	Time between successive characters (μsec)
Drum	2,000,000	0.5
Disc	500,000	2
Magnetic Tape	25,000	40
Line Printer	1,250	800
Card Reader	1,250	800
Card Punch	500	2,000
Paper Tape Reader	500	2,000
Paper Tape Punch	100	10,000
Teletype	10	100,000

Table 10.1   Typical speeds of computer peripherals

- The start/stop type of communication employed by the terminal is not used within a central computer system.

- The seven unit information code used by the terminal will be different to the internal code of the computer.

- If parity checking is used, some kind of error message must be assembled and returned which can be understood by a terminal user.

By merely adding one simple terminal to a system, it, therefore, becomes necessary to:

- Convert serial data from the terminal into parallel form for communication over the input/output channel and vice versa.

- Provide buffer storage to compensate for the different speeds of the terminal and the high speed input/output channel.

- Strip off incoming start/stop signals incoming from the terminal and add them on in the reverse direction.

- Convert information arriving from the terminal from the communication code to the internal code of the computer and reverse this process for information flowing in the other direction.

- Check parity on incoming characters from the terminal and assemble some kind of error message when necessary for transmission back to the terminal.

The first approach to these problems was to provide a line terminating unit (LTU) between the modem and the computer. The functions of the LTU were to provide the necessary electrical interface between the computer and the line and to convert the data from serial into the necessary parallel form on incoming messages and vice versa. Buffering was provided in the main store of the computer and the other functions listed above were performed by a combination of hardware logic and a rudimentary communications central program (CCP) again resident in the main store. The division of the functions between hardware and software varied considerably. In these circumstances, a central processor was involved in a number of small but time consuming routine tasks and the addition of one terminal could seriously degrade the efficiency of the whole system. The reasons for this can be seen if we consider the additional load on the valuable central processing resource which is caused by adding a terminal.

Before a character arrives from the terminal, the central processing unit (CPU) will be performing batch processing work under the direction of a master control program or operating system. The operating system deals with 'housekeeping' functions and handles all input/output requests in priority order, controls the queuing of those requests waiting to be handled, allocates store areas and other tasks necessary in a multi-programming system. Some computers have direct memory access (DMA) which enables data to be sent direct from a peripheral into core store to await processing. In many cases, however, the program being processed is interrupted by an input/output (I/O) routine which controls the transfer of a character or word into store; after the transfer takes place, control is handed back to the processing program – if no other work of higher priority has to be done. In order to give good service to the terminal, it will almost certainly be given the highest priority for CPU resource allocation, so that when a character from the terminal arrives all other work requiring the CPU will be inhibited until all the work associated with the incoming character from the terminal is finished. Before the CPU can begin processing the character, there is other work to be done. Because another job has been interrupted, it is necessary for the computer system to remember what the particular job was and at what point to start again. The operating system must, therefore, store the status of the program and the address of the next instruction to be performed. In order to know what to do with the oncoming character from the terminal, the CPU must then operate under the direction of the communications control program. As only one terminal is involved in this case and there are no complex line protocols, this program would be fairly simple dealing only with message assembly, code conversion, error checking and so on.

Nevertheless, it will be seen that the 'interrupt' caused by each incoming character from the terminal will occupy a sizeable slice of CPU time and a similar portion of time will be required when information is transmitted in the reverse direction – this, of course, is in addition to the time required to execute the instructions in any application program which is being accessed.

As more terminals are added, the number and complexity of the tasks necessary to handle them grows. The additional work involved will vary between different types of system but some of the more general ones are given below:

   – Line protocols or line control procedures become more complex. This is particularly true when the activity of terminals is controlled by the use of polling techniques.

   – Different methods are required for synchronous and asynchronous terminals. Additional problems are involved if both types of terminal are to be handled.

   – Communications may be required with terminals using different codes which adds to the code conversion problem.

   – As the number of terminals on a network grows, it becomes increasingly necessary to gather statistical information on the level of terminal activity, the number of errors which occur, etc.

– Where contention is used on a network, the efficient handling of queues must be arranged.

– In order to facilitate recovery from a failure in a large network, it is often necessary to provide a running record or 'audit trail' of terminal activity.

– Some systems require extensive editing facilities to assist terminal operators in checking a message before transmitting it. In some cases, an operator may be provided with a prepared format printed on a page or displayed on a screen. Data compression might be needed in these cases to suppress blanks to give more efficient transmission.

– Security reasons may dictate that some programs are only available to certain terminal users. Similarly, it might be decided that some terminals should have priority over other terminals for use of a communications line or a particular program.

– Systems using communications over the public switched telephone network may require automatic dialling and automatic answering facilities.

Having looked at some of the problems which are involved, we can now return to the earlier question of where these different functions should be performed.

One solution, which was widely adopted by main frame computer manufacturers, was to supply a 'hard-wired' or non-programmable communications control unit (CCU) to perform the simpler logical operations and reduce the load on the main processor. A typical configuration is shown in figure 10.1.

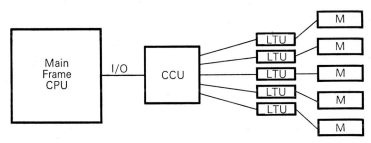

CPU — Central Processing Unit
I/O — Input/Output Channel
CCU — Communications Control Unit
LTU — Line Terminating Unit
M — Modem

Figure 10.1 A communications control unit (CCU) used to 'front end' a 'main frame' central processor

The typical functions performed by a CCU are as follows:

– Error detection, commonly by the use of character and block parity checking.

– The identification of control characters.

– The insertion and deletion of synchronising characters when synchronous communication is used.

– Character framing with start/stop bits for asynchronous communications.

– The parallel to serial and serial to parallel conversion of bits within a character.

– Providing the necessary interfaces with the communications lines via modems or line adaptors, and with the main processor input/output channel.

– Automatic dialling and automatic answering of calls, where necessary, on the public telephone network.

– Automatic polling.

The manufacturers of CCUs supplied a communications control program (CCP) which provided a number of special facilities which included:

– Line control

– Code conversion

– Buffering and queuing

– Error control

– The collation and analysis of statistics related to terminal or line activity, errors and failures.

The user was, therefore, provided with a general purpose package which would handle a variety of different communications facilities. As each application differs in its requirements, he was obliged to write his own application program to suit his particular purposes. Generally, this program exercised control over the CCP and performed those functions not provided by the manufacturer's software such as the editing or vetting of incoming messages, handling message queues and of course the actual processing of the incoming messages. This approach has a number of weaknesses:

– The central processor is still committed to perform a number of simple but time consuming data communications control functions, which can considerably reduce the system performance in terms of the response time given to users and the number of messages or transactions per second which can be handled. As the storage in CCUs is usually limited to a few characters, the central processor is interrupted whenever a line buffer is full. Many computer systems were designed primarily for batch processing work and are not really suited to the hurly burly of data communications with the numerous unscheduled demands made on the central processor. Not surprisingly, in some systems using hard-wired, front end units a large percentage of CPU time is occupied with communications control. As such a system grows, there is increasing pressure on the user to obtain a more powerful and expensive CPU.

– Communications control programs may occupy large areas of costly core store in some cases exceeding 50K bytes. Further core memory is needed when message buffers are provided in the main memory. Where the maximum size of the immediate access core store available is limited, the memory demands of data communications may prevent other data processing work from being carried out.

– Hard-wired, front end units are inflexible devices. Data communications is in a highly volatile state. There are an ever increasing number of new terminal devices being produced; conventional communications facilities are being extended and completely new ones introduced; line control procedures are being improved; rapid changes in semi-conductor technology are reducing costs of logic and mass storage while the price of communications equipment is remaining fairly constant. In this changing environment, it is becoming increasingly necessary to design systems which have the flexibility to adapt to changing conditions and this can only be achieved by programmable devices.

– In the event of a main processor failure, a hard-wired CCU cannot maintain any kind of back-up service to the terminals. The effects of such a failure in a single processor system are, therefore, likely to be serious and, as message queues cannot be maintained, recovery from failure is difficult. The reliability of telecommunications-based computer systems has always been an important factor in system design. Today, when throughout the world there is an increasing risk of militant industrial or political action, there is an even greater emphasis on ministering the risks involved when failures occur. System designers are looking for economic solutions to the problems of failure and although in very large systems the duplication of main-frame computers can sometimes be justified this solution does not satisfy the majority of users. More often the solution lies in isolating the purely communications elements of a system from the main-frame computer which gives a 'fail soft' capability maintaining a degraded service to terminals while the central computer is down.

Front-end Processors

There are a number of different ways in which a small processor can be used to front-end a central computer. These processors, which are often made by manufacturers other than the main-frame manufacturer, are frequently more powerful than a large central processor for performing those functions such as line control, data buffering, message processing, error checking and recovery which are associated with data communications. Front-end processors fall into two main categories, 'passive' and 'active'.

The 'passive' front-end processor

A passive or 'transparent' front-end processor is a replacement unit which merely emulates a communications control unit and performs those functions normally performed by a CCU which were discussed earlier. No changes are made to the communications control central software or application programs and consequently there are no reductions in the number of interrupts on the main processor.

The immediate advantage of using a front-end processor in this way is a gain in flexibility which enables a user to use communications facilities and terminals made by other manufacturers which could not normally be handled by a CCU; as CCUs tend to be costly there may also be a considerable saving in cost.

Replacing a CCU in this way gives the user the capability to develop his system in phased steps and the initial emulation of the CCU is often only a transitional stage.

The 'active' front-end processor

An 'active' front-end processor generally takes over the data communications control from the central computer. The generalisation is necessary because the implementation of an active front-end processor can be an extremely complex operation particularly when it is of different manufacture to the main-frame, and it is for the system designer to decide which functions it should actually take over from the main processor. Typically, an active front-end will do many of the basic control functions such as line control procedures, character to message assembly and dis-assembly, polling, message queuing, code translation, collection of error statistics and error control and recovery.

Figure 10.2 shows a typical system using an active front-end processor. The communications control program (CCP) is removed from the main memory of the central computer and is stored in the smaller processor.

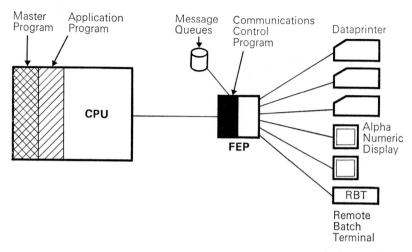

Figure 10.2 Example of a system using an 'active' front end processor (FEP)

The use of an active front-end processor has the following advantages:

– There is a considerable reduction in the load on the central processing unit.

– A substantial amount of main storage is saved in the main frame, freeing it for other tasks. Storage in the small processor is relatively cheap and there may also be a cost advantage.

– In the event of failure on the main frame, it is possible to give a degraded service to the terminals. Recovery from such a failure is much easier if queues are handled by the front-end. The front-end itself being much smaller with fewer parts to go wrong is likely to be more reliable than the central computer.

– Being a programmable device, the front-end processor can readily be adapted to suit changing conditions. The modular communications software in the front-end may be modified without interfering with the operating software at the main frame.

– The ease of maintenance or 'maintainability' of a data communications network can be improved by providing special diagnostic software in the front-end.

'Intelligent' Terminals, Concentrators and Controllers

A good system design will provide processing power where it is of optimum value in a network. There are three main reasons why it may be desirable to provide small programmable processors at the terminals themselves or in concentrators placed at strategic points within a network. These are:

- To bring computing power closer to the user and provide a local processing capability.
- To provide local file storage and easy access to these files.
- To reduce communications costs through data concentration.

Where the intelligence should reside will depend on what functions are to be performed and the number and geographical location of the terminals.

Intelligent terminals

An intelligent terminal is defined here as "a terminal which has its own processor and which provides a user with a local facility for processing his own programs". Other terminals which include a processor which the user cannot 'get at' and those which perform logical operations in hardware are not discussed here.

Although there are circumstances where a user's processing needs are unique and cannot possibly be provided in any other way, the two main reasons for providing an intelligent terminal are:

- This is the most economic way of meeting the particular user's needs for processing.
- The user likes intelligent terminals and has sufficient influence to get one.

Leaving the second point for the psychologists, we might dwell for a moment on the first. A decade ago it would have been unthinkable to have provided a remote terminal with a processor. Apart from the high cost of the processor, the availability and cost of suitable air conditioned accommodation of sufficient size would have horrified most users. Today a mini computer with 8K bytes of store is relatively inexpensive and will work in normal office conditions; the prospect is therefore far less daunting than it was.

'Intelligent terminals' are not a specific terminal category but can be regarded as the clever relations of those different types of terminal discussed in Chapter 5. Thus we may have an intelligent dataprinter, an intelligent remote batch terminal and so on.

Plate 10.1 shows a typical intelligent graphics terminal used for computer-aided design work. The graphic display system includes a small but powerful mini computer and is linked to a central processor using a 2400 bit/s dial-up service.

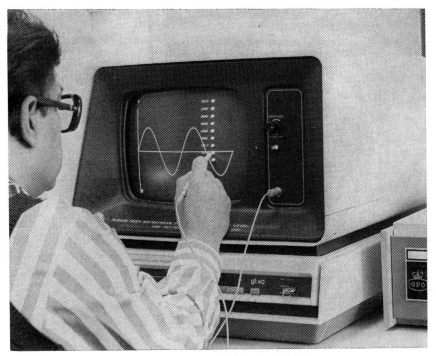

Plate 10.1 An intelligent graphics terminal

A typical use of this system is in the design of printed circuit boards. After an engineer has completed the design of an electronic circuit (usually a computer-aided task in itself) he is faced with the problem of laying out the components and interconnections. To minimise the size of a layout, printed circuit boards are normally used which are made of insulating material; copper tracks making the connections between the various components.

The position of the tracks and components on a board are variable and it is a difficult and tedious task to design the optimum layout. The use of the computer graphics system makes this work very much easier. The designer first codes his design in a form required by a specially prepared program, together with other information such as the size of the board. The coded information is fed into the system and is processed to provide a visual image of the printed circuit board with all the electrical inter-connections and components.

By using a light pen, which enables lines to be drawn and deleted on the screen, the designer can make modifications to the displayed layout. When the designer is satisfied with the result, he types a command for the computer to output the design on to paper tape. This tape is fed into an automatic plotter which draws the printed circuit board design on photographic material with a light beam.

The drawing is developed as a negative and subsequently used for preparing the copper track layout on a board. The mask is placed over a board which initially is completely covered with copper and light is exposed to the un-masked parts. Chemical processes are then used to etch away the masked areas, leaving only the required copper tracks on the board.

In this particular application, the program for the layout is held at the central computer and is 'called in' by a designer when he wishes to use it; the program is then 'dumped' into the local processor using the data link. The designer then uses the terminal in 'stand alone' mode, only calling for the assistance of the central computer when he needs it. When the design is completed, the information shown on the screen is returned to the central processor for further processing. In this way, a designer gets the very fast response he needs when working interactively with the system.

To give the same response time, if a central rather than a local processor were used, a data signalling rate of over 48K bit/s would be necessary. The delay in feeding in programs from the central computer and sending results back is not nearly so time critical and the data signalling rates of the data link need be no more than 2400 bit/s to give a satisfactory service.

Hence, we have a typical example of where the provision of an intelligent terminal is now economically feasible. The example system can be bought for less than £8,000 and gives a remote facility which can save hundreds of hours of key staff time per year. The obvious alternative of providing an 'un-intelligent' terminal with all the processing done in a central computer is usually either too costly or is simply impractical to provide. Until recent times, the very high data signalling rates necessary to provide remote graphic facilities has meant that graphic terminals have only been provided within the same building as a main-frame computer.

The value of intelligent terminals has been seriously questioned in the past. There are fewer sceptics today, but the question of what an intelligent terminal should do is still the subject of much debate. Generally, the smaller routine jobs will be best handled at the intelligent terminal which leaves three main reasons why the central processor should also be used:

    – To handle very large problems or jobs which cannot be handled by the terminal.

    – To access a large database. It is still more economic to share mass storage; also the accurate maintenance of large files needs careful control which is more likely to be achieved on a central installation.

– Expensive peripherals such as microfilm output devices, high speed line printers and plotters may be too costly to be justified at individual terminal locations.

So we find that at a particular site an intelligent, remote batch terminal is used for the local processing of small jobs while the bigger jobs are processed on a central computer – in many cases, the large machine's time being rented from a computer bureau. Intelligent data printers such as those frequently used in banking are polled by a central computer for on-line data collection but are also used locally for routine computations.

Intelligent concentrators
Chapter 9 described how intelligent concentrators could be used for line switching, message switching and polling. They can also be used to share a local processing resource amongst a number of 'unintelligent' terminals enabling terminal users to share programs stored at the concentrator for routine functions such as computation.

Intelligent terminal controllers
Terminal controllers are usually provided in circumstances where a number of terminals situated in one location can economically share common equipment or facilities. The clustered alphanumeric display terminals described in Chapter 5 are linked to a common terminal controller and, typically, share buffer storage, and character generation circuits provided in the controller. An intelligent or programmable controller is similar to an intelligent concentrator in that it provides a local processing resource as well as controlling communication between the terminals and the central processor.

Of all the arguments for using small computers in a data communications system perhaps the most persuasive is that which advocates using distributed intelligence as a means of separating the planning functions of the communications and computing elements in a system. The strength of this argument lies in the different pace of development in the communications and computing fields. Although technological developments in communications in recent years have been rapid, new techniques have to be gradually absorbed into an existing system in which thousands of millions of dollars/pounds/D marks/etc are invested internationally. In communications, the accent must, therefore, be on expansion with gradual improvements, rather than scrapping an existing system when newer and better techniques emerge. The pattern of advancement in communications is, therefore, steady rather than dramatic and the cost of communications facilities tends to be fairly stable. This is in sharp contrast to the situation in computing where the position is much more fluid. In the last ten years, for example, we have seen the cost of mini computers for a given performance ratio decreasing by about 60 per cent per year. The whole pattern of competition in the industry has changed also in recent years and users are now able to shop around for an ever increasing variety of plug-compatible equipment, and software which will interface with that supplied by the main-frame manufacturers.

There are, therefore, convincing reasons why the planning of the more volatile computing elements in a data communications system should be separated from those of the relatively quiescent communications. This is more readily achieved by using a front-end processor; severing the umbilical cord between the operating software in the main frame and the communications software. The use of an active front-end processor is perhaps the most important step towards a rational distribution of intelligence in a system and gives the flexibility which many users feel is essential for efficient system development.

Switching of Message Traffic

Any problem involving the transmission and reception of messages involves an analysis of the following factors:

- The number and geographical locations of the terminals to be used.
- The speed of delivery required.
- The response time required.
- The volume of the message traffic derived from the number of messages, their average length and deviation from the mean. (This not only involves a careful analysis of the source and destination of messages over periods in a day, but the identification of peak periods of activity which may take place over a year. A key result of the analysis must be to show clearly the peaks of traffic which are required to be carried by the system.)
- The degree of reliability and security which is required in the system.
- The types of terminals which exist already or are required to be used.

Although designers of data communications systems will recognise those factors listed as being fundamental to their network design requirements, they are not exclusively related to data messages. Studies of this type have been done for many years in designing systems for communicating messages of a telegraphic nature. Historically, communication of these messages over private networks has fallen into two basic categories, 'circuit' switching and 'message' switching. Today, these methods are also used for data communications and some networks are required to carry both telegraph and data messages. A third important method must now be added – packet switching, and the remainder of this chapter will seek to distinguish between these switching methods and describe the principles involved.

Circuit Switching

The simplest method of providing inter-connection economically between a number of points is to provide some form of circuit switching. The PSTN and the Telex networks are both examples of this type of switching whereby circuits are connected together by switching for the duration of a call and then released.

The economies to be gained by this method are fairly obvious and it will be seen from figure 10.3 (a) and (b) that line costs can be saved in this way even in small networks.

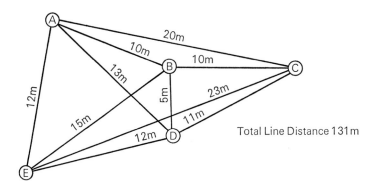

Figure 10.3a Point to point system

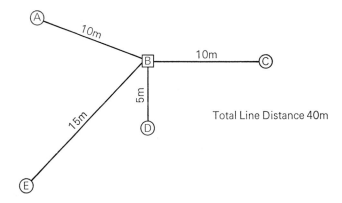

Figure 10.3b Circuit switched system

There is clearly a trade-off between the saving in line costs and the costs of switching. However, total savings can be considerable where many points are to be connected over long distances. A major disadvantage of circuit switching is the poor circuit utilisation – particularly where single circuits are used. A good deal of personal and circuit time may be wasted trying to establish a connection, particularly in busy periods. For example, in figure 10.3(b) A may have a number of messages for C but may have difficulty getting through, having no indication when C becomes free. Indeed, while A is trying to reach C, C might be trying to call A; circumstances which are familiar to all telephone users. An advantage of circuit switching is that once a call is established instant communication can be given between operators for the duration of a call.

Message Switching

Unlike circuit switching, no 'call' is established in a message switching system. In principle a message, suitably addressed, is entered into the message switching system irrespective of whether the called station is free or busy; the message is stored in the system in some way and delivered later. Message switching systems have, therefore, the following advantages over circuit switching:

- No time need be wasted in entering messages into the system if the receiving terminal is busy.

- Terminals, which could not communicate in a circuit switching system because of speed difference or code incompatibility, are able to exchange messages; the necessary conversion being performed at the switching centre.

- A message input by one terminal can be 'broadcast' to a number of other terminals, avoiding the setting up of several connections.

- More control over the network is possible; the type, format and volume of messages can be monitored at the switching centre.

- Messages stored in the system can be re-transmitted if errors occur.

- More efficient circuit utilisation is achieved.

- Messages may be delivered in priority order.

Evolution of Message Switching

Whilst the development of message switching is towards computer control, message switching already has a long history. Public telegram systems, essentially message switching, have been in operation since the early developments of telegraphy. Many efficient private systems have also been designed, the development of which can be traced through three main stages.

Torn paper tape switching systems

These are manually operated, the incoming messages to the centre being received on paper tape receivers. On the completion of the incoming message, an operator tears off the tape, reads the destination and transfers the tape to the appropriate paper tape transmitter connected to the called terminal. In periods of peak traffic, queues of messages may build up for a particular terminal. Usually, they are queued in arrival order, being cleared during a slack period. Priority messages can be speeded up by jumping the queues. In this way, the centre absorbs the peaks yet still has the flexibility to build into the system a hierarchy of priorities.

Whilst such manual systems may appear unsophisticated in relation to modern computerised systems, their strength lies in simplicity, reliability and good manual operating. Increasing operator costs has, however, led to a gradual reduction in the number of torn paper tape systems.

Figure 10.4 shows the network of the torn tape message switching or 'tape relay' system used until 1973 by the National Freight Federation Ltd in

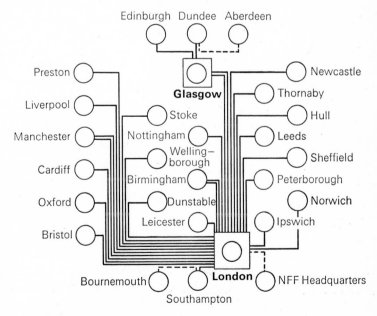

Figure 10.4   National Freight Federation torn tape network

Britain. This system gave extremely good service and was developed over a number of years. The average propagation time for a message through the system was two and a half minutes with an objective delivery time of less than 30 minutes. The system, using tape transfer centres in London and Glasgow, handled over a million messages a year – more than 65 million words.

Duplex telegraph private circuits were used between the tape transfer centres and the 28 teleprinter terminals. The latter served as feeder stations for several thousand National Freight Federation depots and offices. The method of transmitting messages into the feeder stations varied depending on the location of the depot or office and the message volume, but Telex, local simplex private wire teleprinters, facsimile, telegrams and pneumatic tube were all used.

Semi-automatic switching systems

In semi-automatic switching systems, the paper tapes are handled automatically at the switching centre. Typically, a continuous paper tape loop is

(Courtesy of Freight Computer Services Ltd)

Plate 10.2   The London torn tape relay centre

formed presenting the messages to an operator at a control console, who mechanically directs the message to the appropriate outgoing transmitter. A further refinement leads to the bulk of 'normal' messages being automatically read and routed leaving the operator to deal only with exceptions and errors.

Computerised message switching

With the increase in the size of systems and the growing need for more accurate and faster message handling, the use of a digital computer to control the system was a natural development. Computer control offers the following advantages.

Speed

Computerisation does not merely provide faster switching – although there are dramatic improvements over manual methods. Computer control brings a new awareness – an *instant* knowledge of what is happening in all parts of the system. Dynamic adjustment to changes in traffic flow are possible and more efficient queuing methods result in a general speeding up of the whole system.

Accuracy

The inclusion of error control minimises delays caused by errors. Errors are made apparent more quickly and in the case of requests for re-transmission the storage system enables the speedy identification and retransmission of messages. In certain cases, automatic error correction is in-built reducing the need for re-transmission.

Volume

As a manual or a semi-automatic system grows, the size and complexity of the switching centre begins to offset some of the advantages of centralised message switching. A computerised system reduces the need for physical expansion. Additionally, the increasing complexity of routings and the increase in the volume of messages can be handled with the greater flexibility which computer control brings.

Multi-termination messages

The transmission of a message to a number of terminals on a network can be built into the capability of a computerised system. Whilst these facilities can be available on manual and semi-automatic systems, they tend to be cumbersome. On a computerised system, the holding of address lists eases multi-destination messages; broadcast commands can be held by the computer or individual lists of addresses can be entered by the calling terminal.

Statistical and control information

The extraction of statistical information is eased in a computerised system. The increased awareness of what is happening in the system in terms of traffic volume, failures, errors, etc, provides a basis for good system control and development. Queue reports and fault reports can be provided quickly so that remedial action can be taken faster than would be possible in earlier systems.

Flexibility

A computerised system can be designed to react dynamically to failure conditions; for example, a faulty terminal can be quickly identified, a fault report issued and any messages addressed to the terminal can be referred back to the source with a notification of the fault. Extremely sophisticated systems have been designed to give automatic re-routing of messages in the event of line failure on key routes. The routine changes, which are inevitable in any system, such as changes in address or message priorities, can be made simply and quickly via the operating console.

Storage

The problems involved in the physical storage of paper tape are simply overcome in a computerised system. Although messages in transit may be held on disc, copies may be output to magnetic tape and held as long as is necessary.

The SITA (Société Internationale de Telecommunications Aeronautique) computerised message switching system

The computerised SITA message switching system has been developed from earlier torn paper tape systems and is a good example of a comprehensive data communications network. It provides the main intercommunication facility for the world's airlines. A 'high level' 4800 bit/s network links computer nodes in London, Amsterdam, Brussels, Paris (the major centre), Madrid, Frankfurt, Rome and New York.

Each computer node serves airline terminals at airports, ticket and administrative offices. In some cases, direct access may be given into the high level network from computer centres.

The system has been designed to handle the following types of traffic:

		Priority
QS	— 'Life and Death'	1
QU	— Double Rate (urgent)	2
QK	— Ordinary Rate	3
QD	— Cheap Rate (non-urgent)	4

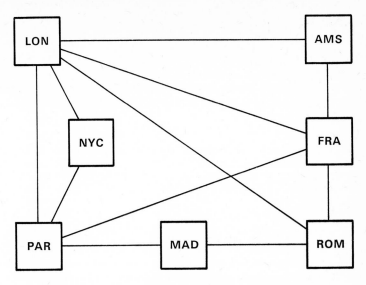

Figure 10.5   The 'high-level' 4800 bit/s SITA network

Four levels of priorities are provided within the system and alternative routings can be arranged under congestion or failure conditions. File changes at the nodes involve some 2700 individual codings per year.

Computer equipment for message switching

The hardware provided for a computerised message switching system will vary. However, there are a number of, usually small, machines which have been designed primarily for message switching and they share a number of common features. A 'typical' small, message switcher might have:

Central processing system

This comprises a central processing unit (CPU) and a main store (not usually more than 250,000 characters in size). The functions required include the processing of message headers, the routing of messages, maintenance of queues, the transfer of information to and from peripheral devices and error checking. Programs concerned with the overall system control, or application programs which are frequently used, are permanently resident in main storage.

Multiplexor

The CPU may be linked to a communications multiplexor over a high speed input/output (I/O) channel. The main function of the multiplexor is to transfer information between the relatively low speed lines and the central processing system.

Storage

Normally, there are three levels of storage. Messages, which are in transit and awaiting despatch, are queued on fast access backing storage such as a fixed head disc or drum; application programs which do not need to be held in the main store are also held in this area being called into main storage when required. There is also a longer term storage system (usually magnetic tape) which stores messages previously handled in case of a retrieval request. Statistics regarding system usage are also kept in this store.

System control facilities

These provide supervisory controls over the total message switching system. They often include a teletype control console or VDU, with the functions of correcting messages diverted to the console, because of errors. Additionally, the console acts as a fault reporting and systems performance centre with access to reports on queues, traffic levels, fault occurrences and the like. From this console, remedial action can be co-ordinated, such as the diversion of traffic, information on system status to users, queue control and the resetting of serial numbers.

Whilst these facilities control day-to-day operational adjustments, longer term alterations such as software development may be handled by a sub-system. This sub-system typically consists of a line printer and punch card or tape input/output equipment.

Message formats

All messages to be handled by a computer controlled system must provide sufficient information for the switching system to route the call to one or more addresses, to identify the message source, and to identify any special characteristics of the message. The text of a message is of no direct interest to message switching systems, except as a quantity to be stored. Each message must, therefore, have a header section which meets the needs of the switching system and which also satisfies the requirements of the originator, the recipient and the terminal operators. The message header should therefore provide:

- Start pattern. (To alert the message switcher.)
- Start of message indicator.
- Transmission indicator. (Originator's code and serial number.)
- Priority indicator.
- Address coding. (Routing information.)

The information in the header must be in fields that are clearly identifiable, either by using a fixed format or by using special characters indicating the beginning and end of each field.

Similar requirements are needed to identify the completion of transmission.

To illustrate these message formats, two examples are given from the system used by the UK Automobile Association (AA). This developed from a torn tape system but now uses a computer controlled store-and-forward procedure to feed 64 duplex telegraph lines operating at 50 or 75 bauds in IA 2, linking 44 AA offices (*see* plate 10.3).

(Courtesy of ITT Business Systems)

Plate 10.3 The message switching system of the Automobile Association, Basingstoke, Hampshire

The system was designed to meet a busy hour traffic loading of about 850 received messages and 2,200 retransmitted messages, and can considerably exceed these figures if necessary. A simple format helps the routing of messages by using three-letter address codes to cover individual or group messages. Out-of-format messages or those bearing an invalid code are automatically referred back to the originator for correction and to the system supervisor. Four levels of teleprint precedence are provided. Up to 3000 messages can be held on magnetic disc while awaiting retransmission or because a route has been 'closed' and such messages can be retrieved if required for a 'rerun'.

Example of message into the AA Message Switching Centre

Line 1 —

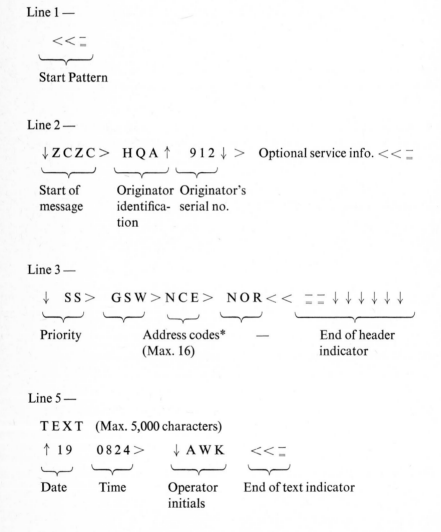

Last line —

NNNN

End of message indicator
16 Line feeds

KEY:
↓ — Letter shift
↑ — Figure shift
< — Carriage return
= — Line feed
> — Space

The message switching system, on accepting the incoming message, will then select the routings based on the routing information. Assuming the message has been correctly received, the system stores the message then relays it in priority order when the distant station is free.

The header of the onward message from the message switching centre is changed so that the receive terminal is provided with all the necessary information regarding the message.

Example of message transmitted from the AA Message Switching Centre

Line 1 —

< < =

Start pattern

Line 2 —

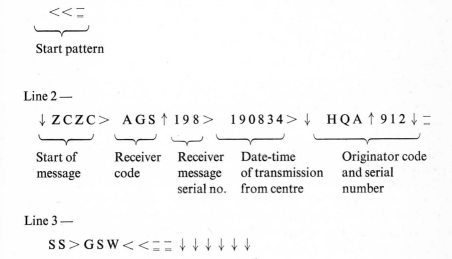

↓ ZCZC > AGS ↑ 198 > 190834 > ↓ HQA ↑ 912 ↓ =

Start of message / Receiver code / Receiver message serial no. / Date-time of transmission from centre / Originator code and serial number

Line 3 —

SS > GSW < < = = ↓ ↓ ↓ ↓ ↓ ↓

Priority / Originator's routing info. / End of header

Line 5 —

T E X T

↑ 1 9 0 8 2 4 > ↓ A W K < < ⁼ ↓
‿‿‿‿‿‿‿‿‿‿‿‿‿‿‿‿‿‿

Originator's date, time, initials

Last line —

N N N N
‿‿‿‿‿‿‿‿

End of message
16 Line feeds

(NB: Example shows a message from the AA headquarters at Basingstoke for Glasgow)

Packet Switching

Packet switching can be defined as 'the routing of data in discrete quantities called packets, each of controlled format and with a maximum size'. It differs fundamentally from circuit switching in that circuits are not switched and dedicated to the user for the duration of a 'call'. Although there are similarities between packet switching and the conventional message switching techniques from which it was conceived, the different units of information transmitted, ie packets and messages, demand a totally different approach to the problems of switching.

A packet consists of a 'header' section which contains control information such as the network address of the destination terminal, a data section containing the information to be transferred and a 'tail' section containing checking information. Any data 'message' is, therefore, split up into a number of packets when packet switching techniques are employed. Although all packets are 'delivered' to the destination address, they may be handled separately in the network and may follow completely different routes depending on network conditions. Internationally, there are two different approaches to the delivery of packets. One approach regards the packet switching network as a simple packet transfer system and does not set out to deliver packets in the order they were initially transmitted. The other approach provides sequencing such that packets are delivered in transmission order. The latter is adopted by the UK Post Office Experimental Packet Switching Service (EPSS).

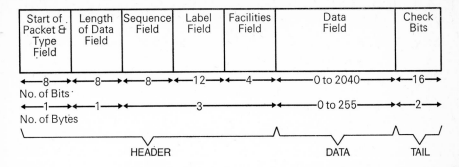

Figure 10.6 Example of packet used in EPSS

The advantages of packet working

The heading begs the question 'advantages over what?' Certainly, if we compare an efficient public packet switched system for data with the current facilities for data on speech type private circuits and the PSTN, there are a number of potential benefits well worth exploring. The UK Post Office has identified the following areas in which packet working appears to offer benefits to data communications users:

(a) Simplification of communication control equipment and procedures

The philosophy of interspersing packets from a number of sources lends itself to increasing the utilisation of communication channels and control equipment at computer centres. For instance, overall economic advantage may be obtained by replacing a large number of low capacity connections and associated control equipment with a single, high capacity communication link into a computer centre.

This mode of operation offers another inherent advantage: data from all terminals arrives at the computer centre in the same transmission format, irrespective of the nature of the originating terminal, thus simplifying the communications control aspects of the computer system.

(b) Utilisation of communication links

The techniques, which have generally been employed on UK Post Office networks and customer data communications systems to date, have made relatively inefficient use of the total data transfer capacity of the communications links between terminal devices. This inefficiency arises because, whilst a dedicated connection or circuit switched connection provides a continuously held path for the duration of the call, in practice, user's data is generated spasmodically, interspersed with periods in which no data is transmitted.

With packet switching, individual packets are sent into the network which then routes the packet to the destination terminal. Thus, the setting up of a continuously held communications path for a particular call is avoided. The links interconnecting packet switching exchanges may, therefore, intersperse packets originating from many customers, thus taking advantage of the intervals between packets making up a particular call.

(c) Error protection

Each packet transmitted contains a polynomial check, which provides a high degree of protection against line errors. This form of error control is not uncommon on data communications links, but for a packet switched network there is the added advantage that a packet is checked for errors at each packet switching exchange (PSE) along its route, ie link-by-link checking, so improving the undetected error rate compared with an end-to-end check.

(d) Automatic route protection

In the event of interference adversely affecting the performance of a link between packet switching exchanges, any packets in transit are safeguarded and may, under the control of the appropriate packet switching exchange, be re-transmitted via an alternative route. At any stage of a call the packet switched system is capable of quickly adapting to and re-routing data on a particular link, thus ensuring minimal disturbance to customer's data.

(e) Interworking between terminals operating at different data transmission rates

In conventional systems, the transmitter must send data at a speed which the receiver can accept. In a packet switching system, the transmitted packets received at the originating PSE are conveyed at a higher speed through the network and then, at the destination PSE, transmitted at a suitable speed to the destination terminal which need not, however, operate at the same speed as that of the terminal originating the packet.

The Experimental Packet Switched Service (EPSS)

A considerable amount of research has been undertaken by the UK Post Office, and other organisations within the UK and abroad, to examine the potential benefits of a public packet switched service. Although far from being conclusive, the evidence has been sufficiently encouraging for the Post Office to introduce an experimental packet switched service on a limited basis in close co-operation with a number of important data users. Packet switching over a public data network is a completely different method of working to that required in sending data over the PSTN or private data networks and the experiment is intended to provide both users and the

Post Office with the experience necessary for proper evaluation. If the experiment proves technically and economically viable, the Post Office intend to provide a service on a continuing basis. The objectives of the EPSS are to set up a packet switched data communications experimental service of sufficient capacity, flexibility and geographical extent to satisfy the following requirements:

– To enable customers to evaluate the overall benefits of packet working within the data processing and data transmission environments.

– To enable the Post Office to evaluate operational aspects of a packet switched service.

– To obtain an indication of likely future demand for a packet switched service.

– To define and prove procedures and interfaces with customers and manufacturers of customer equipment and, hence, to provide a basis for national and international standardisation.

– To assist in determining tariffs for such a service, taking into consideration customer and Post Office requirements.

The EPSS Network

The Packet Switching Exchanges (PSEs) used in the EPSS will be situated in London, Manchester and Glasgow, interconnected by 48K bit/s links.

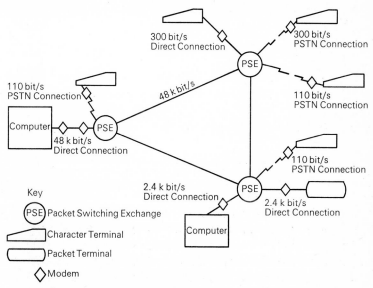

Figure 10.7   EPSS network structure

Switching

The EPSS does not employ conventional store and forward message switching techniques, only a limited amount of storage being provided in the system.

Plate 10.4   EPSS processor (Ferranti Argus 700E)

The storage capacity is employed for buffering a limited number of packets to enable terminals of differing speeds to communicate and make maximum use of the high speed links by transmitting synchronously at 48K bit/s. The system is protected against overloading its storage capacity. For example, call originating packets will be accepted for any valid address but further packets will not be accepted by the EPSS network until a first response packet has been received from the destination terminal and returned to the caller. The flow of subsequent packets is controlled by the use of the Extra Buffers Transferred Field but for one particular call no more than eight packets can be transferred without a packet being returned in response. This method limits considerably the amount of storage required in the network. In cases where a local PSE is unable to accept another packet from a packet terminal due to congestion, the PSE will return a 'Packet Hold' signal to the terminal. Character terminals will be sent special 'hold off' characters when local packet buffers are full and are 'called in' again when free capacity becomes available. If a local PSE can accept a packet but is unable to deliver it for some reason, it will send a network information packet to the calling terminal with an indication of the problem.

Access to the PSEs can be by dialling over the PSTN or by private circuits depending on the speed and mode of operation of the particular terminal; in all cases, Post Office modems will provide the appropriate interface with the terminal equipment.

Data terminals, operating at defined data rates, may be connected to the EPSS. There are, however, two fundamentally different modes of operation available – character terminal access and packet terminal access.

Character terminal access
Character terminals on the EPSS use normal asynchronous working with the following character structure:

110 bit/s terminals	300 bit/s terminals
one start element	one start element
seven character elements	seven character elements
one parity element	one parity element
two stop elements	one stop element

Characters are assembled into packets by the originating PSE and these packets are then transmitted synchronously between PSEs to the destination PSE. If the destination terminal is a packet terminal, the packets are delivered to the terminal: if the destination terminal is a character terminal, the packets are disassembled at the PSE and delivered a character at a time to the terminal.

Packet terminal access

Packet terminals work in a synchronous mode on the EPSS. Byte synchronisation is maintained on the network and all transmission between packet terminals and PSEs is in the form of contiguous bytes (eight bit units).

When no packets or acknowledgements are being transmitted, contiguous idle bytes must be transmitted.

Error control

A 16 check bit polynomial is used to check each packet on the EPSS. The polynomial used is defined in CCITT Recommendation V41, $x^{16}+x^{12}+x^5+x^1$, and is discussed in Chapter 8. The check bits are used by the EPSS to provide a link-by-link error check between consecutive PSEs and a terminal operating in the packet mode. A packet terminal, on sending a packet, waits for an acknowledgement signal from the PSE. If an acknowledgement is not received when it is expected, the packet will be retransmitted.

The 'closed user group' facility

A closed user group within the EPSS enables a customer to restrict intercommunication between terminals to those which are members of his particular group. In this way, the privacy of a private network is retained while taking advantage of the facilities and potential economies to be gained on a public packet switched system. The closed user group facility is achieved by using 'interlock' code procedures which are controlled entirely by the packet switching exchanges serving the particular terminals. Interlock codes are not accessible to terminal users and cannot be altered except by prior arrangement with the Post Office. A variant of this is the 'partially closed user group' facility which allows nominated terminals to communicate additionally to other terminals on the EPSS. For example, in a network comprising a computer centre and a number of terminals, the partially closed user group facility could restrict the terminals so that they could communicate only with each other and the computer centre whereas the computer itself, as well as communicating with its own terminals, would also communicate with other terminals on the EPSS.

11 Data Transmission Services in the UK

The Datel Services

The Post Office data transmission services are given the generic title Datel Services. A Datel Service consists of a suitable line, modems where necessary, and maintenance support. A description of each of the services available at time of print is given, but the already extensive range of those services is being continually extended. Up-to-date information and advice on facilities and prices of the Datel and other supporting services can be readily obtained from General Managers' offices; details are given in the Post Office Telephone Directories.

Datel 100 (CCITT V10)

Service	Signal Path	Speed (bit/s)		Operating Mode	Remarks
		Assured	Possible		
Datel 100	Private Telegraph Circuit (Tariff H)	50		Asynchronous	The PO can provide a tele-printer for 50 bit/s working
	Private Telegraph Circuit (Tariff J)	110		Asynchronous	The PO can provide a tele-printer for 75 bit/s working
	Public Telex Network	50		Asynchronous	Telex terminal equipment is supplied by the PO

This service was first introduced in 1964. It is the slowest service providing up to 50 bit/s on the Telex network and up to 110 bit/s on private telegraph circuits using private equipment. Although the speed of the service is slow by comparison with others, Datel 100 is inexpensive and is often very suitable for applications where small quantities of data are sent and received. The service is particularly attractive when a company has a need to transmit ordinary message traffic in addition to data. Datel 100 is used for reservations, stock control, payrolls, data collection and for time sharing computer bureau operation.

A range of facilities is provided within the service which comprises a Telex connection or a private telegraph circuit and terminal equipment to suit a customer's requirement. As telegraph type circuits are used on the service, digital transmission is employed throughout and *no* modems are required.

Figure 11.1 (schematically) shows a typical Datel 100 installation with a Post Office teleprinter No. 15 with automatic transmission (paper tape reader) being used on the Telex service to transmit data.

In an ordinary message (using IA 2) between terminal 'A' and terminal 'B', a 'local copy' or 'local record' would be produced at terminal 'A' by a connection between the transmitter and receiver. However, any five unit code can be used by a slight modification to both teleprinters. This includes the provision of 'local record disconnect' keys which are thrown manually at each end after the Telex call has been established and the operators are ready to transmit and receive the data. These keys have a different function at each

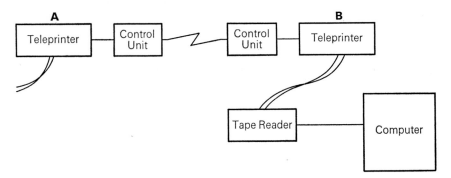

Figure 11.1   Established telex connection using Datel 100 service

end of the connection. At terminal 'A', the key prevents the production of a local record. This record would be useless to the user as it would merely represent the teleprinter 15's interpretation of the data. As the teleprinter is designed to use IA 2 and the data being sent is in a different code, the printer characters would have no significance. At terminal 'B', the transmitted data is reproduced by the reperforator (tape reader) and a useless page copy is produced – this is inescapable as the printing mechanism is an integral part of the receiver. The local record key at the 'B' end is to prevent mutilation of the received data. This can occur if the data transmitted from terminal 'A' includes characters equivalent to 'who are you' (character D) in IA 2. When such a character is received, the receive terminal transmitter will automatically respond with its own answer back code. This is not only sent back to terminal 'A' in a normal message but is also leaked to the terminal 'B' receiver. The local record disconnect key in severing the path between the terminal 'B' transmitter and receiver prevents interference caused by the answer back code.

A further part of the modification enables all the codes used to be punched into the paper tape at terminal 'B'. Under normal message conditions using punched paper tape, characters in IA 2 such a 'J bell' (used to attract a distant operator's attention) and 'figure D' (who are you) are not punched by the reperforator. However, if data is transmitted using some other five unit code it is important that all the characters transmitted are reproduced at the receivers; this is achieved by the 'all codes modification'. Although the example described uses a Telex connection, the same facilities are available on private point-to-point tariff 'H' circuits.

It is, of course, possible to transmit and receive data over unmodified Post Office teleprinters if IA 2 is used. In these circumstances, the message is encoded into punched paper tape by preparing the data 'off-line' using the teleprinter keyboard and a reperforated attachment. If the standard code is used, then code conversion is required beyond the receive terminal before the data can be processed. However, the need for code conversion is not confined to IA 2. Most of the data transmission information codes in use (with the notable exception of EBCDIC) are incompatible with computer codes and if no more than 58 characters are required there is very little to be gained by using non-standard five unit codes in preference to IA 2.

In chapter 1, the need for six, seven and eight unit codes was discussed and the majority of data communications codes in use are of this order. These can be sent using the Datel 100 service but private apparatus (normally paper tape reading and punching equipment) is required. This equipment, which requires Post Office permission to connect, is joined to the Telex lines by a Post Office switching unit provided at each end of the line. This arrangement is shown in figure 11.2.

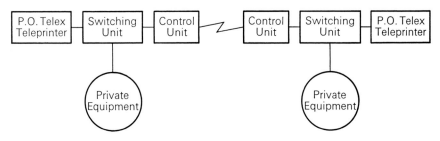

Figure 11.2   Private equipment arrangement using Datel 100 service

The call is established by dialling in the usual way and by pressing buttons on the switching units the private apparatus is connected to line. When the calling party releases the call, normal Telex service is restored by automatic restoration to the Post Office equipment at both ends of the connection. It should, of course, be remembered that the number of characters transmitted per second will be less with say a seven unit code than with a five unit code. If we assume that the seven unit ASCII is used on Telex with one start and two stop elements, only five characters per second are transmitted (the modulation rate of Telex is 50 baud maximum) against 6.66 characters per second using IA 2.

The Post Office teleprinter 15 can be used which gives ten, five unit, IA 2 characters per second on 75 baud Tariff 'J' circuits. Tariff 'J' circuits are available giving a modulation rate of 110 baud which allows ten characters per second to be transmitted using private teleprinter apparatus (these machines normally use seven unit ASCII with one start, one parity and two stop elements).

Error detection

Error detection facilities are available on the Datel 100 service with 'Telex' circuits (not internationally). An information feedback or 'echo checking method' is used; the arrangements are shown in figure 11.3.

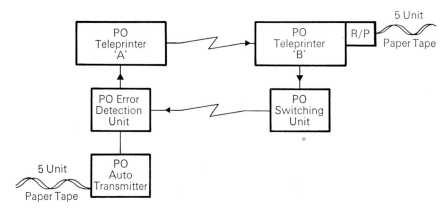

Figure 11.3   Error detection configuration for Datel 100

Although the average error rate on Telex is between five characters in 10^5 and two characters in 10^6, the errors tend to occur in long bursts and, therefore, are usually easily identified without recourse to error detection. The Post Office Error Detection Unit (EDU) is provided to ensure that the very few users requiring additional protection can get an inexpensive and reliable error detection system.

Data control equipment No. 3 (DCE3)

We have seen that private apparatus can be connected to Telex by the use of switching units which restore the line to the teleprinters on completion of the data transmission.

Both the Post Office teleprinter and the switching unit can be dispensed with altogether by using a DCE3. This enables a Telex line to be connected to a computer, a communications control unit, front end processor or a store and forward message switching device.

In replacing the standard Telex station, the DCE3A has four main functions. It provides:

(i) A suitable terminal impedance so that it will 'look like' a normal station to the Telex network.

(ii) A response to 'who are you' by the transmission of an answer back code.

(iii) The ability to detect the absence of terminal equipment and return the standard symbol ABS to the calling customer.

(iv) Conversion of the incoming telegraph signals to the voltage levels required by the terminal equipment and vice versa.

Facilities are also available which allow a computer to dial calls over the Telex network. These facilities are provided by the DCE3A/2 which has the ability to convert instructions from the computer (or other terminal device) into the Strowger pulses necessary to route the call. The DCE3A/2 can also interpret incoming supervisory signals during the setting up and clearance of a call and provide the necessary responses.

Datel 200 (CCITT V21)

Service	Signal Path	Speed (bit/s) Assured	Possible	Operating Mode	Remarks
Datel 200	Public Telephone Network	200	300	Asynchronous	
	Private Circuit	200	300	Asynchronous	

This service was introduced in 1967. Facilities are provided which enable keyboards and similar machines to communicate over the public switched telephone network and private speech band circuits using the PO Modem No. 2.

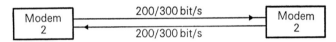

Figure 11.4   Datel 200 – modem arrangements

Public Switched Telephone Network (PSTN)

By setting up a normal telephone call and, when contact has been established, switching over to the modem and terminal equipment, data can be transmitted to any similarly equipped telephone installation. Transmission in both directions can take place simultaneously if required. There are no extra charges for data transmission calls; customers pay only normal telephone call charges and, of course, full use can be made of cheap rates. STD services, where available, enable speedy connections to be set up to a wide selection of places.

Private speech band circuits

These circuits are provided for customers' exclusive use between their premises for data transmission and in addition can also be used for speech at no extra charge dependent upon customers' particular requirements. Two-wire circuits are suitable for the Datel 200 Service.

Operational characteristics of Datel Modem No. 2

The modem is designed to accept dc signals from the data input equipment and use them to modulate a voice-frequency carrier signal generated within the modem. The modulated signal is fed to line and reconverted to dc pulses by the demodulator in the modem at the distant location. The modem provides two transmission channels, one to transmit data at any rate up to 300 bit/s, and the other to receive data at any rate up to 300 bit/s. The signals produced by the modem to represent the binary '0' (space) and binary '1' (mark) conditions of the data have the following frequencies:

Channel 1	Binary '0'	1180 Hz
Channel 1	Binary '1'	980 Hz
Channel 2	Binary '0'	1850 Hz
Channel 2	Binary '1'	1650 Hz

At rest, the modem is conditioned to transmit on Channel 1 and receive on Channel 2. For data to be exchanged between two terminals, however, one modem must be conditioned to receive on Channel 1 and transmit on Channel 2, and by international agreement this must be the modem associated with the called terminal.[1]

Switching at the receive modem will not take place unless automatic ringing is applied to the line. If the modem at 'B' were to be connected to a manual

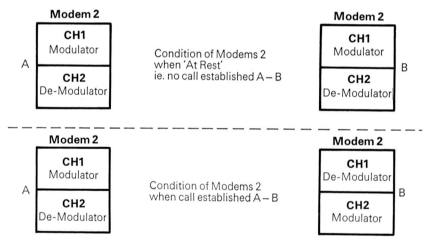

Figure 11.5   Datel 200 – operational characteristics of Datel modem No 2

---

[1] By international agreement, it is always the modem at the receive terminal that changes. Modems 2 at a computer bureau are usually modified so that they are permanently in a receive condition (ie, channel 1 de-modulates and channel 2 modulates). Since Duplex facilities are available, terminals operating in a conversational mode can use 'echo checking' for error control.

telephone exchange or to an extension from a **PBX** with manual ringing, switching would not take place. In these circumstances, a 'receive call' button is provided on the telephone associated with the modem so that the channel switching can be done manually.

Automatic switching of channel functions enables any Datel 200 user to call any other, and many more users are now making use of this facility. One difficulty which can occur is when a customer tries to call a distant terminal and fails – commonly, because the called terminal and exchange line is busy for a long period. In cases like this, it is natural for the caller to seek the assistance of an operator and this he will probably do by dialling '100' and 'booking' the call. The operator will dial the distant terminal and, when this is free, it will automatically switch channel functions. Holding the called customer on the line she will then dial the originator of the call and his modem will also change channels. This places both modems in a receive condition on channel 1 and a transmit condition on channel 2 and data cannot be exchanged. To guard against this eventuality, a 'booked call' button may be provided on the telephone associated with the modem, at the calling station. When depressed it will restore the modem at the calling station to its original condition.

The majority of keyboard machines operate at 10/30 characters per second (*see* Chapter 7) and many of these are used by customers of time sharing computer bureau operators (*see* figure 11.6).

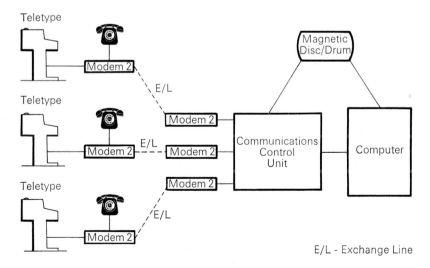

Figure 11.6   Computer bureau arrangements – Datel 200

Control 200A

Any installation faced with a large and possibly growing requirement for data transmission has the problem of maintaining ease of control and the saving of costly space. Control 200A is a specially designed termination and modem racking unit for Datel 200. (*see* figure 11.7)

Public switched circuits and private circuits can be answered manually or automatically, test access is provided to all modems and flexibility between circuits and modems is possible. The initial capacity of the unit is 12 circuits and as the system grows modules of 12 can be added.

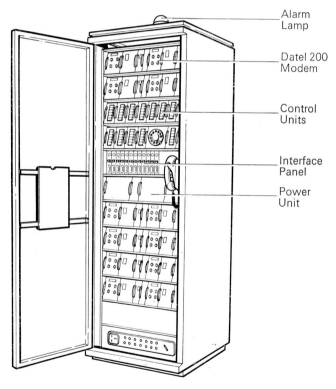

Figure 11.7   Control 200A – termination and modem racking unit for Datel 200

Datel 400

Service	Signal Path	Speed (bit/s)		Operating Mode	Remarks
		Assured	Possible		
Datel 400	Public Telephone Network	600 or 300 Hz (Analogue)		Asynchronous	Transmission direction out-station to instation only
	Private Circuit	600 or 300 Hz (Analogue)		Asynchronous	Transmission direction out-station to instation only

The Datel 400 Service was introduced in 1973 and uses the Datel Modulator No. 10 to provide one-way digital or analogue transmission facilities for data collection or telemetry applications.

Datel 400 is intended for use in almost any situation where variables need constant or intermittent monitoring and is especially suitable in cases where the outstations are scattered and unmanned. An example of a typical operation is the measuring of the quality of water at sewage outfalls.

Public Switched Telephone Network (PSTN)
The service can be operated over the public switched telephone network, the instation originating all calls to activate the outstation modulator into sending the sensor readings back to the instation. The operation is one-way only and can be either digital at up to 600 bit/s or analogue at 0 to 300 Hz.

Private speech band circuits
Private speech band circuits can be provided to connect the instation and out-station giving identical characteristics of operation to the public switched network.

Operation of Datel 400
The Modulator No. 10 operating in a digital mode is fully compatible with the Datel 600 Modem No.1. Transmission frequencies of 1300 Hz (Binary '1')

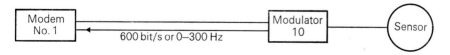

Figure 11.8   Datel 400 – modem and demodulator arrangements

and 1700 Hz (Binary '0') are used. In the analogue mode, it is necessary for a modified type of Modem No. 1 to be fitted at the central station which has the capability of receiving analogue signals. The analogue mode has a 300 Hz frequency spread.

In general, it is expected that calls will be set up from the central station either manually or automatically using a DCE1 (*see* page 304) and that these calls will be answered automatically by the terminal.

Since this service does not provide both-way transmission facilities, the outstation modulator is arranged to transmit a nominal six second period of Binary '1' tone (1300 Hz) following call connection, after which the terminal may transmit data. In the event of a normal speech call misrouting to a Datel 400 terminal arranged for automatic answering, the automatic answering sequence will be followed by data transmission and the terminal will not be aware that it is a false call.

Where a call is answered manually or originated from the outstation, the Modulator No. 10 can be connected to line.

Environmental considerations

The Modulator No. 10 can be accommodated in either a plastic case, where normal office conditions apply, or in a weatherproof case for external siting.

Datel 600 (CCITT V23)

Service	Signal Path	Speed (bit/s)		Operating Mode	Remarks
		Assured	Possible		
Datel 600	Public Telephone Network	600	1200	Asynchronous	
	Private Circuit (4-wire)	1200		Asynchronous	A 4-wire private circuit is required for Duplex transmission

This service was introduced in 1965. Facilities are provided which enable data to be transmitted over public switched telephone network and private speech band circuits using the PO Modem No. 1. (Model numbers are shown in the boxes below.)

Facility

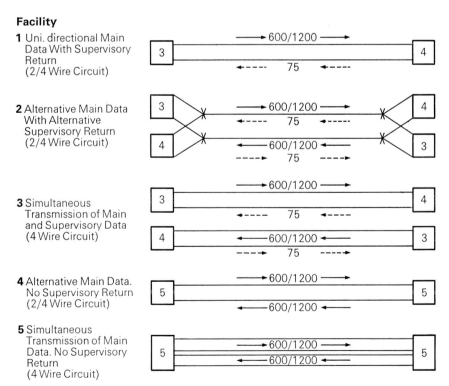

1 Uni. directional Main Data With Supervisory Return (2/4 Wire Circuit)

2 Alternative Main Data With Alternative Supervisory Return (2/4 Wire Circuit)

3 Simultaneous Transmission of Main and Supervisory Data (4 Wire Circuit)

4 Alternative Main Data. No Supervisory Return (2/4 Wire Circuit)

5 Simultaneous Transmission of Main Data. No Supervisory Return (4 Wire Circuit)

Figure 11.9   Datel 600 – facilities offered (PO Modem No 1)

Public Switched Telephone Network (PSTN)

By setting up a normal telephone call and, when contact has been established, diverting the line to the modem and terminal equipment, data can be transmitted in one direction at a time to any similarly equipped installation. There are no additional call charges for data transmission calls and, of course, full use can be made of cheap rates. STD services, where available, enable speedy connections to be set up to a wide selection of places.

Private speech band circuits

These circuits are provided for customers' exclusive use between their premises for data transmission and they can also be used for speech at no additional charge. Circuits can be installed exclusively for data or for alternative speech or data dependent upon customers' particular requirements. Two-wire circuits into a customer's premises can be used for data transmission in one direction at a time (ie half-duplex). To enable the transmission of data in both directions simultaneously, a 4-wire circuit will be necessary.

Unlike the Modem 2 used on the Datel 200 service, different models of Modem No. 1 are not always compatible with one another. There are a wide range of facilities offered on the Datel 600 service which have been provided by constructing the Modem No. 1 in modular form and providing those modules which meet a particular requirement. The service is therefore 'tailor made' for each individual customer and it is necessary to determine all the points between which data communication is required so that arrangements to ensure compatibility between modems (*see* figure 11.9) can be made.

Operational characteristics of Datel Modem No. 1

The modem is designed to accept from the input equipment dc signals of specific characteristics and use them to modulate a voice-frequency carrier signal generated within the modem. The modulated signal is fed to line and reconverted to dc signals by the demodulator in the modem at the distant terminal. The signals produced by this process to represent the binary '0' and binary '1' conditions of the data have the frequencies shown below. The selection from the two ranges available, viz up to 600 bit/s and up to 1200 bit/s, is controlled from a switch on the customer's terminal equipment via a connection on the interface cable.

Data Signalling Rate	*Frequency used for Data Channel*	
Up to 600 bit/s	binary '1'	1300 Hz
	binary '0'	1700 Hz
Up to 1200 bit/s	binary '1'	1300 Hz
	binary '0'	2100 Hz

The optional slow speed return channel, operating at up to 75 bit/s enables supervisory and control signals to be returned to the sending station. The frequencies used for this channel are:

binary '1' — 390 Hz
binary '0' — 450 Hz

The need to widen the difference between the frequencies with higher rates of transmission, when using frequency shift keying transmission, was referred to earlier in chapter 4. This widening of the difference is arranged in the Modem 1 by replacing the 1700 Hz frequency by one of 2100 Hz when operating in the higher range. The selection from the two ranges available is controlled from a switch on the customer's terminal equipment via the interface cable. In Chapter 5, the relative quality of private circuits and random PSTN connections was discussed. Although the majority of PSTN established connections will respond to the 2100 Hz binary '0' frequency, in some cases attenuation will be too great and will, therefore, prevent effective 1200 bit/s operation. It should always be possible, however, to obtain a connection giving 600 bit/s, as the 1700 Hz (binary '1') is unlikely to be severely attenuated. The 75 bit/s return or 'supervisory' channel uses frequencies of 450 Hz for binary '0' and 390 Hz for binary '1', the lower rate allowing closer spacing of the frequencies. The use of filters enables these frequencies to be returned simultaneously with the frequencies of the data being sent even on a 2-wire circuit. This is illustrated in figure 11.10. The term 'asymmetrical duplex' is used to describe the situation where data is sent in both directions simultaneously but not at the same rate.

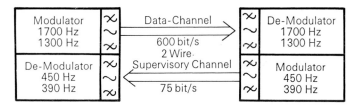

Figure 11.10   Datel 600 — asymmetrical duplex transmission

Although half-duplex transmission of data is possible on 2-wire private circuits and the PSTN, duplex transmission requires a 4-wire private circuit. This is illustrated in figure 11.13. A 600 bit/s operation is shown for simplicity.

During data transmission, the operation of the Modem No. 1 is remotely controlled from the private terminal equipment and control signals are

Figure 11.11   Simultaneous transmission of data using the same frequencies
is not possible on a 2-wire circuit

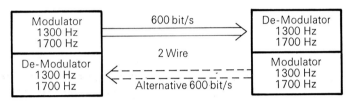

Figure 11.12   Alternative transmission of data using the same frequencies
(Datel 600)

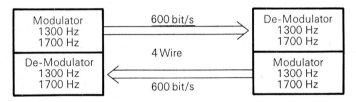

Figure 11.13   Duplex transmission of data using the same frequencies on
4-wire private circuit (Datel 600)

provided by the modem to the terminal equipment enabling line disconnection,
etc, to be brought to notice quickly.

The frequency shift keying, two state, system employed by the modems on the
Datel 600 service does not in itself require synchronisation of the modulator
at the transmit station and the demodulator at the receive station. The
Modem No. 1 is 'transparent' both to the rate of transmission between the
two ranges described earlier and also code transparent as any data transmission code may be transmitted. This enables a wider variety of terminals
to be connected to the Datel 600 service. Some kind of synchronisation is
always necessary between terminals connected by the modems and the line
to keep the terminals in step. This may be done asynchronously by using start/
stop signals separating characters or blocks, or synchronously by using
electronic clocks in the terminals. If synchronous operation is employed, the

transmitted bit stream will be clocked at a fixed speed and the receiver will be kept in step by comparing the incoming bit rate from the modem against the receive clock timing and continuously adjusting for any drift which occurs.

Datel 600 is widely used throughout industry and commerce for both off-line and on-line applications. In the banking sector, a large number of nationwide multipoint circuits (*see* Chapter 9) have been provided to give bank branches direct on-line access to computers.

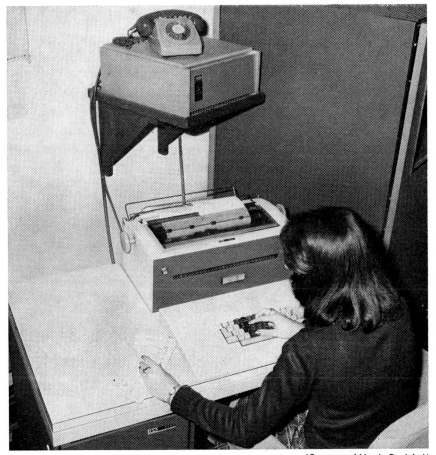

(Courtesy of Lloyds Bank Ltd)

Plate 11.1   A bank terminal and Modem No 1 at a bank branch

(Courtesy of Lloyds Bank Ltd)

Plate 11.2   A bank computer centre with Datel 600 Modems No 1 and racking

Control 600

The control 600 facilities have been designed to provide a convenient and efficient means of accommodating the modems and circuit terminations of the Datel 600 service. Up to eight Datel 600 terminators and modems can be accommodated in one unit, but the units can be extended on a modular basis.

Datel 2400 (CCITT V26A)

Service	Signal Path	Speed (bit/s)		Operating Mode	Remarks
		Assured	Possible		
Datel 2400	Private Circuit	2400		Synchronous	A 4-wire private circuit is required
	Public Telephone Network (Standby)	600	1200	Synchronous	

This service was introduced in 1968 and provides the fastest assured PO Datel service over private speech band circuits, using the Datel Modem No. 7.

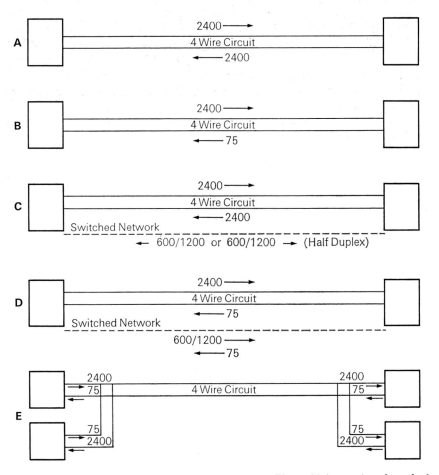

Figure 11.4 – continued overleaf

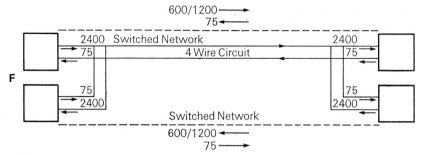

Note
A Post Office Datel Modem No. 7 will be
provided at each end of the line. To
meet the facilities offered in E and F
two Datel Modems No. 7 will be required
at each end of the line. Each Datel Modem
No. 7 must have access to an exchange line,
except in E where single exchange line
access will serve two modems.

A   2400 bit/s both-way simultaneously.

B   2400 bit/s forward channel and 75 bit/s on the backward channel
simultaneously

C   2400 bit/s both-way simultaneously plus alternative working 600/1200
bit/s in either direction but not simultaneously. Unattended answering
is available on the public telephone network.

D   2400 bit/s forward channel and 75 bit/s on the backward channel
simultaneously, plus alternative working 600/1200 bit/s forward channel
and 75 bit/s backward channel simultaneously — unattended answering
is available on the PSTN.

E   2400 bit/s and 75 bit/s in both directions simultaneously.

F   2400 bit/s and 75 bit/s in both directions simultaneously, plus alternative
working 600/1200 bit/s and 75 bit/s in both directions simultaneously
using two public telephone circuits — unattended answering is available
on the PSTN.

Figure 11.14   Datel 2400 – facilities offered (PO Modem No 7)

Public Switched Telephone Network (PSTN)

For maintenance purposes, the Datel Modem No. 7 must have access to the
public switched telephone network via a direct exchange line. This access
can also be used for alternative working, at 600 or 1200 bit/s, whenever this
is required. Unattended answering facilities can be provided when the data
terminals are connected to the public switched telephone network in their
standby mode of operation.

Private speech band circuits

The circuits necessary for Datel 2400 are 4-wire private telephone circuits provided by the Post Office.

These circuits are provided for customers' exclusive use between their premises and in addition to data transmission can also be used for speech communication.

There are a wide range of facilities offered on the Datel 2400 service and it is similar to Datel 600 in this respect. The service is 'tailor-made' for the individual customer's requirement and therefore close attention is required in the determination of the Datel 2400 configuration.

Operational characteristics of Datel Modem No. 7

The technique of 4-phase differential modulation is employed by the Modem No. 7 on the Datel 2400 service (*see* Chapter 4).

The alternative 600 or 1200 bit/s facility is provided by means of frequency shift keying (FSK) techniques at present but may be replaced by a two-phase modulation method in the future.

The modem is designed to accept from the input equipment dc signals of specific characteristics and use them to modulate a voice frequency carrier signal generated within the modem. The modulated signal is fed to line, and reconverted to dc pulses by the demodulator in the modem at the distant terminal. The modem accepts data from the input equipment at a rate of 2400 bit/s and by means of a 4-phase differential modulation technique modulates the carrier signal at a rate of 1200 bauds.

The modulated carrier signal is accepted by the receiving modem and demodulated as data at the fixed rate of 2400 bit/s, for acceptance by the output equipment. The system may be used in the full duplex mode or alternatively with an optional return channel, operating at up to 75 bit/s, which enables supervisory and control signals to be returned to the sending station. The frequencies employed for this channel are:

binary '1' — 390 Hz
binary '0' — 450 Hz

Optional facilities are available to allow alternative working at 600/1200 bit/s over the public switched telephone network. This may be selected by means of a control on the customer's terminal equipment via a connexion in the interface cable. These alternative facilities are identical to those provided by the Modem No. 1 for the Datel 600 service, except that the forward channel is restricted to operation at *fixed rates* of either 600 or 1200 bit/s and the received data is regenerated — transmitter and receiver signal element timing being provided. During data transmission, the operation

of the modem is remotely controlled from the private terminal equipment.
Control signals are provided by the modem to the terminal equipment,
enabling line disconnections, etc, to be brought to notice quickly.

Control 2400

Reflecting the philosophy of control systems, Control 2400 has been
designed to provide an efficient and space saving method of accommodating
the modems and associated equipment used in the Datel 2400 service. Each
unit has been produced to take up to four Datel 2400 terminations and as
these units are modular they can be linked to provide the required accommodation and control.

Datel 2400 Dial Up

Service	Signal Path	Speed (bit/s)		Operating Mode	Remarks
		Assured	Possible		
Datel 2400 Dial Up	Public Telephone Network	600	2400	Synchronous	The Post Office can give no assurances for satisfactory transmission at 2400 bit/s. The modem can be switched to operate at 600 and 1200 bit/s

This service was introduced in 1972 and provides on an unassured basis 2400 bit/s over the public switched telephone network using a modified version of the PO Modem No. 7.

Figure 11.15   Datel 2400 Dial Up – facilities offered (PO Modem 7C)

Public Switched Telephone Network (PSTN)

As the title suggests, the Datel 2400 Dial Up service offers 2400 bit/s transmission over the public switched telephone network. Synchronous communication facilities are provided at 2400 bit/s or at a reduced rate of 600/1200 bit/s between any two points on the UK telephone network. Simultaneous transmission in both directions cannot be given at either of these rates but both way alternative working is provided. When the service is operated in the 600 or 1200 bit/s mode, it is compatible with the fall-back mode of the Datel 2400 service and communication between these services is, therefore, possible. No 75 bit/s channel is provided with 2400 Dial Up.

Datel 48K

Service	Signal Path	Speed (bit/s)	Operating Mode	Remarks
Datel 48K	Special Quality Circuit	40.8K, 48K, 50K	Synchronous	

Datel 48K was introduced in 1970 and provides facilities for the simultaneous bothway transmission of serial binary data at fixed rates of 40.8K bit/s, 48Kbit/s and 50Kbit/s over special circuits using PO Modems No. 8 and No. 9.

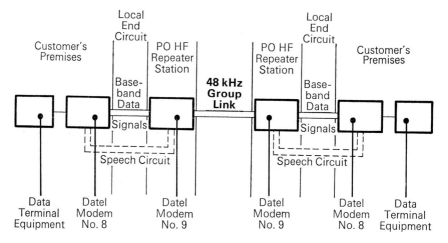

Figure 11.16   Datel 48K – modem and circuit arrangements

Private circuits

The special circuits have a bandwidth of 48kHz and are provided for customers' exclusive use between their premises. The actual arrangement made for the provision of a Datel 48K link may vary depending upon the locations to be connected and the facilities required. Terminations within about 25 cable kilometres may be provided throughout by physical cable. (Modem No. 9 will not be necessary in these circumstances.)

To optimise on line plant arrangements, two modulator/demodulator equipments have been developed – the Datel Modem No. 8 which is sited at the customer's terminal premises and the Datel Modem No. 9 which is normally sited at the nearest suitable PO repeater station. A typical Datel 48K link comprises two Datel Modems No. 9 inter-connected in the PO high frequency network and two Datel Modems No. 8 which are connected to the respective Datel Modems No. 9 by suitably engineered plant; one 4-wire cable will be provided at each local end to facilitate simultaneous bothway data transmission (*see* figure 11.16).

The transmission of data occupies a bandwidth of only 44kHz (60-104kHz). This allows the provision of a telephone channel in the 104-108kHz band. An additional 4-wire circuit is necessary between the Modems 8 and 9 (*see* figure 11.16) to prevent analogue speech signals interfering with the baseband digital signals.

There may be also a requirement to use the special quality links alternatively for high speed data transmission at night and for channelling the special quality link into a number of speech circuits during the day. The Post Office can provide both Modems 8 and 9 in the customer's premises at each end of the link to enable the customer to switch from the Modem No. 9 to the channelling equipment.

Operational characteristics of PO Modems Nos. 8 and 9

A Datel 48K Link consists of:

– Two Datel Modems No. 9 sited at the nearest Post Office repeater (amplifying) station and inter-connected by a 48kHz special circuit; and

– Two Modems No. 8 situated at the customer's terminal premises and connected by suitably engineered plant to the Modems No. 9.

The function of the Datel Modem No. 8 is to accept the serial binary data signals from the terminal equipment at fixed rates of 40.8, 48 or 50Kbit/s and to convert them into a suitable form for onward transmission to the Datel Modem No. 9. In the Modem No. 8, the digital signals are encoded to produce a pseudo-random data pattern. This encoding superimposes a pre-determined binary pattern in the digital data which spreads the signal energy over a frequency spectrum independent of that produced by the data input. The signals are digital and are sent at baseband (alternate '0's and '1' would produce a baseband frequency of 24kHz at 48Kbits). If this pseudo-random pattern was not inserted, there could be periods when long strips of binary '0's or '1's would be transmitted producing direct current signals unsuitable for transmission over local lines. This technique of pro-ducing a pseudo-random data pattern so that baseband signals in the required frequency range may be transmitted over local cables is known as a suppressed dc binary (SDCB).

At the Datel Modem No. 9 in the repeater station, the pseudo-random binary signal is re-shaped and used to amplitude modulate a 100kHz carrier. The modulated signal is then filtered and a single sideband between 60 to 104kHz is transmitted together with the 100kHz carrier frequency which is transmitted at a lower level. In the repeater station at the receive end, the Modem No. 9 produces a carrier which is synchronised in phase and frequency with the received suppressed carrier. This synchronous carrier is used to demodulate the 60-104kHz signal and reproduce the suppressed dc binary signal. In the Modem No. 8 at the receive terminal, the signal is decoded to present the originated data signals to the customer's terminal equipment.

During transmission, the operation of the Datel Modem No. 8 is controlled from the customer's terminal equipment. Datel 48K is a synchronous service and the timing may be provided by the Modem No. 8 or the customer's data terminal equipment.

Automatic Calling and Answering on the Public Switched Telephone Networks (CCITT V25)

There is increasing demand for data calls to be originated and received over the public switched telephone network without the need for human intervention. The Post Office has introduced Data Control Equipments which enable these facilities to be provided.

Data Control Equipment No 1 (DCE1)

The DCE1 can be provided in association with most standard facilities offered by Datel 200, 600, 2400 and 2400 Dial Up using the public switched telephone service. The installations may be arranged for manual or automatic answering. The facilities offered are as follows:

- automatic calling and manual answering;
- automatic calling and inland automatic answering;
- automatic calling and international automatic answering.

The DCE1 will be under the control of customers' computer equipment during all stages of the call (ie setting up, switching the modem to line and call clearance). The telephone numbers are stored within the terminal equipment in binary coded decimal form and are transmitted one digit at a time to the DCE1 which converts them into pulses, for operation of exchange equipment. Provision is made in the DCE1 for operation from a PABX extension where a prefix digit is required to gain access to the public exchange.

Data Control Equipment No 2 (DCE2)

The DCE2 has been designed to enable data terminals using Datel 200, 600, 2400 or 2400 Dial Up to answer automatically calls from overseas data terminals. The facilities provided by the DCE2 enable the disablement of echo suppressors, which are used on some intercontinental circuits, and, therefore, permit transmission of data both ways simultaneously. Once disabled, an echo suppressor will remain inoperative provided a tone (ie data signal) is maintained in at least one direction of transmission. Any cessation of tone occurring in both directions of transmission simultaneously, and exceeding 100 ms in duration, will allow an echo suppressor to become operative for the remainder of that call. Facilities for the automatic answering of inland data calls are available within PO modems 1, 2 and 7, but these are only suitable where operation is entirely within the UK.

The DCE2 conforms to CCITT V25 recommendations and employs the internationally agreed 2100 Hz tone for answering and echo suppressor disabling. Where a DCE2 is used, it will facilitate automatic answering on both inland and overseas calls.

Dataplex Services

The Post Office first introduced the Dataplex Service in 1971 primarily to meet the needs of time sharing computer bureaux to enable their remote users to access the computer via the public switched telephone network at local call charge rates. Since that time, additional facilities have been provided and two main services are now available: Dataplex 1 and Dataplex 2 using FDM and TDM techniques respectively. Dataplex Services are provided on a package basis; that is to say, a customer rents a complete system including multiplexors, lines and modems. Dataplex may be limited to use by one organisation or may be available on a wider basis with access to the system being gained over the public switched telephone network and/or low speed private circuits. Access to a Dataplex system is normally via standard Datel Services although in some cases where terminals and the remote multiplexor are sited in the same customer's premises, they may be directly connected. Usually, only the computer end multiplexor is sited on customers' premises with the remote multiplexor being housed in a Post Office Telephone Exchange or Repeater Station – this approach leads to an 'on the spot' maintenance service, a saving on line plant required for PSTN access circuits and avoids customers having to provide accommodation for the remote multiplexor, thus offering reduced cost and improved maintenance service. In practical terms, a Dataplex *Channel*[2] can be regarded as extending a Datel Service

---

[2] Although strictly speaking a *Channel* is defined as transmission only from A to B and a circuit provides a bothway transmission capability, ie A to B and B to A, we will for convenience use the term *Channel* to define a duplex transmission path derived from a multiplexor system to avoid confusion between the derived paths and the physical bearer or access circuits.

interface to a remote point, such as a distant computer interface. Because a number of Dataplex Channels are sharing one long distance circuit some limitations have to be accepted. For example, unlike Datel Services, alternate speech/data or outgoing call access on to the public switched network is not possible. However, these are very slight constraints when compared with the cost savings that can be achieved by the use of Dataplex compared with use of individual Datel Circuits.

Dataplex 1

The Dataplex 1 Service employs Frequency Division Multiplexing (FDM) techniques and enables up to six or twelve separate channels, each operating up to 110 bit/s to be derived from a 4-wire speech band circuit. The Dataplex 1 package is shown at figure 11.17. This Service is accessible only by terminals

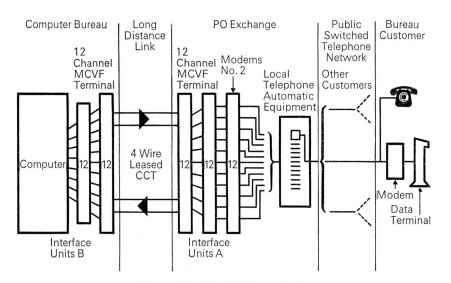

Figure 11.17   PO Dataplex 1

using the Datel 200 Service and thus the principle of a Dataplex 1 Channel is to extend an interface (CCITT V21) from a Post Office Datel Modem 2 situated at the remote exchange to the computer input port. This is achieved by serialising the parallel interchange circuit conditions produced at the Modem 2 and extending these in telegraph signalling form to the computer end where the signals are re-converted into parallel form for presentation to the computer. The method of operation imposes additional delays in timings on the various interchange circuits during setting up and clearance of a call.

Facilities

Six or twelve channel systems are available enabling up to six or up to twelve simultaneous duplex transmissions between user terminals and a computer, comprising public switched telephone network connections extended over a 240 Hz spaced Multi Channel Voice Frequency (MCVF) System.

Data transmission at data signalling rates of up to 110 bit/s only is provided. Computer bureau controlled backward busying of any channel is given by key operation.

Busying can be effected whilst a call is in progress so that when the caller clears down the channel is busied. This facility enables a computer port to be taken out of service without being seized by an incoming call.

'Lamps' at the computer site to indicate the state of each channel at any instant. The lamps indicate:

- calling signal — 'Data Set Ready';
- carrier detected;
- channel backward busied.

A 'reserve bearer circuit' is available between appropriate terminal repeater stations in case of failure.

Each Channel provides what is virtually a code independent transmission medium in each direction.

Because no speech facilities are available, unattended automatic answering mode of operation must be employed by the computer. It should be noted that 'Connect Data Set to Line' method of line switching must be used (*see* Chapter 6).

Equipment

Included within the Dataplex 1 Service is:

At the computer site —

- a group of Interface Units B
- MCVF equipment   } provided within one
- a control module with lamps and keys   } equipment rack

Between multiplexor sites —

- a 4-wire speech band circuit
- a reserve circuit between terminal repeater stations that can be switched in by the Post Office

At Post Office premises at the remote end —

- a group of Interface Units A
- MCVF equipment
- 6 or 12 Datel Modems 2 connected by local circuits to outlets of a final selector in the local exchange.

Dataplex 2

Dataplex 2 overcomes the limitations of Dataplex 1 in terms of Channel speed and Channel capacity. It employs character interleaved Time Division Multiplexing (TDM) techniques and can, typically, enable up to 51 simultaneous transmissions from terminals operating at 110 bit/s to be carried over a 4-wire speech band circuit; alternatively, it can handle a fewer number of channels operating at speeds up to 1200 bit/s (*see* Table 11.1). Access to Data-

Signalling rate of asynchronous inputs bit/s	Character Format (Signalling, elements)			Character Rate (char/s)	Circuit capacity of system	
					Signalling rate of Circuit T (Kbit/s)	
	START	DATA	STOP		2·4	4·8
110	1	8	2	10	25	51
134·5	1	7	1	14·8	18	38
150	1	8	2	13·6	16	33
200	1	8	2	18·2	12	25
300	1	8	1	30	7	16
600	1	8	1	60	3	7
1200	1	8	1	120	1*	3

*Other channels at lower signalling rates can be inserted

Table 11.1   Circuit capacity of PO Dataplex 2

plex 2 is usually via Datel Services (100, 200 or 600 service) operating over the public switched telephone network or speech or telegraph private circuits (*see* figure 11.18); exceptionally, where the remote multiplexor is sited on customer's premises, terminals incorporating a CCITT V24 interface may be directly connected.

The Dataplex 2 multiplexor system is designed to handle data only from character terminals, ie those using start-stop transmission. As explained in Chapter 9, the multiplexor strips off the start and stop bits to improve the efficiency of the system and these are re-applied at the demultiplexing stage. To enable interface control information to be passed over each channel and yet preserve full transparency for the data transmission, a single 'control'

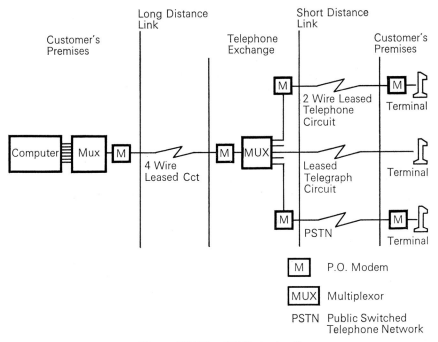

Figure 11.18   PO Dataplex 2

bit is added to each character or control code passed over the channel, the state of which determines whether it should be regarded as data or control.

The multiplexor can be regarded as comprising three parts:

- low speed input/output transmission units;
- processor and central control unit;
- high speed transmission modules.

The low speed transmission units consist of channel cards together with shelves of 16 or 32 card capacity. Each card is capable of operating at each of the low speed signalling rates available with Dataplex 2, and the speed required is selected by strapping.

Two types of card are available, one catering for normal duplex operation and the other where particular Datel 600 facilities are required to be extended over Dataplex 2. The Processor or Central Control Unit has a memory capacity to handle a maximum of 64 low speed channels independent of speed or code of the low speed transmissions. The processor can be programmed to handle a single transmission speed on all channels or a mix of speeds and transmission codes up to a maximum of seven. The object of this unit is to control the transfer of transmissions between the low speed input/output channels and related time slots on the high speed line(s) and vice-

versa. Additionally, the processor can be programmed to transfer transmissions in a particular time-slot on one high speed line to a given time-slot
on another high speed line without involving a low speed input/output
channel (*see* 'Through Circuit Facility'). A high speed transmission module
is required for each bearer circuit connected to the multiplexor and up to six
of these can be handled simultaneously by the processor unit. The data
transfer rate of each bearer circuit may be 2400 bit/s or 4800 bit/s as required
depending on whether a Post Office Datel Modem 7 or 15 is used.

Facilities

- Bearer rates of 2400 bit/s or 4800 bit/s.

- Data rates of 50, 75, 110, 134.5, 150, 200, 300, 600 or 1200 bit/s can be
multiplexed. The maximum number of channels at a given speed that can
be multiplexed on to a 2400 bit/s or 4800 bit/s bearer circuit is shown
in Table 11.1.

- Ability to handle up to seven different low speed data rates and/or
transmission codes per system.

- Connection to all Standard Datel 200 and 600 facilities together with
Datel 100 leased line facilities.

'Automatic bit rate and code selection (ABR)' — This facility is similar to that
described under Adaptive Speed Control in Chapter 9. The provision of an
ABR module at the remote node enables each one of a group of channels to
adapt its speed to match the speed of an incoming transmission. Character 'H'
is transmitted at the beginning of the message and the information received
by the multiplexor is sampled to determine the speed of that transmission.
The channel speed is then suitably adjusted and a similar process must next
take place in the computer equipment. Because this adaptive capability is not
dynamic, it is necessary when determining the bearer circuit capacity to
assume that all of the channels concerned are operating at the maximum of
the range of data rates to be handled. For example, a system with ABR
catering for 110, 134.5 and 300 bit/s terminal rates would have the bearer rate
capacity limited to X-300 bit/s channels.

'Hubbing' — This is the term used to describe the ability of Dataplex 2
multiplexor to serve up to six high speed bearer circuits: *see* figure 11.19.

'Through circuits' — This facility permits an intermediate multiplexor in a
Dataplex 2 network to pass data through without de-multiplexing. The use
of this facility can result in reduced circuit charges: *see* figure 11.20.

'Synchronous intermix' — Dataplex 2 has the capability of providing a single
synchronous 2400 bit/s channel together with asynchronous data. This
facility is provided within the Post Office Datel Modem 15 which can provide

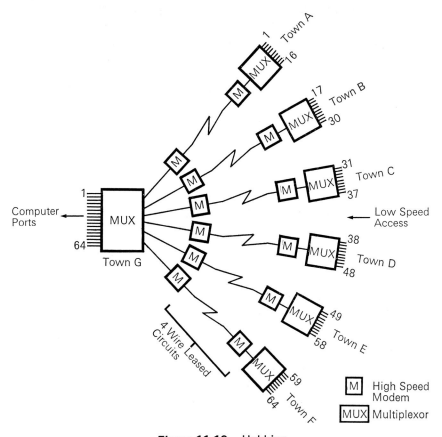

Figure 11.19 Hubbing

2×2400 bit/s channels (dual port mode) as an alternative to a single 4800 bit/s data stream: *see* figure 11.21.

'Backward busying' on channels connected to the public switched network by key control or control via the interface at the computer centre — This facility allows a busy condition to be applied during a call but which takes effect at the clearance of that call. Because no speech facilities are available, unattended automatic answering must be employed at the computer end.

'System test module' — Comprehensive customer controlled diagnostics are available without the need for external test equipment. This unit functions both as a monitor of system errors and as a channel by channel tester.

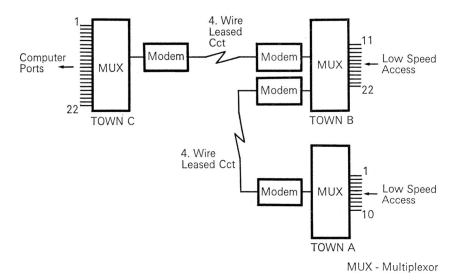

Figure 11.20   Through circuits

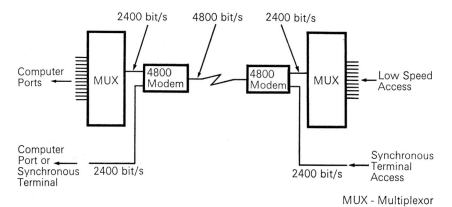

Figure 11.21   Synchronous intermix

Equipment

Included within the Dataplex 2 Services is:

On the computer site —

- – a multiplexor unit
- – a system test module ⎫
- – one or more 2400 or 4800 bit/s modems ⎬ mounted in a rack
⎭

Between multiplexor sites —

- – a four-wire speech band circuit

At the remote node, usually on PO premises —

- – a multiplexor unit
- – a 2400 or 4800 bit/s modem
- – an ABR module (optional)
- – low speed Datel Modems
- – connections to final selector outlets and/or low speed speech or telegraph circuits

Attachments of Private Apparatus to Post Office Lines

The British Post Office has the responsibility to provide and maintain an efficient telecommunications system. Whilst actively encouraging the use of data communications within the United Kingdom and playing a leading role in international data communications, it has, nevertheless, a responsibility towards all users of the system and for the safety of its own maintenance personnel.

The Post Office conditions for the attachment of private apparatus to the UK network reflects this responsibility. Before examining these conditions, it should be clearly understood that the Post Office cannot be responsible to the user for the efficiency or otherwise of the private apparatus connected to the network. The attachment of non-Post Office equipment may be permitted provided that it fulfils the conditions specified by the Post Office. These conditions do not cover the efficiency of the equipment from the user's point-of-view, and the Post Office's permission to connect equipment is in no way a guarantee that it will work satisfactorily.

The first condition laid down by the Post Office is that all private equipment connected to the network should be intrinsically safe. This means that the electrical conditions produced by the equipment are within clearly defined safety limits and cannot endanger the Post Office engineers, who maintain the telecommunications system. Secondly, the signals produced by the private apparatus must not cause interference to the service of other users of the system. Thirdly, the Post Office must be satisfied that there are adequate arrangements for maintaining the apparatus.

There is a fourth condition which only applies to apparatus connected to exchange lines. The Post Office employs two types of voice frequency signalling systems for dialling over 25 miles. It must, therefore, guard against interference with these systems by ensuring that the signals passing over the public switched telephone network are controlled by the Post Office. This sometimes results in a situation where a device is given permission to be connected to a private circuit but not to an exchange line.

Like most other PTTs the Post Office asks that should a fault develop on a circuit with private apparatus connected to it, that the fault is proved to be on the line before it is reported. The Post Office has a nationwide maintenance organisation and if this condition was not imposed there could be abortive and costly maintenance visits by Post Office staff.

12 International Data Communications

The development of long distance international communications was a natural step following in the wake of technological advances and progress in national telecommunications. Additionally, with the pressures generated by greater international interaction, international telecommunications have developed at a rapid rate, striving to meet the demands.

International data communications at present have to utilise the existing telecommunications systems, namely telephone and telegraph plant and techniques. In this respect, data transmission has to be tailored to the appropriate system. As a consequence, a review of the international telecommunications system is justified, in order to appreciate the manner in which international data transmission rides on the back of international telecommunications.

International Telecommunications
A historical review produces definite technological cycles, each contributing major advances for international communications. Some cycles may seem to undermine previous advances, but overall each enhances the system, quickening the pace as shown in figure 12.1 overleaf.

Telegraphy (cable)
The first attempt to breach the international barrier was across the English Channel in 1850; technically it was a success. Unfortunately, shortly after

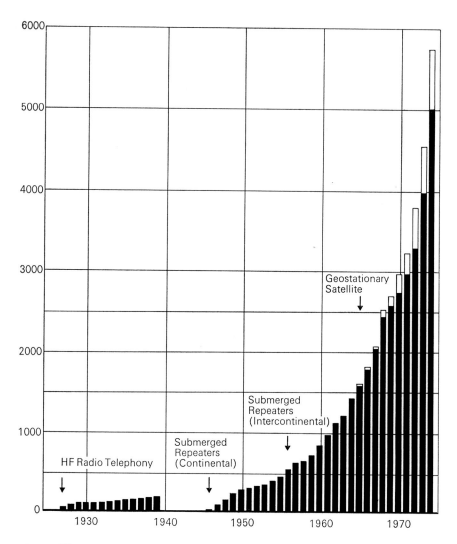

Figure 12.1   Total international public telephone circuits – UK

being made operational the cable had an argument with a French fisherman's trawl, and lost! However, the technical success encouraged further attempts, fortunately with longer term survival.

This relatively small step led to the next natural step, trans-Atlantic. August 1858 saw the first trans-Atlantic telegraphic messages. More permanent telegraphy across the Atlantic did not materialise until the successful laying of a cable in 1866 by the 'Great Eastern' cable ship. From 1866 onward, telegraph companies from both sides of the Atlantic invested in telegraph cables and provided a network of cables across the North Atlantic.

On other routes, the need to communicate to the British Empire hastened the development of a complex network of telegraph cables. The Eastern Telegraph Company, a forerunner of Cable and Wireless Limited, was formed to undertake the development of the networks. Their success is summed up in figure 12.2 overleaf.

Telegraphy (radio)
The challenge to cable telegraphy came just as it was reaching a dominant position. In 1901, Marconi and Kemp successfully transmitted across the Atlantic using the new technology of radio. The ensuing developments were rapid, building upon the flexibility that was not available to the physical point to point cable telegraphy. By 1907, radio telegraphy had developed into a commercial service under the control of Marconi, with plans for a worldwide system of short-wave Marconi wireless telegraph beam stations.

Telephony (radio)
As the radio telegraph cycle gradually undermined the further development of cable telegraphy, the complementary development of radio telephony enhanced radio transmission techniques. Success in radio telephony came in a trans-Atlantic call in 1926. Further technical developments using high frequency (HF) carriers and, in 1937, single side band (SSB) techniques encouraged the development of the trans-Atlantic telephony service.

Telephony (cable)
Whilst there were substantial improvements in the quality of radio telephony, there was a limit to its improvement relative to the quality offered by inland (ie national) trunk systems. As a result of the technical development of inland multi-channel carrier systems and coaxial cables, a 12-channel coaxial cable was laid between England and Holland in 1937.

The expansion of cable telephony was dependent upon the solution of several technical problems related to the long distances involved. Firstly, repeaters,

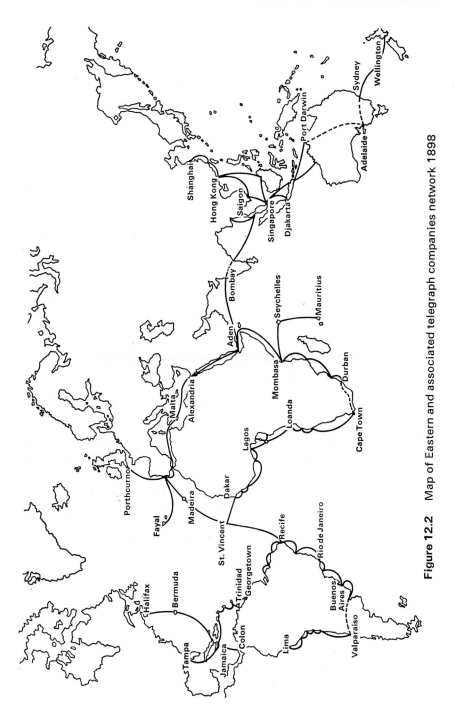

Figure 12.2   Map of Eastern and associated telegraph companies network 1898

which could be easily accessed for maintenance on land, had to be developed in order to withstand the harsh sea-floor environment for substantial periods without attention. Secondly, component reliability was essential to maintain the stability of the amplifiers. Thirdly, power feeding, and finally the physical problems related to accurately laying cable with bulky repeaters.

Success was gradual but definite; 1943 saw the first repeatered cable, which was laid across the Irish Sea, 1945 a repeatered coaxial cable to Germany and in 1950 a cable across the English Channel with four repeaters in tandem. The Atlantic was traversed in 1956 by TAT1, a 36 circuit cable with 51 repeaters.

Plate 12.1   PO cable laying ship – *CS Alert*

Each step brought with it further technical improvements which resulted from close collaboration in technical research on both sides of the Atlantic. The confidence generated by the above success led to a large and quickening programme of cable laying which is still continuing today (*see* plate 12.1). The improvements and their scale is exemplified in the comparative table on the following page.

Canada/UK – Cantat I & Cantat II

	Cantat I	Cantat II
Date	1961	1974
Number of speech channels	80	1840
Number of repeaters	90	490
Cost per circuit between cable terminals	£100,000	£16,500

Telephony (satellite)

Less than two years after the successful laying of TAT1 (1956) a new techno-logical cycle was heralded with the launching of the Russian satellite, Sputnik, in October 1957. The ensuing telecommunications developments, envisaged by Arthur C Clarke in 1945,[1] have materialised from the 'spin-off' of advances made in space technology.

July 1962 marked the date of the launch of Telstar, an experimental tele-communications satellite that was a forerunner of the present day geo-stationary satellites owned and operated by Intelsat. The pace of development has been very rapid; in the space of 10 years commercial communications satellites have provided over 60 per cent of the world's inter-continental circuits. Additionally, because of the wide bandwidths available, colour television has been provided on a global basis.

The most attractive feature of satellite communications is that it provides a flexible communications medium enabling direct communications on low density routes that would have been uneconomic on a physical cable basis. With additional flexibility offered by continuing technical advances, such as the spot beams on the Intelsat IV satellites which concentrate power into smaller areas on the earth's surface and so give greater circuit capacity; and such as SPADE,[2] which enables circuit flexibility between countries on a demand assigned rather than a pre-assigned basis satellites promise a great future. The improvements made since Early Bird's day are shown by the following table:

	Early Bird (Intelsat I)	Intelsat IV
Date of launch	April 1965	March 1971
Design life	$1\frac{1}{2}$ years	7 years
Number of circuits per satellite	240	5,000
Cost per $\frac{1}{2}$ circuit per year	$32,000	$9,000

---

[1] A. C. Clarke – 'Extra Terrestrial Relays', *Wireless World,* October 1945.

[2] SPADE – Single Channel per Carrier, Pulse Code Modulation, Multiple Access, Demand Assignment Equipment.

With continual advances in space, complementary development on the ground is vital to exploit the maximum benefits. For example, the latest UK ground station aerial, Goonhilly No. 3, was made operational in August 1972. This latest addition complements the two other existing aerials at Goonhilly. Their respective utilisations are as follows:

Aerial	Satellite	Coverage
Goonhilly 1	Indian Ocean	Australia, Far East, Middle East, E Africa
Goonhilly 2	Atlantic Major Path	North America
Goonhilly 3	Atlantic Primary	N and S America, Middle East, Africa

Plate 12.2   Goonhilly satellite earth station – Aerial 3

The attractiveness of investment in satellite communications may, at first sight, seem to undermine any further investment in submarine cables. However, they are better regarded as a complementary rather than competitive means of transmission.

On high density routes, and also as a safeguard against failure, satellite and cable systems will operate hand in hand. The parallel expansion of the North American satellite routes and the laying of TAT6 (1976 – 4000 circuits) reflects this complementary development.

For operational reasons, there will always be a need for submarine cables. Satellites have a limitation resulting from the propagation time of about a quarter second caused by the 70,000 km leg to the satellite and back. A reply on a two-way voice circuit will, therefore, take a half second to arrive back. A 'double hop' making use of two satellites in turn will give a one second delay, making conversation extremely difficult. Hence, for speech conversations, only a one satellite link in a connection is practicable. Thus, for some calls a cable link is required to extend the calls beyond the range of one satellite. In this respect, they are truly operationally complementary.

International Subscriber Dialling (ISD)

As the telecommunications systems of the world become more sophisticated, so countries are able to extend the range of services offered. A major development has been the extension of subscriber dialling facilities to the international service (ISD). This is a relatively new service in all countries and is being introduced as the appropriate equipment and capacity is installed. ISD has been available in the UK since 1964, when it was introduced in London, and it is now being extended throughout the UK. The range of services enables, at present, subscribers with ISD to dial about 65 per cent of the telephones in the world through most exchanges in 22 countries.

Future developments

In 1973/74, the UK originated some 61 million international calls; should the current annual growth rate of approximately 22 per cent continue, as is expected, the influence of international telecommunications will gather momentum. There will be a gradual extension of the services to other countries and it is anticipated that by 1980 some 85 per cent of all UK international calls will be subscriber dialled. Technical progress will continue to contribute to the expansion of international telecommunications. The promise of new transmission plant, such as waveguides, optical fibre cables, and electronic switching, will support the current potential of space communications.

International Organisations

The need for co-operation, guidance and standards in telecommunications was recognised a long time ago and is exemplified by the establishment of the International Telecommunications Union (ITU) in 1863. The expansion of international telecommunications and the resulting interaction between telecommunications authorities produced the gradual evolution of inter-national organisations, having the common aim of easing the business of international telecommunications. Three of the most important of these are described in the following paragraphs.

International Telegraph and Telephone Consultative Committee (CCITT)

The ITU conference of 1925, held in Paris, decided that the increasing complexity of international telephone services deserved more regular study than was possible at the periodic ITU conferences. As a result, the 'Comité Consultatif International des Communications Telephoniques a Grande Distance' (CCIF) was established as an integral part of the ITU. The overall objective was 'the study of standards regulating technical and operating questions for international long distance telephony'.

In 1956, the CCIF joined its telegraph partner CCIT, also established in 1925, to form a single committee, CCITT. Their specialised secretariats were amalgamated and utilised the same working methods.

These were to study questions, raised by the CCITT members at plenary assemblies, using specialised study groups and joint working parties. (*See* figure 12.3.) These groups were to report back to the committee at the

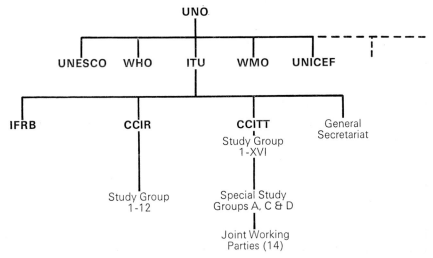

Figure 12.3 Organisation structure of CCITT

appropriate plenary sessions, held every four years, with the results of their investigations.

The plenary sessions of the committee are then charged with the responsibility of deciding the appropriate standard based upon the presented evidence. The resulting decision is then endorsed as a CCITT Recommendation; not a mandatory decision, strictly a recommendation. Naturally, as a corporate recommendation, there are positive benefits in adopting the recommendations and, generally, they are adopted by the member countries throughout the world.

Some of CCITT recommendations at 1972 (fifth plenary session) applying to data transmission

V Series
V2   – Power levels for data transmission over telephone lines
V3   – International Alphabet Number 5
V10 – Use of the telex network for data transmission at the modulation rate of 50 bauds
V15 – Use of acoustic couplers for data transmission
V21 – 200 baud modem standardised for use in the general switched telephone network
V22 – Standardisation of data signalling rates for synchronous operation in the general switched telephone network
V23 – 600/1200 baud modem standardised for use in the general switched telephone network
V25 – Automatic calling and/or answering on the general switched telephone network including the disabling of echo suppressors on manually established calls
V26 – 2400 bit/s modem standardised for use on four-wire leased circuits
V26 – BIS 2400/1200 bit/s modem standardised for use in the general switched telephone network
V27 – 4800 bit/s modem standardised for use on leased circuits
V35 – Data transmission at 48 kilo bit/s using 60 to 108kHz group band circuits
V51 – Organisation of the maintenance of international telephone type circuits used for data transmission.

X Series
Data transmission over Public Data Networks
Section 1 – Services and Facilities (X1, X2)
Section 2 – Data Terminal Equipment and Interfaces (X20, X21, X30, X31, X32, X33)
Section 3 – Transmission Signalling and Switching (X40, X50, X70)
Section 4 – Network Parameters
Section 5 – Charging Methods and Accounting.

European Conference of Postal and Telecommunications Administrations (CEPT)

A more recently established international organisation, the CEPT, was formally inaugurated in 1959. The organisation consists of European administrations working together on a consultative basis (26 member administrations). The scope and objectives of CEPT are intentionally expressed in terms capable of wide interpretation so that it may develop in a flexible and co-operative manner.

'The essential aims of the Conference are the establishment of closer relations between member administrations and the harmonising and practical improvement of their administrative and technical services' (Article 4.1 CEPT provisions).

The plenary assembly of CEPT meets approximately every two years, being supported by two main committees, Postal and Telecommunications (*see* figure 12.4). They generally convene to coincide with the plenary assembly,

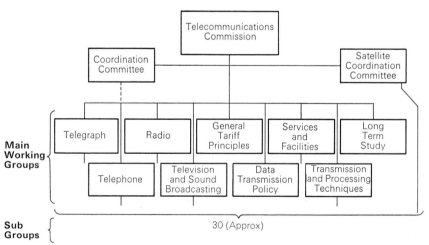

Figure 12.4 Organisation structure of CEPT

though the telecommunications committee hold meetings in the intervening years. It has been the practice that the head of the delegation to the plenary assembly be a member of the respective administration's Ministry of Posts and Telecommunications or equivalent government department. The two major committees are supported by working parties and sub-groups who meet or exchange information on a regular basis. There is no permanent secretariat or headquarters, the management of CEPT being undertaken in turn by the member administrations.

The scope of the CEPT telecommunications committee can be seen from the organisation chart, the responsibilities of the working groups naturally break down the general areas for detailed discussions. The recommendations set out by CEPT tend to be strictly for the development of European telecommunications, though they may have influence at CCITT when they are involved in discussions on the same topic. CEPT, in this case, gives an alternative to CCITT for a European oriented development, with the additional flexibility of shorter plenary terms.

Apart from its role for setting codes of practice for European PTTs, in parallel with CCITT, CEPT can also act as a sounding board for telecommunications development. In the data communications field, the most notable example has been the Eurodata study. This study, which was suggested within the services and facilities committee, was established under the aegis of CEPT. Those CEPT members (17 in all) who were interested contributed to a detailed study of data communications in Europe up to 1985. The specific objectives of Eurodata were:

' – to establish the nature and future characteristics of those activities giving rise to the need for data communication, both within and between European countries and between those countries and the other main communications centres of the world.

– to provide forecasts up to 1985 of all relevant characteristics of data traffic.'

The study report was published in 1973 and provided those CEPT PTTs who financed the study with information to assist in development of data communications facilities.

International Telecommunications Satellite Organisation (INTELSAT)

The development of satellite communications systems brought about an essential parallel development of international co-operation. Intelsat was established in 1964 to organize a commercial satellite communications system. The initial membership was 11, but this now stands at 85 member nations (March 1974).

The financial investment and voting quotas of Intelsat members are directly related to the amount of use made of the system. The US is the largest user of the system, with an investment share of 37.5 per cent, followed by the UK with a share of 10.8 per cent.

Intelsat's policy issues and overall direction are controlled largely by the Board of Governors, a body which represents 60 of the 85 member nations. Day-to-day matters are looked after by an internationally composed executive organ and also by Comsat, the US Communications Satellite Corporation which is responsible for technical and operational functions. Figure 12.5 illustrates the relationship of these bodies and various other organs of Intelsat.

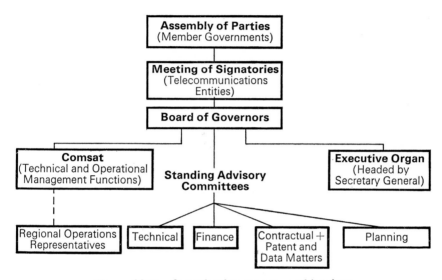

Figure 12.5   Organisation structure of Intelsat

Users, for example, the British Post Office, lease satellite capacity from Intelsat and in turn collect revenue from their own subscribers.

The satellites, launched by NASA, are manufactured by US firms but some work is sub-contracted out to non-US firms (BAC in UK). However, the earth stations are owned and controlled by the local telecommunications authorities.

International Data Communications Services (Available from UK)

Prior to 1965, data transmission between the UK and countries abroad was carried on private leased circuits, usually point to point 50 baud telegraph type. Post 1965, with the development of more attractive data transmission services for national needs and with the pressures from users it became technically feasible and appropriate to introduce International Datel Services. Additionally, speech grade private circuits were made available for data transmission.

In order to achieve an international service, mutual agreement of feasibility and willingness was required between the appropriate countries. To this end, the introduction of a series of CCITT Recommendations eased the implementation of these services.

> CCITT V10 – 50 bauds (telex)
> CCITT V21 – 200 bauds (telephone)
> CCITT V23 – 600/1200 bauds (telephone)

International Datel Services

In the international service, the term Datel has been adopted to refer only to data transmission using the public telephone or telex systems. In addition to International Datel, data transmission may be arranged with other countries over leased telegraph type or telephone circuits, whether or not International Datel Service is available to the country concerned.

International Datel 100 Service

(Introduced April 1968.)

This service is designed to allow serial transmission of digital data at speeds of 50 bit/s using the public telex network without the need for modems. Calls are set up and cleared with an exchange of answer-back codes. When either party wishes to introduce data transmission equipment into the connection a signal 'SSSS' needs to be transmitted.

Terminal equipment can include the following:

– A teleprinter with a tape punching attachment which forms an integral part of the telex installation.

– Automatic transmitter.

– A switching device which allows connection of customer's data processing equipment for which permission has been granted by the Post Office to the international telex network.

For the majority of countries in Europe, the only restriction in the codes used for International Datel 100 is that no more than seven elements of start polarity may be transmitted consecutively.

To some countries, Datel 100 transmission is restricted to the use of five unit code with stop-start signals according to the structure of International Alphabet Number 2. Users may, however, decide how combinations of characters should be used for various components of the data information. Where this restriction exists and users wish to use data equipment capable of responding to codes other than five unit code with start-stop signals, the difficulty may be overcome by using user-provided regrouping converters at the sending and receiving terminals.

International Datel 200 Service

(Introduced May 1969.)

International Datel 200 calls to Europe may be set up either by using International Subscriber Dialling (ISD) over the international telephone network or via the appropriate international telephone operator. In the latter case, in order to minimise possible sources of error arising on calls connected via the switchboard, for example, timing 'pips', users should advise the operator that they are making a Datel call and ask for the 'Uninterrupted Facility'.

The Post Office Modem Number 2 has been designed in accordance with internationally agreed standards for the serial transmission of data over the international telephone network.

International Datel 600 Service

(Introduced July 1965.)

This service provides half duplex serial transmission within the speed range up to 600 to 1200 bit/s using the public telephone network.

Calls to Europe may be set up either by using ISD or via the international telephone operator in the same manner as for International Datel 200. For calls outside Europe, even if ISD facilities are available for speech calls, the user on reaching the International exchange must ask for the International Datel operator.

The Post Office Modem Number 1 for Datel 600 conforms with the CCITT recommendations for serial transmission up to 600 to 1200 bit/s and can be provided with a 75 bit/s return channel for control purposes.

Restrictions to International Datel Services

As a result of utilising a network designed for voice communications to transmit data, there are certain drawbacks. On an international level these restrictions can be compounded by other factors.

Echo suppressors

On satellite and long distance inter-continental cable circuits, (ie beyond Europe), in order to offer a satisfactory quality of voice communication, echo suppression is inserted. The operation of the equipment is designed to block the return channel to prevent the time-delayed echo which will impair the quality of speech communications.

For the data communications user, it may be essential to have the return channel open (eg for 75 bit/s control procedures). To offer this facility, it is necessary to allow the customer to disable the echo suppressor; this is done by utilising the disabling facility in the echo suppressor unit. On switching a data set to line, 2100 Hz tone is transmitted which activates the disabling facility prior to the transmission of data. This may be done automatically on answer (in the UK by a DCE2A) or manually during the call. The return path is held open throughout the transmission. At the end of transmission, following a 100 ms pause, the echo suppressors are brought back into operation.

Not all echo suppressors have the disabling facility, which is one of the reasons why all inter-continental calls must, at present, go via the International Datel operator.

Time assignment speech interpolation (TASI)

Due to the pressure generated by the demand for international telephony, a successful attempt was made to utilise the existing plant more efficiently. TASI was the result of the venture; it was designed to enable 74 telephone circuits (cable) to be connected internationally using 37 channels (*see* figure 12.6).

The dynamic allocation of channels in response to actual conversational periods was based upon 'normal' speech characteristics over telephone links.

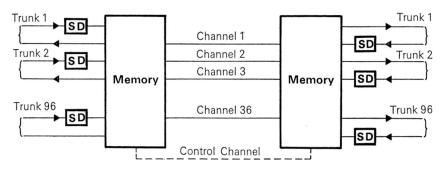

Maximum of 96 Trunks into 36 Channels—
in practice only about 74 Trunks connected at a time

SD =Speech-Detectors

Figure 12.6 TASI – Time Assignment Speech Interpolation

The equipment samples, in time, a telephone conversation many thousand times a second. When making a call, a caller only takes up about 50 per cent of the time and is silent for the remainder. By fast electronic switching, it is possible to utilise these silent periods to interleave other conversations.

Data transmission, unfortunately, does not conform with the 'normal' speech pattern. In fact, because data transmission usually contains no pauses, a call would normally lock out one of the channels for the duration of the call. In doing so, it has repercussions on the balance of TASI equipment which may effect the quality of speech communication.

As it is the responsibility of the Post Office to protect all users of their services, data transmission calls are routed via non-TASI circuits. Because of TASI problems and the operational requirements for echo-suppressor disabling equipment, data calls are established by an operator. In this way, it is possible to route the calls on the designated circuits to give the required transmission path. This is schematically shown in figure 12.7.

(NB   TASI equipment is restricted to inter-continental, ie non-European, circuits.)

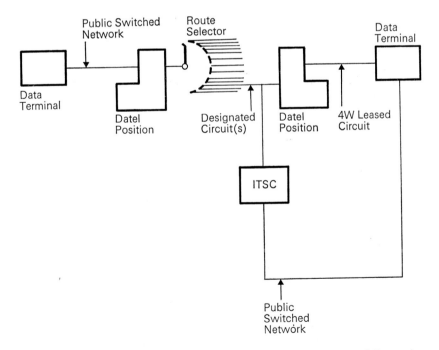

Figure 12.7   Example of international Datel 600 call (beyond Europe)

International Datel Service – USA

Because of the different telecommunication organisation in the USA, the development of the International Datel Services to the USA have been restricted.

Historically, the Federal Communication Commission (FCC) granted monopoly rights for international telegraphy to three private companies. (Western Union International (WUI), RCA Global Communications and ITT World Communications). These rights were extended to the data transmission field in 1965. The outcome for the UK Post Office was that they were precluded from using the trans-Atlantic public switched telephone network for Datel calls.

Consequently, international Datel calls to the USA must be manually connected at the international exchange via a dedicated data circuit to one of the three carrier companies. The carriers extend the call either over their own, or other private-wire networks, or over the Bell Dataphone network. In the case of the Dataphone network, calls are not permitted direct connection. When the data communications subscriber wishes to make an International Datel call to the USA, the operator must be advised of the carrier facilities required (*see* figure 12.8).

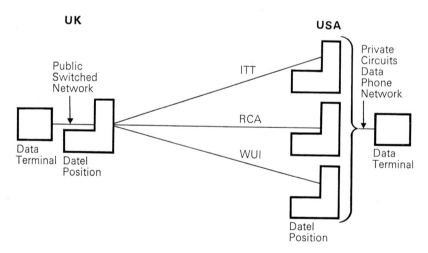

Figure 12.8   International Datel service to USA

International Leased Circuits for Data Transmission

Leased circuits play an important role in the field of international data communications. The attractiveness of leased circuits may be based on an economic loading against switched dialled services, or because users require higher speeds than those offered by the current International Datel Services, or, lastly, because of the need for speedy reliable access to distant users. In addition, there has been the development of more complex international leased systems. Private networks comprising high and low speed circuits to link a number of countries, together with multi-access points within the country, has enabled airlines, banks, hotels, shipping, computer time sharing organisations and the like to operate their data communications efficiently. The use of multiplexing equipment on leased circuits has also been permitted by a number of PTTs.

International leased circuits are provided for a customer's exclusive use between the selected premises. Arrangements for providing the various types of international leased circuits naturally vary from location to location. Depending on the tariffs, circuits can be used exclusively (eg for data transmission or for alternate speech/data and speech/facsimile), and can provide data transmission equivalent to Datel 200 and Datel 600; but, in practice, with a special quality circuit and with other modulation techniques, higher speeds than the current Datel Services can be achieved. In addition, telephone circuits grouped to give 48 kHz bandwidth can be made available for high speed data up to 72Kbit/s approximately. In general, 48 kHz circuits cannot be made available at short notice.

Future Developments

Datel services
Negotiations are continuously being undertaken to extend the International Datel Services to other countries. The expansion will be tailored in step with technical developments in the international telecommunications system and with the demand of users for additional Datel connections.

The range of International Datel Services offered on existing and new routes is likely to be extended, reflecting the developments of data transmission services, nationally and internationally.

Leased circuits
Leased circuits and leased circuit networks will grow in those areas where it is seen that the facilities offered by the public networks do not meet the requirements of a particular user; or, alternatively, where the level of activity in voice, data and message content is such as to make leased circuits an economic proposition. The growth of leased circuit networks is likely to continue to be hindered by the limited capabilities of interworking with public and other

private networks. The restrictions may be due to physical incompatibility of the networks or due to the objections of telecommunications authorities to the multi-user and common carrier aspects of interworking.

Data Communications Services Available Internationally

The basic information given was correct as at January 1975. However, detailed and up-to-date information is available from the points of contact shown. Information on the USA is at the end of this section.

Australia

Public tele-graph up to 50 bit/s	Private tele-graph up to 50 bit/s	Private tele-graph up to 110 bit/s	Private tele-graph up to 200 bit/s	Public tele-graph up to 200 bit/s	Public tele-phone up to 200 bit/s	Public tele-phone up to 300 bit/s	Public tele-phone up to 600 bit/s	Public tele-phone up to 1200 bit/s	Public tele-phone up to 2400 bit/s	Public tele-phone up to 4800 bit/s	Public tele-phone up to 9600 bit/s
✓	✓		1		1	1	1	1			

Private tele-phone up to 200 bit/s	Private tele-phone up to 300 bit/s	Private tele-phone up to 600 bit/s	Private tele-phone up to 1200 bit/s	Private tele-phone up to 2400 bit/s	Private tele-phone up to 4800 bit/s	Private tele-phone up to 9600 bit/s	Other public switched services	Other private services	Wide-band services	Special data network plans	PTT condi-tions for service
1	1	1	1	1	1				1	5	5

Key:

1 – PTT modem only
2 – PTT or private modem
3 – Unguaranteed speed
4 – Special conditions
5 – Details from PTT
6 – Approved private modem

Point of contact:

Data Communications Section
Telecommunications Division, PMG Department
199 William Street, Melbourne, Victoria 3001
Telephone No: 6307833
Telex No: AA 30146

Belgium

Public tele-graph up to 50 bit/s	Public tele-graph up to 200 bit/s	Private tele-graph up to 50 bit/s	Private tele-graph up to 110 bit/s	Private tele-graph up to 200 bit/s	Public tele-phone up to 200 bit/s	Public tele-phone up to 300 bit/s	Public tele-phone up to 600 bit/s	Public tele-phone up to 1200 bit/s	Public tele-phone up to 2400 bit/s	Public tele-phone up to 4800 bit/s	Public tele-phone up to 9600 bit/s
✓	4	✓	✓	✓	1	1	1	1	1		

Private tele-phone up to 200 bit/s	Private tele-phone up to 300 bit/s	Private tele-phone up to 600 bit/s	Private tele-phone up to 1200 bit/s	Private tele-phone up to 2400 bit/s	Private tele-phone up to 4800 bit/s	Private tele-phone up to 9600 bit/s	Other public switched services	Other private services	Wide-band services	Special data network plans	PTT condi-tions for service
1	1	1	1	1	6	6		1	5	5	5

Key:
1 – PTT modem only
2 – PTT or private modem
3 – Unguaranteed speed
4 – Special conditions
5 – Details from PTT
6 – Approved private modem

Point of contact:
Régie des Télégraphes et des Téléphones
Rue des Palais, 42 Department RN
1030 Bruxelles
Telephone No: 02 2184787
Telex No: 25130 DEP RN B

Canada (TCTS)

Public tele-graph up to 50 bit/s	Public tele-graph up to 200 bit/s	Private tele-graph up to 50 bit/s	Private tele-graph up to 110 bit/s	Private tele-graph up to 200 bit/s	Public tele-phone up to 200 bit/s	Public tele-phone up to 300 bit/s	Public tele-phone up to 600 bit/s	Public tele-phone up to 1200 bit/s	Public tele-phone up to 2400 bit/s	Public tele-phone up to 4800 bit/s	Public tele-phone up to 9600 bit/s
✓			✓		2	2	2	2	2	2	2

Private tele-phone up to 200 bit/s	Private tele-phone up to 300 bit/s	Private tele-phone up to 600 bit/s	Private tele-phone up to 1200 bit/s	Private tele-phone up to 2400 bit/s	Private tele-phone up to 4800 bit/s	Private tele-phone up to 9600 bit/s	Other public switched services	Other private services	Wide-band services	Special data network plans	PTT condi-tions for service
2	2	2	2	2	2	2	5	5	5	5	5

Key:

1 – PTT modem only
2 – PTT or private modem
3 – Unguaranteed speed
4 – Special conditions
5 – Details from PTT
6 – Approved private modem

Point of contact:

The Market Support Centre
Computer Communications Group
Trans-Canada Telephone System
160 Elgin Street, Ottawa, Ontario
Telephone No: 613 237 6540
Telex No: 610562 8969

Denmark

Public tele-graph up to 50 bit/s	Public tele-graph up to 200 bit/s	Private tele-graph up to 50 bit/s	Private tele-graph up to 110 bit/s	Private tele-graph up to 200 bit/s	Public tele-phone up to 200 bit/s	Public tele-phone up to 300 bit/s	Public tele-phone up to 600 bit/s	Public tele-phone up to 1200 bit/s	Public tele-phone up to 2400 bit/s	Public tele-phone up to 4800 bit/s	Public tele-phone up to 9600 bit/s
✓		✓	✓	1	1	1	1	1	1		

Private tele-phone up to 200 bit/s	Private tele-phone up to 300 bit/s	Private tele-phone up to 600 bit/s	Private tele-phone up to 1200 bit/s	Private tele-phone up to 2400 bit/s	Private tele-phone up to 4800 bit/s	Private tele-phone up to 9600 bit/s	Other public switched services	Other private services	Wide-band services	Special data network plans	PTT condi-tions for service
1	1	1	1	1	1	2	5	5	1	5	5

Key:

1 – PTT modem only
2 – PTT or private modem
3 – Unguaranteed speed
4 – Special conditions
5 – Details from PTT
6 – Approved private modem

Point of contact:

General Directorate of Posts and Telegraphs
Telecommunications Service
17 Farvergade, DK 1007 København
Telephone No: 45 111 6605 360
Telex No: 22999

Finland

Public tele-graph up to 50 bit/s	Public tele-graph up to 200 bit/s	Private tele-graph up to 50 bit/s	Private tele-graph up to 110 bit/s	Private tele-graph up to 200 bit/s	Public tele-phone up to 200 bit/s	Public tele-phone up to 300 bit/s	Public tele-phone up to 600 bit/s	Public tele-phone up to 1200 bit/s	Public tele-phone up to 2400 bit/s	Public tele-phone up to 4800 bit/s	Public tele-phone up to 9600 bit/s
✓		✓	✓	✓	1	1	1	1	1		

Private tele-phone up to 200 bit/s	Private tele-phone up to 300 bit/s	Private tele-phone up to 600 bit/s	Private tele-phone up to 1200 bit/s	Private tele-phone up to 2400 bit/s	Private tele-phone up to 4800 bit/s	Private tele-phone up to 9600 bit/s	Other public switched services	Other private services	Wide-band services	Special data network plans	PTT condi-tions for service
2	2	2	2	2	2	2					5

Point of contact:

General Direction of Posts and Telegraphs
Telegraph Division, Box 527
SF 00101 Helsinki 10
Telephone No: 90 7041
Telex No: 12 517

Key:

1 — PTT modem only
2 — PTT or private modem
3 — Unguaranteed speed
4 — Special conditions
5 — Details from PTT
6 — Approved private modem

France

Public tele-graph up to 50 bit/s	Public tele-graph up to 200 bit/s	Private tele-graph up to 50 bit/s	Private tele-graph up to 110 bit/s	Private tele-graph up to 200 bit/s	Public tele-phone up to 200 bit/s	Public tele-phone up to 300 bit/s	Public tele-phone up to 600 bit/s	Public tele-phone up to 1200 bit/s	Public tele-phone up to 2400 bit/s	Public tele-phone up to 4800 bit/s	Public tele-phone up to 9600 bit/s
✓	✓	✓	✓	✓	6	6	2	2			

Private tele-phone up to 200 bit/s	Private tele-phone up to 300 bit/s	Private tele-phone up to 600 bit/s	Private tele-phone up to 1200 bit/s	Private tele-phone up to 2400 bit/s	Private tele-phone up to 4800 bit/s	Private tele-phone up to 9600 bit/s	Other public switched services	Other private services	Wide-band services	Special data network plans	PTT condi-tions for service
6	6	2	2	4	4	4	5	5	5	5	5

Key:

1 – PTT modem only
2 – PTT or private modem
3 – Unguaranteed speed
4 – Special conditions
5 – Details from PTT
6 – Approved private modem

Point of contact:

Ministere des PTT, Sous Direction de la
Téléinformatique et des Réseaux Spécialises
20 Avenue de Segur, 75700 Paris
Telephone No: 551 46 46
Telex No: 25310

Greece

Public telegraph up to 50 bit/s	Public telegraph up to 200 bit/s	Private telegraph up to 50 bit/s	Private telegraph up to 110 bit/s	Private telegraph up to 200 bit/s	Public telephone up to 200 bit/s	Public telephone up to 300 bit/s	Public telephone up to 600 bit/s	Public telephone up to 1200 bit/s	Public telephone up to 2400 bit/s	Public telephone up to 4800 bit/s	Public telephone up to 9600 bit/s
√		√	√		6	6	6	6			

Private telephone up to 200 bit/s	Private telephone up to 300 bit/s	Private telephone up to 600 bit/s	Private telephone up to 1200 bit/s	Private telephone up to 2400 bit/s	Private telephone up to 4800 bit/s	Private telephone up to 9600 bit/s	Other public switched services	Other private services	Wide-band services	Special data network plans	PTT conditions for service
6	6	6	6	6	6	6			4		5

Key:

1 – PTT modem only
2 – PTT or private modem
3 – Unguaranteed speed
4 – Special conditions
5 – Details from PTT
6 – Approved private modem

Point of contact:

The Hellenic Telecommunications Organisation SA (OTE)
Telex Data Division
Data Communications Section, 5 Stadiou Str, Athens 124
Telephone No: 3231099
Telex No: 215558

Ireland

Public tele-graph up to 50 bit/s	Public tele-graph up to 200 bit/s	Private tele-graph up to 50 bit/s	Private tele-graph up to 110 bit/s	Private tele-graph up to 200 bit/s	Public tele-phone up to 200 bit/s	Public tele-phone up to 300 bit/s	Public tele-phone up to 600 bit/s	Public tele-phone up to 1200 bit/s	Public tele-phone up to 2400 bit/s	Public tele-phone up to 4800 bit/s	Public tele-phone up to 9600 bit/s
✓		✓	✓	✓	1	1	1	1			

Private tele-phone up to 200 bit/s	Private tele-phone up to 300 bit/s	Private tele-phone up to 600 bit/s	Private tele-phone up to 1200 bit/s	Private tele-phone up to 2400 bit/s	Private tele-phone up to 4800 bit/s	Private tele-phone up to 9600 bit/s	Other public switched services	Other private services	Wide-band services	Special data network plans	PTT condi-tions for service
2	2	2	2	2	2	2					5

Point of contact:

Department of Posts and Telegraphs
Telecommunications Branch, Telephone House
Marlborough Street, Dublin 1

Key:

1 – PTT modem only
2 – PTT or private modem
3 – Unguaranteed speed
4 – Special conditions
5 – Details from PTT
6 – Approved private modem

Italy (SIP)

Public tele-graph up to 50 bit/s	Private tele-graph up to 50 bit/s	Private tele-graph up to 110 bit/s	Private tele-graph up to 200 bit/s	Public tele-phone up to 200 bit/s	Public tele-phone up to 300 bit/s	Public tele-phone up to 600 bit/s	Public tele-phone up to 1200 bit/s	Public tele-phone up to 2400 bit/s	Public tele-phone up to 4800 bit/s	Public tele-phone up to 9600 bit/s
	√		√	1	1	1	1	1		

Private tele-phone up to 200 bit/s	Private tele-phone up to 300 bit/s	Private tele-phone up to 600 bit/s	Private tele-phone up to 1200 bit/s	Private tele-phone up to 2400 bit/s	Private tele-phone up to 4800 bit/s	Private tele-phone up to 9600 bit/s	Other public switched services	Other private services	Wide-band services	Special data network plans	PTT condi-tions for service
1	1	1	1	1	1	1			1	5	5

Key:
1 — PTT modem only
2 — PTT or private modem
3 — Unguaranteed speed
4 — Special conditions
5 — Details from PTT
6 — Approved private modem

Point of contact:

SIP Direzione Generale
SATS Via Gianturco. 2-00196
Roma
Telephone No: 3877

Japan (NTT)

Public telegraph up to 50 bit/s	Public telegraph up to 200 bit/s	Private telegraph up to 50 bit/s	Private telegraph up to 100 bit/s	Private telegraph up to 200 bit/s	Public telephone up to 200 bit/s	Public telephone up to 300 bit/s	Public telephone up to 600 bit/s	Public telephone up to 1200 bit/s	Public telephone up to 2400 bit/s	Public telephone up to 4800 bit/s	Public telephone up to 9600 bit/s
√		√	√		2	2	2	2			

Private telephone up to 200 bit/s	Private telephone up to 300 bit/s	Private telephone up to 600 bit/s	Private telephone up to 1200 bit/s	Private telephone up to 2400 bit/s	Private telephone up to 4800 bit/s	Private telephone up to 9600 bit/s	Other public switched services	Other private services	Wide-band services	Special data network plans	PTT conditions for service
2	2	2	2	2	2		5		5	5	5

Point of contact:

Circuits Section
Commercial Bureau NTT
1-6 Uchisaiwai-cho, Chiyoda-Ku
Tokyo, Japan
Telephone No: 509 3544
Telex No: 222 5300

Key:
1 – PTT modem only
2 – PTT or private modem
3 – Unguaranteed speed
4 – Special conditions
5 – Details from PTT
6 – Approved private modem

Netherlands

Public tele-graph up to 50 bit/s	Public tele-graph up to 200 bit/s	Private tele-graph up to 50 bit/s	Private tele-graph up to 110 bit/s	Private tele-graph up to 200 bit/s	Public tele-phone up to 200 bit/s	Public tele-phone up to 300 bit/s	Public tele-phone up to 600 bit/s	Public tele-phone up to 1200 bit/s	Public tele-phone up to 2400 bit/s	Public tele-phone up to 4800 bit/s	Public tele-phone up to 9600 bit/s
√		√	√	√	6	6	6	6	3		

Private tele-phone up to 200 bit/s	Private tele-phone up to 300 bit/s	Private tele-phone up to 600 bit/s	Private tele-phone up to 1200 bit/s	Private tele-phone up to 2400 bit/s	Private tele-phone up to 4800 bit/s	Private tele-phone up to 9600 bit/s	Other public switched services	Other private services	Wide-band services	Special data network plans	PTT condi-tions for service
6	6	6	6	6	6	6			5		5

Point of contact:

Centrale Directie der PTT
Centrale Telegraph Traffic and Tariffs Branch
Kortenaerkade 12 Gravenhage
Telephone No: 70753394

Key:

1 – PTT modem only
2 – PTT or private modem
3 – Unguaranteed speed
4 – Special conditions
5 – Details from PTT
6 – Approved private modem

New Zealand

Public tele-graph up to 50 bit/s	Public tele-graph up to 200 bit/s	Private tele-graph up to 50 bit/s	Private tele-graph up to 110 bit/s	Private tele-graph up to 200 bit/s	Public tele-phone up to 200 bit/s	Public tele-phone up to 300 bit/s	Public tele-phone up to 600 bit/s	Public tele-phone up to 1200 bit/s	Public tele-phone up to 2400 bit/s	Public tele-phone up to 4800 bit/s	Public tele-phone up to 9600 bit/s
✓		✓	✓		1	1	1	1			

Private tele-phone up to 200 bit/s	Private tele-phone up to 300 bit/s	Private tele-phone up to 600 bit/s	Private tele-phone up to 1200 bit/s	Private tele-phone up to 2400 bit/s	Private tele-phone up to 4800 bit/s	Private tele-phone up to 9600 bit/s	Other public switched services	Other private services	Wide-band services	Special data network plans	PTT condi-tions for service
6	6	6	6	6	6	6					5

Key:
1 – PTT modem only
2 – PTT or private modem
3 – Unguaranteed speed
4 – Special conditions
5 – Details from PTT
6 – Approved private modem

Point of contact:

Director General, Telegraph Division
PO Headquarters, Wellington
New Zealand
Telephone No: 59976

Norway

Public tele-graph up to 50 bit/s	Public tele-graph up to 200 bit/s	Private tele-graph up to 50 bit/s	Private tele-graph up to 110 bit/s	Private tele-graph up to 200 bit/s	Public tele-phone up to 200 bit/s	Public tele-phone up to 300 bit/s	Public tele-phone up to 600 bit/s	Public tele-phone up to 1200 bit/s	Public tele-phone up to 2400 bit/s	Public tele-phone up to 4800 bit/s	Public tele-phone up to 9600 bit/s
√		√	√	1	1	1	1	1	1		

Private tele-phone up to 200 bit/s	Private tele-phone up to 300 bit/s	Private tele-phone up to 600 bit/s	Private tele-phone up to 1200 bit/s	Private tele-phone up to 2400 bit/s	Private tele-phone up to 4800 bit/s	Private tele-phone up to 9600 bit/s	Other public switched services	Other private services	Wide-band services	Special data network plans	PTT condi-tions for service
1	1	1	1	1	1	4			√	5	5

Point of contact:
Norwegian Telecommunications Administration Headquarters
Datel Services Office
PO Box 6701, St Olavs Pl
Oslo 1, Norway
Telephone No: 02 48 89 90
Telex No: 11203

Key:
1 – PTT modem only
2 – PTT or private modem
3 – Unguaranteed speed
4 – Special conditions
5 – Details from PTT
6 – Approved private modem

Portugal

Public tele-graph up to 50 bit/s	Public tele-graph up to 200 bit/s	Private tele-graph up to 50 bit/s	Private tele-graph up to 110 bit/s	Private tele-graph up to 200 bit/s	Public tele-phone up to 200 bit/s	Public tele-phone up to 300 bit/s	Public tele-phone up to 600 bit/s	Public tele-phone up to 1200 bit/s	Public tele-phone up to 2400 bit/s	Public tele-phone up to 4800 bit/s	Public tele-phone up to 9600 bit/s
				6	6			6			

Private tele-phone up to 200 bit/s	Private tele-phone up to 300 bit/s	Private tele-phone up to 600 bit/s	Private tele-phone up to 1200 bit/s	Private tele-phone up to 2400 bit/s	Private tele-phone up to 4800 bit/s	Private tele-phone up to 9600 bit/s	Other public switched services	Other private services	Wide-band services	Special data network plans	PTT condi-tions for service
6			6	6	6						5

Point of contact:

Direccao dos Servicos de Telecomunicacoes
2a Divisao R Conde Redondo, 79
Lisboa 1
Telephone No: 59101

Key:

1 – PTT modem only
2 – PTT or private modem
3 – Unguaranteed speed
4 – Special conditions
5 – Details from PTT
6 – Approved private modem

Spain (CTNE)

Public tele-graph up to 50 bit/s	Public tele-graph up to 200 bit/s	Private tele-graph up to 50 bit/s	Private tele-graph up to 110 bit/s	Private tele-graph up to 200 bit/s	Public tele-phone up to 200 bit/s	Public tele-phone up to 300 bit/s	Public tele-phone up to 600 bit/s	Public tele-phone up to 1200 bit/s	Public tele-phone up to 2400 bit/s	Public tele-phone up to 4800 bit/s	Public tele-phone up to 9600 bit/s
			✓	✓	1	1	1	1	1	1	4

Private tele-phone up to 200 bit/s	Private tele-phone up to 300 bit/s	Private tele-phone up to 600 bit/s	Private tele-phone up to 1200 bit/s	Private tele-phone up to 2400 bit/s	Private tele-phone up to 4800 bit/s	Private tele-phone up to 9600 bit/s	Other public switched services	Other private services	Wide-band services	Special data network plans	PTT condi-tions for service
1	1	1	1	1	1	4	5	5	5	5	5

Key:
1 – PTT modem only
2 – PTT or private modem
3 – Unguaranteed speed
4 – Special conditions
5 – Details from PTT
6 – Approved private modem

Point of contact:

Servico de Marketing
Division de Informatica CTNE
Avda Brazil No 17, Planta 17, Madrid 20
Telephone No: 4 55 87 84
Telex No: 27320

Sweden

Public tele-graph up to 50 bit/s	Public tele-graph up to 200 bit/s	Private tele-graph up to 50 bit/s	Private tele-graph up to 100 bit/s	Private tele-graph up to 200 bit/s	Public tele-phone up to 200 bit/s	Public tele-phone up to 300 bit/s	Public tele-phone up to 600 bit/s	Public tele-phone up to 1200 bit/s	Public tele-phone up to 2400 bit/s	Public tele-phone up to 4800 bit/s	Public tele-phone up to 9600 bit/s
✓		✓	✓	1	1	1	1	1	4		

Private tele-phone up to 200 bit/s	Private tele-phone up to 300 bit/s	Private tele-phone up to 600 bit/s	Private tele-phone up to 1200 bit/s	Private tele-phone up to 2400 bit/s	Private tele-phone up to 4800 bit/s	Private tele-phone up to 9600 bit/s	Other public switched services	Other private services	Wide-band services	Special data network plans	PTT condi-tions for service
1	1	1	1	1	1	1			5	5	5

Point of contact:

Data Sales Office
Central Administration of Swedish Telecommunications
S 123 86 Farsta, Sweden
Telephone No: 46 8 7132881
Telex No: 19290

Key:

1 – PTT modem only
2 – PTT or private modem
3 – Unguaranteed speed
4 – Special conditions
5 – Details from PTT
6 – Approved private modem

Switzerland

Public telegraph up to 50 bit/s	Public telegraph up to 200 bit/s	Private telegraph up to 50 bit/s	Private telegraph up to 110 bit/s	Private telegraph up to 200 bit/s	Public telephone up to 200 bit/s	Public telephone up to 300 bit/s	Public telephone up to 600 bit/s	Public telephone up to 1200 bit/s	Public telephone up to 2400 bit/s	Public telephone up to 4800 bit/s	Public telephone up to 9600 bit/s
√		√	√	√	1	1	1	1	1	6	

Private telephone up to 200 bit/s	Private telephone up to 300 bit/s	Private telephone up to 600 bit/s	Private telephone up to 1200 bit/s	Private telephone up to 2400 bit/s	Private telephone up to 4800 bit/s	Private telephone up to 9600 bit/s	Other public switched services	Other private services	Wide-band services	Special data network plans	PTT conditions for service
2	2	2	2	2	6	6		5	6	5	5

Key:

1 – PTT modem only
2 – PTT or private modem
3 – Unguaranteed speed
4 – Special conditions
5 – Details from PTT
6 – Approved private modem

Point of contact:

PTT General Directorate - Telecommunications Services
Coordination Office for Data Transmission
21 Viktoriastrasse, Ch 3000, Berne 33
Telephone No: 031 62 11 11
Telex No: 32011

U.K.

Public telegraph up to 50 bit/s	Public telegraph up to 200 bit/s	Private telegraph up to 50 bit/s	Private telegraph up to 110 bit/s	Private telegraph up to 200 bit/s	Public telephone up to 200 bit/s	Public telephone up to 300 bit/s	Public telephone up to 600 bit/s	Public telephone up to 1200 bit/s	Public telephone up to 2400 bit/s	Public telephone up to 4800 bit/s	Public telephone up to 9600 bit/s
✓		✓	✓		1	1	1	1	3	6	6

Private telephone up to 200 bit/s	Private telephone up to 300 bit/s	Private telephone up to 600 bit/s	Private telephone up to 1200 bit/s	Private telephone up to 2400 bit/s	Private telephone up to 4800 bit/s	Private telephone up to 9600 bit/s	Other public switched services	Other private services	Wide-band services	Special data network plans	PTT conditions for service
2	2	2	2	2	6	6	5	5	2	5	5

Key:

1 — PTT modem only
2 — PTT or private modem
3 — Unguaranteed speed
4 — Special conditions
5 — Details from PTT
6 — Approved private modem

Point of contact:

Data Communications - Marketing
Freepost
London EC2B 2TX
Telex No: 885425 (Datel THQ LDN)

W. Germany

Public tele-graph up to 50 bit/s	Public tele-graph up to 200 bit/s	Private tele-graph up to 50 bit/s	Private tele-graph up to 100 bit/s	Private tele-graph up to 200 bit/s	Public tele-phone up to 200 bit/s	Public tele-phone up to 300 bit/s	Public tele-phone up to 600 bit/s	Public tele-phone up to 1200 bit/s	Public tele-phone up to 2400 bit/s	Public tele-phone up to 4800 bit/s	Public tele-phone up to 9600 bit/s
✓	✓	✓	✓	✓	1	1	1	1	1		

Private tele-phone up to 200 bit/s	Private tele-phone up to 300 bit/s	Private tele-phone up to 600 bit/s	Private tele-phone up to 1200 bit/s	Private tele-phone up to 2400 bit/s	Private tele-phone up to 4800 bit/s	Private tele-phone up to 9600 bit/s	Other public switched services	Other private services	Wide-band services	Special data network plans	PTT condi-tions for service
6	6	6	6	6	6	6	5		5	5	5

Point of contact:

Fernmeldetechnisches Zentralamt
Referat B12
D61 Darmstadt, Postbox 800
Telephone No: Darmstadt 6151 83 2826
Telex No: 4 19 511

Key:

1 – PTT modem only
2 – PTT or private modem
3 – Unguaranteed speed
4 – Special conditions
5 – Details from PTT
6 – Approved private modem

USA

All telecommunications activity in the USA is under the overall control of the Federal Communication Commission (FCC). Following a series of events (MCI – 1963) and decisions (Carterfone, Specialised Carriers and Domestic Satellite Proceedings) the FCC has allowed common carrier operations to be opened to competitive business under the regulatory umbrella of the FCC.

It appears that a substantial number of specialised carriers will be operational during and after 1975, in direct competition with the traditional carrier AT&T (Bell). The expected situation is that there will be about thirteen carriers offering services, either on a regional or national basis.

National Carriers

American Telephone & Telegraph Company (AT&T)
'Bell Current Data Communications Services'

Low speed	– Dataphone 1200 (bit/s) (Data Sets 113A and 407A) (switched)
Network	– Private network, telemetry, telegraph channels, alarm circuits
Terminals	– Touchtone sets, teletypewriter on private line

Medium speed	– Dataphone 2400, 4800 (bit/s) (Data Sets 202 and 203) (switched)
Network	– Switched and private line
Terminal	– Dataspeed 40, Dataspeed magnetic tape

High speed	– Dataphone 50 (303 Wideband Data Service)
Network	– Private line

FUTURE PROPOSALS

The overall approach of the Bell System 'will provide for the varied network facility needs of the country, including data transmission. Bell will selectively participate in the data station and terminal market'.

Construction permits have been issued to construct Digital Data Services (DDS) facilities, which commenced in January 1974. The service will initially be private line, full duplex with synchronous speeds of 2400, 4800, 9600 and 56,000 bit/s. (A switched version is contemplated.)

DDS – End of: 1974 (24 cities), 1975 (60 cities), 1976 (100 cities)

American Satellite Corporation (ASC)

Based upon regional satellite systems, ASC will provide the whole range of telecommunications transmission requirements (voice, data, telemetry, etc). Rates of transmission from 100 bit/s to 60 M/bit/s will be made available.

Currently, earth stations are planned for New York, Chicago, Dallas and Los Angeles, with the extension of the links from the earth station to user premises being via specialised micro-wave carriers associated with ASC and by local Bell telephone companies.

Services can be arranged on a 'wholesaler' basis for other specialised carriers through administrative leasing.

FUTURE PROPOSALS

ASC plan to launch two 12 transponder satellites for their exclusive control. They additionally intend to build further earth stations to physically extend their services.

Data Transmission Company (Datran)

Datran has a digital data transmissions system, currently of leased digital facilities, with proposals to have a nationwide switched digital system operational by 1975. The leased services offered at the present time are from 2400 bit/s through to 1.344 M/bit/s. There will be a very fast set up time (under 0.5 secs) and the main transmission media used will be micro-wave radio.

Supplementing its network 'Datran' will offer customers a total data communications package by providing analysis, evaluation, planning, implementation and management of a user's data communications requirement.

MCI Telecommunications Corporation

The MCI system offers leased-line voice and data service, with separate circuits and test boards for each. Under the '4K plus' service, MCI will undertake full management responsibility for the communications system, including terminal equipment.

The media used is micro-wave radio offering 'raw bandwidths' which can operate from 300 bit/s to 9600 bit/s. In its total management service '4K plus', MCI has no corporate commitment to any manufacturers and can claim to offer objective advice on the total user requirement.

FUTURE DEVELOPMENTS

Plans are under way to broaden the speeds offered up to 50K bit/s. In a horizontal development, MCI plans, under MCI Data Transfer Corporation, to utilise the three way combination of computers, terminal equipment and transmission facilities to provide a fully integrated end-to-end data and message switching and transmission network.

Nebraska Consolidated Communications Company (N – Triple C)

N – Triple C's current system, in the initial stages, is designed for private leased voice and data communications. The system is strictly analogue with a charging structure based on bandwidth steps. Speeds offered over 4kHz, voice grade circuits are 2400, 4800, 9600 bit/s, with additional capability to make up 50K bit/s. There is no restriction on the use made of the bandwidths (voice, data or alternative voice/data) which at present is based on over 100 micro-wave radio site networks.

Packet Communications Inc. (Packet)

One of the latest FCC approved communications companies is 'Packet', a value added network (VAN) carrier whose strategy is to overlay its own network of switching mini-computers on existing wideband transmission lines (leased from the specialised carriers or Bell).

The Company states that it intends to provide dial up and 'full time' connect data services to ten cities initially, rising to sixty cities in time. Users will be charged on a per packet basis dependent upon the time of day and on the volume. The network will allow users to connect to any computer on the network which will support terminals of all types and speeds from the lowest interactive terminals to the highest speed batch devices.

Western Union Telegraph Co.

Western Union (WU) has a long established interconnection agreement with the Bell system. In addition, WU has recently been involved in the develop-ment of its own national microwave system; it is being over built in the Eastern Region with a digital transmission system. WU will also offer a domestic satellite system utilising earth stations in New York, Atlanta, Chicago, Dallas and Los Angeles.

Data transmission services offered include:

– Datacom — a time division multiplexing service permitting derivation of channels for speeds between 75 bit/s and 1200 bit/s.

– Multipoint data service — high quality digitally hubbed data trans-mission service.

– Info Com — a store and forward data transmission service, utilising a WU computer linked to subscribers' premises.

Telenet

As a result of the development of the US Bureau of Defence ARPANET packet switched network an application to FCC is in progress. This value added network (VAN) proposal plans to develop a packet network that will be of 'high performance, low cost and available everywhere'.

Regional Carriers

CPI Telecommunications Inc.

Operating Area – Texas and South Louisiana.

Construction of a network planned for private wire voice and data to fifteen Texas cities with extensions to South Texas and South Louisiana. Inter connection with other specialised common carriers to gain national distribution is being progressed.

South Pacific Communications Company (SPCC)

Operating Area – W Seaboard (USA), Southern USA to St Louis.

Construction of a microwave network planned using the right of way available to its parent company, Southern Pacific Railway, based on the railway track routes. Services will be a tailored point-to-point carrier system for voice and data.

United States Transmission Systems Inc. (USTS)

Operating Area – 4,000 miles corridor, 200 miles wide between New York and Houston, via Atlanta, Washington and Philadelphia.

Construction of a microwave system is planned, utilising the right of way established by the pipeline route of the Transcontinental Gas Pipe Line Corporation (TRANSCO). Services are aimed at the 'under 20' circuit user, avoiding the high volume market.

United Video Incorporated (UVI)

Operating Area – Mid.-west and South-eastern USA.

At present, a microwave network has been established between Dallas and Kansas City offering point-to-point data communications links. To achieve their planned national network extension, interconnection of their network with other specialised common carriers is anticipated.

Western Tele-Communications, Inc. (WTCI)
Operating Area – W and SW USA and Mid-west.

An off-shoot of CATV systems currently being run by WTCI on their microwave transmission system, WTCI is offering point-to-point facilities for data, telemetry and other requirements up to 1.544 megabits. In addition, WTCI intends to offer a store and forward message switched service.

Binary Notation

It is to some extent natural for people to calculate with decimal numbers. Possibly because we have ten fingers, we find it easy to visualise and understand the significance of the 10 symbols 0 to 9 which we use in the decimal system. Although there is a risk that a different image from the one desired might result from the concept of a computer having only two fingers, it is perhaps worth the thought if it only proves that we are imaginative and they are not! The rather comforting fact is that a computer can only understand the difference between two alternatives and the ten alternatives of the decimal system are beyond its capacity to understand.

Before looking at the binary system with its two symbols 0 and 1, it is useful to look a little more closely at our familiar decimal system.

Consider the decimal expression 9321. Although we recognise this as nine thousand, three hundred and twenty-one, we are in fact using a convenient shorthand form of expressing an addition $(9 \times 10^3) + (3 \times 10^2) + (2 \times 10^1) + (1 \times 10^0)$.

The logic behind the expression 9321 can be seen more clearly below:

Thousands		Hundreds		Tens		Units		
10^3		10^2		10^1		10^0		
(9×1000)	$+$	(3×100)	$+$	(2×10)	$+$	(1×1)	$=$	9321

As we have only 10 symbols 0-9, we must carry forward when we exceed the capacity of the notation, ie when we exceed 9 in any column.

10^3	10^2	10^1	10^0	
9	3	2	1	
	4	9	9	$+$
9	8	2	0	
Carry	1	1		

If we only have two symbols, 0 and 1, we must carry when we exceed 1 in any column:

(a)		1	0	1	1	0	
(b)		0	1	1	1	1	$+$
(c)	1	0	0	1	0	1	
Carry	1	1	1	1			

This is an example of a binary addition and is shown again below with the equivalent decimal sum:

	2^5	2^4	2^3	2^2	2^1	units		
Decimal equivalent →	32	16	8	4	2	units		
(a)		1	0	1	1	0	=	22
(b)		0	1	1	1	1	=	15
(c)	1	0	0	1	0	1		37
		1	1	1	1			

Note again that each of the binary numbers in (a), (b) and (c) are also additions. For example in (a) 1 0 1 1 0 = $2^4 + 2^2 + 2^1$ or $(2 \times 2 \times 2 \times 2) + (2 \times 2) + (2 \times 1)$ or in decimals $16 + 4 + 2 = 22$.

Conversions from One Notation to the Other

The two notations of binary and decimal numbers can be regarded as two languages and it is often necessary to convert from one to the other:

Decimal to binary

To convert from decimal to binary, the decimal number is successively divided by two, eg

```
2/932
  466  remainder  0  ⎫
  233     „       0  ⎪
  116     „       1  ⎪
   58     „       0  ⎪
   29     „       0  ⎬  Binary answer =  1 1 1 0 1 0 0 1 0 0
   14     „       1  ⎪
    7     „       0  ⎪
    3     „       1  ⎪
    1     „       1  ⎪
    0     „       1  ⎭
```

Binary to decimal

The decimal value of a binary expression is equal to the sum of the Decimal value of the binary digits, eg

| 1 | 1 | 1 | 0 | 1 | 0 | 0 | 1 | 0 | 0 | Binary |
| 2^9 | 2^8 | 2^7 | 2^6 | 2^5 | 2^4 | 2^3 | 2^2 | 2^1 | Units | Decimal |

$$512+256+128+ 0 + 32 + 0 + 0 + 4 + 0 + 0 = 932$$

Binary Coded Decimal (BCD)

To express decimal numeric information, only four binary digits are required:

'Basic quartet' Bit positions				Decimal equivalent
4	3	2	1	
0	0	0	0	0
0	0	0	1	1
0	0	1	0	2
0	0	1	1	3
0	1	0	0	4
0	1	0	1	5
0	1	1	0	6
0	1	1	1	7
1	0	0	0	8
1	0	0	1	9

Although we could represent numeric information by using this simple code, it will be noticed that there are six combinations of zeros and ones which are not yet utilised. The code we have constructed so far is said, therefore, to be 'redundant'.

To represent letters, two more bits (which we will call a 'control duet') will be used and we can use these to identify three groups of letters in the alphabet.

'Control duet'
Bit positions
   6 , 5
   0   0 (1st group of letters A – I)
   0   1 (2nd group of letters J – R)
   1   0 (3rd group of letters S – Z)
   1   1 (a number)

By combining the six bits, we can now express the ten figures and the twenty-six letters of the alphabet as shown in the following list.

	Control Duet		Basic Quartet				
	0	0	0	0	0	1	A
	0	0	0	0	1	0	B
	0	0	0	0	1	1	C
	0	0	0	1	0	0	D
1st group of letters	0	0	0	1	0	1	E
	0	0	0	1	1	0	F
	0	0	0	1	1	1	G
	0	0	1	0	0	0	H
	0	0	1	0	0	1	I
	0	1	0	0	0	1	J
	0	1	0	0	1	0	K
	0	1	0	0	1	1	L
	0	1	0	1	0	0	M
2nd group of letters	0	1	0	1	0	1	N
	0	1	0	1	1	0	O
	0	1	0	1	1	1	P
	0	1	1	0	0	0	Q
	0	1	1	0	0	1	R
	1	0	0	0	1	0	S
3rd group of letters	1	0	0	0	1	1	T
(NB As there are only 8	1	0	0	1	0	0	U
letters in this group, it is	1	0	0	1	0	1	V
common to represent S by	1	0	0	1	1	0	W
decimal equivalent of 2 in	1	0	0	1	1	1	X
the basic quartet)	1	0	1	0	0	0	Y
	1	0	1	0	0	1	Z

		Control Duet		Basic Quartet				
		1	1	0	0	0	0	0
		1	1	0	0	0	1	1
		1	1	0	0	1	0	2
		1	1	0	0	1	1	3
4th group – numbers		1	1	0	1	0	0	4
		1	1	0	1	0	1	5
		1	1	0	1	1	0	6
		1	1	0	1	1	1	7
		1	1	1	0	0	0	8
		1	1	1	0	0	1	9

Although only 36 characters are shown in the list, a code so structured can give a set of 64 different characters (2^6).

International Alphabet No. 5

Transmission Controls

ACK (*acknowledge*)   This is an affirmative reply from a receiver to a sender.

NAK (*negative acknowledge*)   Indicates a negative reply from a receiver to a sender.

SOH (*start of heading*)   The first character in a heading of an information message.

STX (*start of text*)   This character indicates the start of the text and the end of the heading.

ETX (*end of text*)   A character used to terminate a text.

ETB (*end of transmission block*)   Indicates the end of a transmission block of data where data is divided into such blocks for transmission purposes.

EOT (*end of transmission*)   Indicates the conclusion of transmission of one or more texts.

ENQ (*enquiry*)   A character used as a request for a response from a remote station. It may be used to ask a station to identify itself.

SYN (*synchronous idle*)   This character is used to establish or maintain synchronisation in a synchronous transmission system.

DLE (*data link escape*) A character which will change the meaning of a limited number of the characters which follow immediately behind it. It is used exclusively to provide supplementary data transmission control functions.

Format Effectors

BS (*back space*) Moves the printing mechanism or visual display cursor backwards one position.

CR (*carriage return*) Returns the print mechanism or display cursor to the beginning of the same line.

FF (*form feed*) Moves the printing mechanism or display cursor to the beginning of a new printed or displayed form.

HT (*horizontal tabulation*) Moves the print mechanism or cursor forward to the next predetermined horizontal 'tab' position.

LF (*line feed*) Brings the print mechanism or cursor to the beginning of the next line.

VT (*vertical tabulation*) Moves the printing mechanism or cursor to the next predetermined vertical 'tab' position.

Information Separators

FS (*file separator*)
GS (*group separator*)   These four characters are used to separate
RS (*record separator*)   information as required by the application
US (*unit separator*)

DC1, DC2, DC3 and DC4 (*device controls*) These characters are used to switch on or off a terminal device or special feature.

Other Characters

CAN (*cancel*) An indication to disregard the preceding data in a message or block.

DEL (*delete*) Obliterates unwanted characters by punching holes in every bit position.

EM (*end of medium*) This indicates the end of a card, tape or other medium.

ESC (*escape*) A character which will change the meaning of a specified number of the characters immediately following in order to extend the capacity of the code.

SI (*shift in*)   This indicates that the code combinations, which follow it, have the meaning of the standard character set.

SO (*shift out*)   Indicates that the code combinations, which follow it, have a meaning which is different to the standard character set – until a 'shift in' character is reached.

SUB (*substitute*)   A character which is substituted for one which is invalid or in error.

NUL (*blank tape*)   Used for filling in space on a tape when there is no data.

International Alphabet No. 2

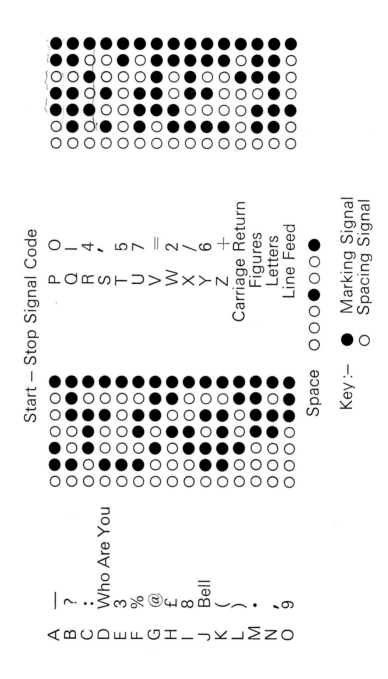

Start – Stop Signal Code

Bibliography

The following bibliography is only a selection of the information sources used, but it will give the reader a link for further sources.

Books

1 *An Introduction to On-Line Systems,* J A T Pritchard (NCC Publications)

2 *Computer Appreciation,* T F Fry (Butterworth)

3 *Transmission Systems Vol I,* M T Hills, B G Evans (G Allen and Unwin)

4 *Data Telecommunications,* R N Renton (Pitmans)

5 *Principles of Data Communications,* R W Lucky, J Salz, E J Welden (McGraw Hill, 1968)

6 *Telecommunications and the Computer,* J Martin (Prentice Hall)

7 *Communication Networks for Computers,* D W Davis, D L A Barber (J Willey and Son, 1973)

8 *Future Developments in Telecommunications,* J Martin (Prentice Hall)

Articles

1 'Why On-Line Computing', J Shergold, *Data Processing*, December 1972

2 'The Design and Planning of The Main Transmission Network', J F Boag, J B Sewter, *POEEJ*, Vol 64, Part 1, April 1971

3 'Certain Factors Affecting Telegraph Speed', H Nyquist, *Trans AIEE*, February 1924

4 'Transmission of Information', R V L Hartley, *Bell System Technical Journal*, 1927

5 'A Mathematical Theory of Communications', C E Shannon, *The Bell System Technical Journal*, Vol XXVII, No. 3, July 1948

6 'High-Speed Voiceband Data Transmission Performance on the Switched Telecommunications Network', M P Balkovic, H W Klancer, S W Klare, & W G McGruther, *The Bell System Technical Journal*, Vol 50, No 4, April 1971

7 'The Characteristics of Telephone Circuits in Relation to Data Transmission', M B Williams, *POEEJ*, Vol 59, Part 3, October 1966

8 'Distributed Intelligence in Data Communications', *EDP Analyzer*, Vol 11, No 2, February 1973

9 'The Design of an Automatic Message Switching Centre', F Lipinski, *Point-to-Point Telecommunications*, Vol 14, No 1, January 1970

10 'Experimental Packet-Switched Data Transmission Service', D E Hadley, D W F Medcraft, *POEEJ*, Vol 67, July 1974

11 'Experimental Packet Switched Service Procedures and Protocols', W Neil, M J Spooner, E J Wilson, *POEEJ*, Vol 67, Part 4, January 1975

12 'Data Communications: Initial Planning', D E Gourley, *Datamation*, October 1972

13 'Software for Telecommunications', J A Bowie, *Data Systems*, December 1972

14 'Computer Communication', *Special issue of 'Proceedings of the IEEE'*, Vol 60, No 11, pp 1243-1466, November 1972

15 'Data Transmission – CCITT Green Book (1972)', *Fifth Plenary Assembly*, Vol VIII (published by ITU 1973)

16 'Sending Data into the 1980s', P T F Kelley, *POTJ*, Vol 26, No 4, Winter 1974/75

Glossary

Many of the terms which follow are precisely defined in the CCITT yellow book.[1] These, however, are phrased in technical language and can be difficult to understand. The aim in this Glossary is to explain the terms used in simple language.

ACOUSTIC COUPLER   A device that permits the transmission of data over telephone circuits without making an electrical connection to the line.

ALPHABET (TELEGRAPHY OR DATA)   A table of correspondence between an agreed set of characters and the signals which represent them.

ALPHANUMERIC   A set of symbols consisting of characters and numbers.

AMPLITUDE MODULATION   *i.* Modulation in which the amplitude of an alternating current is the characteristic varied.

ii. Modulation in which the significant conditions are represented by currents of different amplitude.

ANALOGUE TRANSMISSION   Transmission of a continuously variable signal as opposed to a discretely variable signal. The normal way of transmitting a telephone or voice signal is 'analogue', that is, the physical

---

[1] 2nd Supplement to Part I of List of Definitions of Essential Telecommunications Terms – ITU, Geneva.

speech waves from the human voice are converted into a sympathetic electrical wave for transmission over the telephone system.

ANISOCHRONOUS   The term 'anisochronous' is used in the situation where the signals employed may be of variable duration. Morse code is a simple example of anisochronous transmission where the dots and the dashes are of different durations.

ASYNCHRONOUS TRANSMISSION (START/STOP)   Transmission in which each information character is preceded by a start signal which serves to prepare the receiving mechanism for the reception of a character; this is followed by a stop signal which brings the receiving mechanism to rest in preparation for the reception of the next character. Asynchronous transmission may use start and stop elements between blocks of characters rather than between individual characters.

ATTENUATION   Decrease in magnitude of current, voltage, or power of a signal in transmission between points.

AUDIO FREQUENCY   A frequency within the range audible to the normal human ear.

BACKWARD CHANNEL   A data transmission channel used for supervisory and/or error control signals and associated with the forward channel, but with a direction of transmission opposite to that in which information is being transferred.

BANDWIDTH   The upper and lower limits of a frequency range available for transmission, eg bandwidth of voice grade channel can be 2700 Hz (300 Hz to 3000 Hz).

BAUD   'The unit of modulation rate. It corresponds to a rate of one unit interval per second'.

The term 'baud' is often used loosely in data transmission. It should be used only when describing modulation rate; that is, the rate at which changes can be made in the signalling condition of a circuit. The term is useful to the communications engineer in describing circuit performance.

BAUDOT CODE   A standard five unit code used on most teleprinter machines.

BINARY DIGIT (BIT)   The unit of selective information, ie the amount of information derived from knowledge of the occurrence of one of two equiprobable, exclusive or exhaustive events, 0 or 1, A or B, ON or OFF etc.

BITS PER SECOND (BIT/S)   In most data transmission codes each character is allocated a unique combination of binary digits (bits). For example, in a six unit code the letter 'A' might be represented by the following combination of bits: 010001. As data communications codes vary in the number of bits used to represent each character, it is often more meaningful and more accurate to use the terms 'bits per second' to describe the information transfer rate which is possible on a circuit rather than the alternative term 'characters per second'. For example, the information transfer rate might be, say, 600 bit/s; if a six bit information code were used this could give a rate of 100 characters per second. If, however, an eight bit information code were used the rate would be 75 characters per second – apparently slower (redundancy is ignored in this simplified example).

BLOCK   A group of bits, transmitted as a unit over which an encoding procedure is generally applied for error control purposes.

BUFFER   A storage device used to compensate for a difference in rate of data flow, or time of occurrence of events, when transmitting data from one device to another.

BYTE   A sequence of bits operated on as a unit. (Commonly a character.)

CARRIER   A continuous frequency capable of being modulated, or impressed with a second signal. (Information bearing signal.)

CHANNEL   A means of one-way transmission.

CHARACTER   Letter, figure, punctuation or other sign contained in a text to be transmitted.

CHARACTER CHECK   A system of error control based on a check that some preset rules for the formation of characters are observed.

CHECK BIT   A bit associated with a character or block for the purpose of checking the absence of error within the character or block.

CIRCUIT   A means of bothway communication between two points, made up of associated 'go' and 'return' channels.

CIRCUIT (TWO-WIRE)   A circuit formed of two conductors insulated from each other, providing a 'go' and 'return' channel in the same frequency band.

CIRCUIT (FOUR-WIRE)   A circuit using two pairs of conductors, one pair for the 'go' channel and the other pair for the 'return' channel.

CODE   A method of representing each of a finite number of values or symbols as a particular arrangement or sequence of discrete conditions or events.

CONTENTION   This is a channel allocation system. A request for transmission contends with requests from other terminals, being satisfied in a prearranged sequence when a channel becomes free.

DATA   Any representation, such as digital or analogue signals, to which meaning might be assigned.

DATA SIGNAL   Signal representing a set of digits used to convey information and/or service functions and which may include check digits.

DATA SINK   The equipment which accepts data signals after transmission; it may also check these signals and generate error control signals.

DATA SOURCE   The equipment which supplies data signals to be transmitted; it may also accept error control signals.

DATA TRANSMISSION (TELECOMMUNICATIONS)   Can be described as the movement of information in coded form over an electrical transmission system by breaking down letters and figures, for example, into simple codes in order to send messages by electrical means. The origins of data transmission lie in telegraphy, which is the branch of telecommunications concerned with the process of remote reproduction of documentary matter. Data transmission may be distinguished from telegraphy mainly by the fact that some form of processing is usually involved either prior to or after transmission.

DATEL   The generic title of the UK PO data transmission services, comprising of a suitable line, a modem where necessary and maintenance support.

DIFFERENTIAL MODULATION   A type of modulation in which the choice of the significant condition for any signal element is dependent on the choice for the previous signal element.

DIGITAL TRANSMISSION   With digital transmission, data characters are coded into discrete separate pulses or signal levels. Digital techniques are now being increasingly used for the transmission of speech (using Pulse Code Modulation).

DUPLEX TRANSMISSION   Transmission in both directions simultaneously.

ENTROPHY   A measure of the efficiency of a system (as a code or a language) in transmitting information, being equal to the logarithm of the number of different messages that can be sent by selection from the same set of symbols and then indicating the degree of initial uncertainty that can be resolved by any one method.

EQUALIZATION   A balancing technique to compensate for distortions present on a communication channel.

ERROR CORRECTING CODE   A code in which each telegraph or data signal conforms to specific rules of construction so that departures from this construction in the received signals can be automatically detected, permitting the automatic correction, at the receiving terminal of some or all of the errors.

ERROR CORRECTING SYSTEM   A system employing an error detecting code and so arranged that some or all signals detected as being in error are automatically corrected at the receiving terminal before delivery to the data sink.

ERROR-DETECTING AND FEEDBACK SYSTEM (ARQ)   A system employing an error detecting code and so arranged that a signal detected as being in error automatically initiates a request for retransmission of the signal detected as being in error.

ERROR DETECTING CODE   A code in which each telegraph or data signal conforms to specific rules of construction, so that departures from this construction in the received signals can be automatically detected. Such codes require more signal elements than are necessary to convey the fundamental information.

ERROR DETECTING SYSTEM   A system employing an error detecting code or a data signal quality detector and so arranged that any signal detected as being in error is:

i. either deleted from the data delivered to the data sink, in some cases with an indication that such deletion has taken place.

ii. or delivered to the data sink together with an indication that it has been detected as being in error.

ERROR RATE   The ratio of the number of bits, elements, characters or blocks incorrectly received to the total number of bits, elements, characters or blocks sent.

FORWARD CHANNEL   A data transmission channel in which the direction of transmission coincides with that in which information is being transferred.

FREQUENCY DIVISION MULTIPLEX   A multiplex system in which the available transmission frequency range is divided into narrower bands, each used for a separate channel.

FREQUENCY DIVISION MULTIPLEXING (FDM)   With frequency division multiplexing a relatively wide bandwidth (range of frequencies available for signalling) is divided into a number of smaller bandwidths to provide more channels of communication. For example, the bandwidth required for the transmission of 50 baud telegraph signals is only 120 Hz, while the bandwidth of a good quality speech circuit is about 3000 Hz – using FDM, 24 telegraph channels can be derived from one speech circuit.

FREQUENCY MODULATION   Modulation in which the frequency of an alternating current is the characteristic varied.

FREQUENCY SHIFT KEYING (FSK)   A frequency-change signalling method, in which the frequency or frequencies are made to vary in accordance with the signals and characterised by continuity of phase during the transition from one signalling condition to another.

GAUSSIAN NOISE (WHITE NOISE)   Background noise, naturally present in a conducting material, produced by the normal motion of electrons.

HALF-DUPLEX TRANSMISSION   Transmission in both directions, but not at the same time.

HOLLERITH CODE   Code used to represent data on punched cards.

IMPULSE NOISE   A form of distortion characterised by high amplitude and short duration (peaks). (Manually produced by make and break action of switching.)

INFORMATION FEEDBACK   A method of checking the accuracy of transmission of data in which the received data is returned to the sending end for comparison with the original data, which is stored there for this purpose.

INFORMATION RETRIEVAL   A system or technique concerned with storing and searching large quantities of data for retrieval.

INFORMATION TRANSFER   The final result of a data transmission from one data terminal equipment (source) to another data terminal equipment (sink).

ISOCHRONOUS   The term 'isochronous' is used to describe a modulation system in which each signal is of equal duration.

MODEMS   The term 'modem' is derived from the functions performed, ie modulating/demodulating. Data in the form of letters and figures is changed in a data transmission system into a code comprising binary digits. The direct current output from a data transmission terminal is not suitable for transmission over the existing speech network. These signals are, therefore, converted into voice frequency signals for which the speech system is designed – this is the modulation process. The data now contained in the voice frequency signals transmitted to line have to be converted back again into signals suitable for acceptance by the data transmission terminal at the receive end – this is the demodulation process.

MODULATION   Process by which certain characteristics of a wave are modified in accordance with a characteristic of another wave or a signal.

MULTIPLEX   Use of a common channel in order to make two or more channels either by splitting of the frequency band transmitted by the common channel into narrower bands, each of which is used to constitute a distinct channel (frequency division multiplex) or by allotting this common channel in turn, to constitute different intermittent channels (time division multiplex).

MULTIPOINT CIRCUITS   For data transmission only. In one direction of transmission they distribute signals from a central station to a number of out-stations. In the reverse direction, signals can pass from any individual out-station to the central station. There is no facility for direct communication between out-stations.

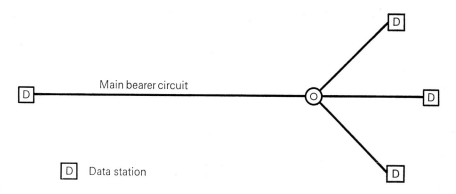

NOISE   Noise is any undesired sound.
By extension, noise is any unwanted disturbance within a useful frequency band, such as undesired electrical waves in any transmission channel or device.

PARALLEL TRANSMISSION   The simultaneous transmission of a certain number of signal elements constituting the same telegraph or data signal.

PHASE MODULATION   Modulation in which the phase angle of a carrier is the characteristic varied.

PULSE CODE MODULATION   Modulation of a pulse train in accordance with a code.

REDUNDANT CODE   A code using more signal elements than necessary to represent the intrinsic information.

RESIDUAL ERROR RATE   The ratio of the number of bits, characters or blocks incorrectly received but undetected or uncorrected by the error-control equipment, to the total number of bits, characters or blocks sent.

SERIAL TRANSMISSION   Using this type of transmission each bit in a character is sent sequentially to line; by convention the least significant bit is usually sent first.

0100011————————————————————————→

SIDEBAND   The frequency band on either the upper or lower side of the carrier frequency within which fall the frequencies produced by the process of modulation.

SIMPLEX TRANSMISSION   Transmission in one direction only.

SYNCHRONOUS TRANSMISSION   In this type of transmission process, synchronisation is maintained (ie the receiver is kept continuously in step with the transmitter, throughout the transmission by electronic clocking devices).

TELEGRAPHY   A branch of telecommunications which is concerned with the movement of information in coded form over an asynchronous two state signalling system.

TELEPHONY   A system of telecommunication set up for the transmission of speech or, in some cases other sounds.

TIME DIVISION MULTIPLEXING (TDM)   Time division multiplexing is a process whereby a channel which is capable of a relatively high information transfer rate (in bit/s) is divided up into a number of time slots to provide a number of lower speed channels. For example, a line which is capable of carrying 2400 bit/s could, by the use of TDM, theoretically be divided into four 600 bit/s channels — or a combination of different speed channels up to a maximum of 2400 bit/s. It will be noticed that in multiplexing there is no 'contention' ie the number of inputs is the same as the number of outputs. This is the primary difference between 'concentrating' and multiplexing.

Abbreviations

AC	Alternating current
ACK	Acknowledgement (positive)
ADCCP	Advanced Data Communications Control Procedure
A/N	Alphanumeric
ARPA	Advanced Research Project Agency
ARQ	Error detecting and feedback system
ASCII	American Standard Code for Information Interchange
ASR	Automatic Send-Receive
AT&T	American Telephone and Telegraph Corporation
BCC	Block Check Character
BCD	Binary Coded Decimal
BSI	British Standards Institution
CANTAT	Canada Transatlantic Telephony Cable
CCITT	The International Telegraph and Telephone Consultative Committee
CCP	Communications Control Programme
CCU	Communications Control Unit
CEPT	European Conference of Postal and Telecommunications Administrations
COMSAT	Communications Satellite Corporation
CPU	Central Processor Unit
CRT	Cathode Ray Tube
CTA	Circuit Terminating Arrangement
dB	Decibel
DC	Direct Current
DCE	Data Communications Equipment or Data Control Equipment
DDS/DDN	Digital Data Service/Network
DTE	Data Terminal Equipment
EBCDIC	Extended Binary Coded Decimal Interchange Code
EDU	Error Detection Unit
ENQ	Enquiry
EOT	End of Transmission
EPSS	Experimental Packet Switching Service
ETB	End of Transmitted Block
ETX	End of Text
FAX	Facsimile
FCC	Federal Communications Commission (USA)
FDM	Frequency Division Multiplex

FEC	Forward Error Control
FSK	Frequency Shift Keying
HZ	Hertz (Cycle per second)
IA	International Alphabet
INTELSAT	International Telecommunications Satellite Consortium
I/O	Input/Output
ISD	International Subscriber Dialling
ITU	International Telecommunications Union
kHZ	Kilo Hertz
KSR	Keyboard Send/Receive
LSI	Large Scale Integration
MCVF	Multi Channel Voice Frequency
MF	Multi Frequency
MHZ	Mega Hertz
MODEM	Modulator/Demodulator
M/S	Milli seconds
MTBF	Mean time between failure
MTTR	Mean time to repair
NAK	Negative Acknowledgement
NTU	Network Terminating Unit
PABX	Private Automatic Branch Exchange
PAM	Pulse Amplitude Modulation
PAX	Private Automatic Exchange
PBT	Push Button Telephone
PBX	Private Branch Exchange
PCM	Pulse Code Modulation
PO	Post Office
POS	Point of Sale
PSE	Packet Switching Exchange
PSTN	Public Switched Telephone Network
PTT	Postal, Telegraph and Telephone Authority
QAM	Quadrature Amplitude Modulation
QSAM	Quadrature Sideband Amplitude Modulation
RBT	Remote Batch Terminal
RJE	Remote Job Entry

RO	Read Only
ROM	Read Only Memory
SDLC	Synchronous Data Link Control
SITA	Société Internationale de Telecommunication Aeronautique
SOH	Start of Heading
SSB	Single Side Band
STD	Subscriber Trunk Dialling
STX	Start of Text
SWIFT	Society for Worldwide Interbank Financial Telecommunications
SYN	Synchronous Idle
TASI	Time Assignment Speech Interpolation
TAT	Trans-Atlantic – Telephony (Cable)
TDM	Time Division Multiplexing
THQ	Telecommunications Headquarters (PO)
TWX	Telex (American Abbr.)
TXE	Electronic Exchange
TXK	Crossbar Exchange
VDU	Visual Display Unit
VSB	Vestigial Side Band

Index